THE DECALOGUE AND A HUMAN FUTURE

The Decalogue and a Human Future

The Meaning of the Commandments
for Making and Keeping Human Life Human

Paul L. Lehmann

With an introduction by
Nancy J. Duff

WILLIAM B. EERDMANS PUBLISHING COMPANY
GRAND RAPIDS, MICHIGAN

© 1995 Wm. B. Eerdmans Publishing Co.

255 Jefferson Ave. S.E., Grand Rapids, Michigan 49503

Printed in the United States of America

00 99 98 97 96 95   7 6 5 4 3 2 1

Library of Congress Cataloging-in-Publication Data

Lehmann, Paul Louis, 1906-1994.
The Decalogue and a human future: the meaning of the commandments for
making and keeping human life human / Paul L. Lehmann.
p.   cm.
Includes bibliographical references.
ISBN 0-8028-0835-2 (pbk.)
1. Christian ethics. 2. Ten commandments. 3. Sociology, Christian. 4. Social ethics.
I. Title.
BJ1251.L37 1994
241.5′2 — dc20   94-23344
                                                  CIP

Unless otherwise noted, Scripture quotations are from the New Revised Version
of the Bible, copyright © 1989 by the Division of Christian Education of the
National Council of Churches in the U.S.A., and used by permission.

Contents

Dedicated to the memory of
John A. Mackay
1889-1983
President of Princeton Theological Seminary
1936-1959

Introduction

On March 26, 1979, Paul Lehmann gave the Annie Kinkaid Warfield Lectures at Princeton Theological Seminary in Princeton, New Jersey. His series of six lectures was entitled, "The Commandments and the Common Life." During his introductory remarks Lehmann described a conversation that he had overheard shortly before beginning his lecture:

> "Have you heard the good news?"
> "No, what is it?"
> "Paul Lehmann is giving the Warfield Lectures on the Ten Commandments."
> "Well, what's so good about that? If Lehmann discusses the Commandments, they'll come out as multiple choice, anyway."

Undaunted by this characterization of his contextual approach to ethics, Lehmann claimed that it is, after all, "the Decalogue itself which forbids single-option living and confronts us with multiple choices that matter."[1] Now some fifteen years later Lehmann's reflections on how the Decalogue provides insights into these "multiple choices that matter" are appearing in this long-promised book. Over the years the title of the project changed from *The Commandments and the Common Life* to *The Decalogue and a Human Future*. The subtitle of this new volume emphasizes his ongoing concern for that which makes and keeps human life human, a concern

---

1. These lectures are available on audiotape from Princeton Theological Seminary's Media Services.

1

that has occupied his attention since the publication of his book *Ethics in a Christian Context* in 1963.[2]

It was in that book *(Ethics in a Christian Context)* that Lehmann first promised a forthcoming volume that would include reflection on the role of the Commandments in Christian ethics.[3] In the meantime another book, *The Transfiguration of Politics,*[4] as well as numerous articles and projects occupied his attention. Now, finally, Lehmann's reflections on the Commandments are made available to us.[5]

Several key concepts employed by Lehmann in this volume are critical for understanding his interpretation of the role of the Commandments for a Christian ethic. In the pages that follow I will briefly describe five aspects of Lehmann's work: (1) the contextual nature of Christian ethics, (2) the descriptive (as opposed to prescriptive) nature of the Commandments, (3) the significance of "apperception" (or discernment) for Christian ethics, (4) the contribution of Luther's thought to this volume of work, and (5) the contribution of sociology to Lehmann's present work. Finally, I will give a brief outline of the book.

The Contextual Nature of Christian Ethics[6]

According to Lehmann, a Christian ethic should embrace neither absolute laws nor utilitarian principles. For him a different direction for Christian ethics is established by the fundamental ethical question, "What am I as a believer in Jesus Christ and as a member of his Church to do?"[7] Neither an ethic of law nor a utilitarian ethic can adequately respond to this question.

2. Paul Lehmann, *Ethics in a Christian Context* (New York: Harper & Row, 1963).

3. Lehmann, *Ethics in a Christian Context,* pp. 148, 223-24, 346.

4. Paul Lehmann, *The Transfiguration of Politics* (New York: Harper & Row, 1975).

5. A bibliography of Lehmann's published work up to 1972 can be found in *Theology Today* 29, 1 (April 1992): 120-32.

6. For a fuller discussion of Lehmann's contextual ethic see my book *Humanization and the Politics of God: The Koinonia Ethics of Paul Lehmann* (Grand Rapids: William B. Eerdmans, 1992).

7. Lehmann, *Ethics in a Christian Context,* p. 45.

Rejection of an Ethic of Absolute Law

Lehmann describes an ethic of law or absolutist ethics in the following way:

> Absolutist ethics declares that the proper answer to the question: 'What am I to do?' is supplied by an 'absolute.' And what is an 'absolute'? Ethically speaking, an 'absolute' is a standard of conduct which can be and must be applied to all people in all situations in exactly the same way. The standard may be an ideal, a value, or a law. Its ethical reality and significance, however, lie in its absolute character.[8]

Lehmann identifies three major weaknesses of the absolutist position.[9] First, it is unable to take seriously the complexity of human life. Even when an ethic of law includes a carefully formulated casuistry (whereby absolute laws are applied to specific situations), adherence to absolute laws often requires one to overlook certain aspects of the particular situation. Life is simply more complicated than application of absolute laws recognizes. Second, adherence to absolute law can lead to a disregard for human welfare, when following the moral law becomes more important than genuine concern for the neighbor. One can maintain a righteous and clear conscience when the dictates of the law are fulfilled even if, as a result of following the law, human suffering increases or is not directly addressed. Third, Lehmann forswears an ethic of absolute law for Christian ethics because it makes one's faith in Jesus Christ peripheral to the ethical enterprise. For Christians, it is our relationship to God and to one another that informs our ethic, not absolute prohibitions or instructions for behavior that can be gleaned from the Bible and/or from reason and then severed from faith.

Rejection of a Utilitarian Ethic

At the same time that Lehmann's contextual approach to ethics was being presented, another ethic that also rejected the absolute character of moral law and concentrated attention on particular situations was widely read — namely, the work of Joseph Fletcher, especially as expressed in his book

---

8. Lehmann, *Ethics in a Christian Context,* p. 125.
9. I have gleaned these three objections from an overview of Lehmann's work; to my knowledge he does not enumerate them in precisely this way.

Situation Ethics. Because Fletcher's term "situation ethics" and Lehmann's term "contextual ethics" are so closely associated, and because both ethicists reject absolute law, it has often been assumed that they are saying the same thing. In fact, their approaches to ethics differ widely, and throughout their careers as teachers and scholars they were in rigorous, albeit friendly, debate with one another. Whereas Fletcher consciously and purposely establishes his ethic upon the principles of utilitarianism, Lehmann rejects utilitarianism as alien to the gospel.[10]

Lehmann objects to both the pragmatic emphasis of utilitarianism and its tendency to make the Christian gospel superfluous to Christian moral decision making (similar to his claim against an ethic of law). Because utilitarianism evaluates the morality of an action based on the consequences of the action, it has a highly practical aspect. One embraces action if it "works." While Lehmann agrees that no one should build a tower without first sitting down to count the cost (see Luke 14:28), he also understands that the Christian does not *always* embrace the most practical solutions to moral dilemmas. In fact, at times the Christian is called upon to do what is foolish in the eyes of the world (see 1 Cor. 1:20-25). Furthermore, just as with an ethic of law, Lehmann believes that utilitarianism marginalizes faith in Christ, even when, as in the case of Fletcher's work, it is presented as a Christian ethic. Once one has identified the greatest good with a biblical theme (in Fletcher's case, *agape*), no further reference to Christ, to the activity of God in the world, or to Christian faith is necessary.

In opposition to an ethic of law and a utilitarian ethic, Lehmann proposes a contextual ethic, which he says is a *koinonia* ethic (*koinonia* being a Greek word referring to the gathering of Christians that we call the church). In describing his understanding of a *koinonia* ethic, Lehmann gives three references to the word *contextual.*[11] By *context* he refers to (1) God's activity in the world, (2) the Christian *koinonia,* and (3) the particular situation in which one is called to make a moral decision. In the first case, Christians are called upon to act in ways consistent with the activity of God. (How one discerns divine activity must be one of the

10. See Lehmann's review of Fletcher's *Situation Ethics* published in the September 1966 issue of the *Episcopal Theological School Bulletin.* A shorter version of the review was published in *The Situation Ethics Debate,* ed. Harvey Cox (Philadelphia: Westminster Press, 1968). See also my discussion of Fletcher and Lehmann in *Humanization and the Politics of God,* pp. 45-51.

11. For further discussion of Lehmann's three interpretations of "context" see my *Humanization and the Politics of God,* pp. 67ff.

questions addressed by Christian ethics.) Second, Christian ethics arises from the Christian *koinonia*. Lehmann never claims that no moral behavior is found outside the *koinonia*, but for Christians ethics is done from the context of the *koinonia*. Finally, one must be acutely aware of the various aspects of the particular situation of moral decision making. Here Lehmann frequently employs Bonhoeffer's claim that Christian ethics must learn to discern "the significant in the factual."

As Christians look toward these three contexts (the activity of God, the Christian *koinonia*, and the particular situation) to understand what they as believers in Jesus Christ and members of his church are to do, they are informed by neither absolute laws nor the principle of utility. Instead, Lehmann emphasizes that the Christian ethos, beliefs, and vision inform Christians of who they are and what they are to do. There is, therefore, an inseparable connection between Christian theology and Christian ethics.

Critics of Lehmann have consistently held two major complaints against his approach. First, they claim that he actually does adhere to absolute principles and laws, although he himself cannot acknowledge or perhaps even recognize such adherence. Second, they say that it is impossible to understand what Lehmann means by the *koinonia*. Many readers of Lehmann's ethics have complained that they have never experienced a church as Lehmann describes it. What exactly does it look like? they ask. Where precisely can it be found? Is he after all appealing to an ideal (an absolute of sorts) that cannot be fully actualized in history?

Lehmann's reflections on the *descriptive* nature of moral law (to which we will turn shortly) provides his response to both of these charges. First, when one understands that moral law describes reality rather than prescribes action, any possibility of the law having an absolute character is thwarted. Second, once one captures sight of the descriptions provided by the Decalogue, one becomes able to discern what the *koinonia* looks like. Furthermore, the *koinonia* is not an impossible ideal that the Christian community is continually and futilely striving to grasp. The Christian *koinonia* is based on and reflects the promises of God. We are called to live within the *koinonia*, engaged in action that also reflects the promises of God, however imperfectly, in this world. Lehmann's ethic, therefore, is based not on an ideal understanding of the *koinonia* but on an eschatological one.[12]

---

12. For further explanation of the role of apocalyptic in Lehmann's thought, see "The Significance of Apocalyptic for Lehmann's Ethics," chap. 4 of my *Humanization and the Politics of God*.

Descriptive Nature of the Commandments

Given that a contextual ethic rejects the absolute character of moral law, one wonders how or even if moral law can function in such an ethic at all. In addressing the function of moral law in this present work, Lehmann claims that the Decalogue, like all moral law for Christians, *describes* (rather than *prescribes*) human life as God would have us live it.

This distinction between description and prescription can be demonstrated by looking at the commandment to honor one's father and mother.[13] (In Luther's numbering of the Commandments this is the fourth.)[14] This commandment, like all of the Ten Commandments, *describes* the way God has ordered the world. In the world of grace and freedom created by God, children honor their parents. However, when this description is turned into *prescription,* strict adherence to the commandment can destroy human freedom and human participation in grace by requiring children to obey abusive parents.

Admittedly there are those ethicists who would advocate an ethic that affirms the prescriptive character of the Decalogue who would at the same time want to avoid a legalistic interpretation that allows for no exceptions. The difference between their opposition to such legalism and Lehmann's, however, is that Lehmann moves away from any affirmation of the *absolute* or *prescriptive* nature of moral law and moves instead to an affirmation of the *contextual* and *descriptive* character of the law. Hence the law to honor one's parents does indeed describe one aspect of the world as God has created and sustained it to be. One cannot, however, fail to recognize situations in which it becomes impossible for children to live according to this description. There are situations in which any possibility of honoring parents has been seriously diminished or actually destroyed by the actions of the parents themselves or by the situation. The children in such cases may need to be entirely removed from the parents, even though such distance makes honoring them impossible. Because of the very nature of the moral law, one cannot make such a move lightly or

13. The following is my explanation of Lehmann's descriptive use of the fourth commandment and is not found in Lehmann's text.

14. As one reads Lehmann's reflections on each commandment it is necessary to remember that Luther numbered them differently from Calvin. Because Luther combines what many of us consider to be the first two commandments into one, he then splits what many of us consider to be the tenth into two. It is Luther's numbering that Lehmann follows throughout this book.

carelessly. The fact that the description of a world where children honor their parents is being thwarted is itself a sign of the brokenness of the situation. The commandment, therefore, is not rendered useless even when one cannot follow the letter of the law. The commandment furthers our ability to discern God's will in the world even as we move beyond strict adherence to it.

Christopher Morse has provided an insightful way of explaining how the law functions descriptively in such a case by suggesting that moral laws serve in a similar way to buoys which indicate to swimmers where the deep waters are.[15] One is at times required to swim past the buoys; in doing so, however, one is made aware that the waters are deep. One is at times required to break the letter of the law; in doing so, however, one is made aware of the brokenness of the situation that requires such action and of the potential danger of swimming in deep moral waters.

One of the advantages in Lehmann's move away from a prescriptive and absolute interpretation of the moral law is that law becomes more dynamic and its application far broader as well as more creative. Hence in this volume one will find that the commandment to keep the sabbath holy leads, among other things, to our understanding of supporting the earth's need for rest and thus for ecologically responsible action. This is a far move away from the trivialization of this commandment found in blue laws and strict rules against any time of work on Sundays. Lehmann's interpretations here are quite consistent with those of Luther, who in his reflections on the Ten Commandments takes each commandment far beyond its limited, literal interpretation.

Lehmann's understanding of the function of moral law is also consistent with Calvin's so-called third use of the law — that is, the law guides repentant sinners in the will and way of God in the world. This guidance comes in the form of discernment or apperception, another significant aspect of Lehmann's ethic.

---

15. Christopher Morse is the Dietrich Bonhoeffer Professor of Theology and Ethics at Union Theological Seminary in New York and the author of *Not Every Spirit: A Dogmatics of Christian Disbelief* (Valley Forge: Trinity Press International, 1994).

Discernment or Apperception

Many critics rightly complain that Lehmann fails to provide clear and concise definitions of terms and concepts. Providing such definitions, however, has never been his primary goal. He strives, rather, to describe the ethos in which Christians are called to live. He wants to cultivate in his readers the gift of discernment — a gift that requires a biblical understanding or vision of God's activity in the world. Lehmann's work is consistent at this point with that of John Calvin, who understood that sin prevents humanity from looking at the world and rightly perceiving the will of God; sin has dimmed our vision, making eyeglasses necessary. Scripture serves as the necessary eyeglasses that allow us to see the world aright. In other words, Scripture is necessary for perceiving God's will and way in the world. While the Ten Commandments make up only one small part of Scripture, they play, according to Lehmann, a significant part in allowing us to see the world as God would have us see it, because they *describe* God's will. This descriptive function of the law therefore serves Christian "discernment" — or as Lehmann prefers to say in this project, "apperception."

As a theme that runs throughout the work, "apperception" will appear enigmatic to many readers on two accounts. First, it is not entirely clear what Lehmann means by the term. His definition reads: "Apperception is the uniquely human capacity to know something without knowing how one has come to know it, and to bring what one knows in this way to what one has come to know in other ways, and, in so doing, to discern what is humanly true or false."[16] Closely tied to the problem of clear definition is the question of whether Lehmann is here proposing a natural theology. Though many of the readers of the original manuscript claimed that it sounded to them like a form of natural theology, Lehmann himself has insisted that this is not the case. In order to understand Lehmann's claim, it is instructive to return to Calvin's position regarding the necessity of Scripture for supplying the lenses necessary to "see" the world correctly.

Many of Calvin's statements sound on first reading like a form of natural theology. In his discussion of the knowledge of God, Calvin says, "There is within the human mind, and indeed by natural instinct, an awareness of divinity." In fact, "God himself has implanted in all

---

16. See Chapter 1, p. 23 below.

men a certain understanding of his divine majesty."[17] In addition to this "seed of religion" or "sense of deity," Calvin believes that there is clear evidence of the presence of God in the universe, as God reveals God's self daily "in the whole workmanship of the universe." All of humankind is "compelled" to see that God exists.[18] It appears, therefore, that Calvin provides a clear notion of natural theology whereby humanity knows that God exists and knows what God requires. However, Calvin states equally clearly that this ability, to which we should indeed have access, is no longer ours by virtue of human sin. The seed of religion is, in fact, totally corrupt.[19] Because of human sin, "all fall away from true knowledge" of God.[20] Calvin's appeal to natural theology goes only so far as to condemn us. Humanity *should* be able to know that God exists and to discern God's will, but "in seeing they see not" (Matt. 13:14-15).[21] What first appears to be natural theology turns out to be Calvin's argument for human depravity and for the necessity of God's grace. Only through divine revelation — not because of any human capacity — do we have true knowledge of God.

This is precisely what Lehmann intends to convey by the concept of apperception. Hence he agrees with Calvin that we need God's revelation as recorded in Scripture in order to make our vision (our apperception) clear. In this project, he will specifically examine that portion of the "eyeglasses" which we call the Decalogue. The Decalogue enables us to focus more clearly on what it means to treat each other as human beings as well as to treat the whole of creation in the way God intended. In turning to the Decalogue, Lehmann takes his cues primarily from Luther's interpretation of the Ten Commandments.

Drawing from Luther

Lehmann first began work on this project during the 450th anniversary of Luther's authorship of *The Large Catechism*. Even though that occasion is

17. John Calvin, *Institutes of the Christian Religion,* ed. John T. McNeill, vol. 1 (Philadelphia: Westminster Press, 1960), 1.3.1, p. 43.
18. Calvin, *Institutes,* 1.3.5, pp. 51-52.
19. Calvin, *Institutes,* 1.4.4, p. 51.
20. Calvin, *Institutes,* 1.4.1, p. 47.
21. Calvin, *Institutes,* 1.4.2, p. 48.

long past, Lehmann's use of Luther's interpretation is instructive. In a day when various forms of liberation and feminist theologies rightly challenge all theology to say a pertinent word regarding human suffering and injustice in today's world, Luther is rarely used by these theologies as a primary source for providing such a liberating word. Lehmann is not ignorant of this fact, nor is he uncritical of the shortcomings of the Reformers, including both Luther and Calvin. He has, however, from the beginning of his vocation as a theologian and ethicist believed that "the faith and thought of the Reformation provide insights into and ways of interpreting ethics which give creative meaning and direction to behavior."[22] Although the Reformers did at times lose the courage of their convictions by not following through on the radical nature of their own thought, and though many of their followers still do the same, this does not mean that we today cannot learn from them while avoiding their errors.

This, I believe, is one of the major contributions of Lehmann's theological ethic. He is able to present a traditional form of theology (Reformed) while listening and incorporating the important criticisms against this tradition. He neither gives up the heart of his faith nor adheres woodenly to traditional interpretations. He teaches his students and readers that traditional interpretations of theology and ethics need not (indeed cannot) be cut off from conversation with the insights of liberation and feminist thought. Hence one can remain loyal to the theological interpretations of Luther as well as Calvin and Barth while reading their work with critical insight and renewed sensitivity.

Drawing from Sociology

In addition to listening critically to different approaches to theology, Lehmann's ethics is able to listen to the wisdom of other disciplines. In agreeing with Bonhoeffer that Christian ethics is to look for the "significant in the factual," Lehmann employs insights from many different types of analysis. In this project he turns specifically to the sociological theories of Peter Blau and Louis Dumont.

Lehmann believes that the "structural realism of the Decalogue" coincides with the insights of sociology offered by these two scholars. In

---

22. Lehmann, *Ethics in a Christian Context*, p. 14. See also the introduction to my *Humanization and the Politics of God*.

a somewhat complicated and technical discussion, he describes the sociological findings of Blau and Dumont in relation to the structure of responsible relationships among human beings. In brief, Lehmann's appropriation of this analysis leads him to reject the hierarchical structure of relationships among human beings that has traditionally been affirmed by both culture and the church. He also rejects the egalitarian structure which has, since the French revolution, been proposed in place of hierarchy. Egalitarianism, argues Lehmann, is not substantial enough to break the bonds of hierarchy and establish right relationships among human beings. Its greatest weakness is found in its inability to acknowledge honestly the real differences that exist among human beings, for fear that once these actual differences are acknowledged, differences in value will also be affirmed. In place of both hierarchy and egalitarianism, Lehmann proposes the idea of "reciprocal responsibility," which emphasizes the differences among human beings (including differences in power) without justifying the privileged status of certain groups, as hierarchy does.

Outline of the Book

This book is divided into two parts. Part I, entitled "Disregard, Disarray, and Discovery," discusses the commandments in a general way while focusing attention on insights from sociology regarding the structure of human life. It consists of three chapters: Chapter 1, "On Not Keeping the Commandments," Chapter 2, "Beyond Hierarchy and Equality," and Chapter 3, "The Structural Realism of the Decalogue."

Part II of the work is entitled "Pathways and Patterns of Reciprocal Responsibility." Following a brief prologue, Part II consists of three chapters: Chapter 4, "Of God and Creation: The Right Tablet of Moses (The First, Second, and Third Commandments)"; Chapter 5, "The Family, Abortion, and Homosexuality (The Fourth, Fifth, and Sixth Commandments)"; and Chapter 6, "Property, False Witness, Vocation, and Belonging (The Seventh, Eighth, Ninth, and Tenth Commandments)." In these chapters Lehmann takes up each commandment for discussion. Following Luther's interpretation both sympathetically and critically, Lehmann uses each commandment as a springboard for discussing critical issues in today's world. It is here that Lehmann's genius for locating the intersection between theological reflection and moral considerations becomes clear. It is also here that his gift for cultivating discernment comes to its best expression. Both scholars and pastors will find his reflections on each of the commandments instructive. Those readers who find Lehmann's description of sociological analysis in Part I too technical may prefer to skim through Part I and pore more carefully over Part II.

Many of Lehmann's friends, colleagues, and former students who have been aware of this project for many years will be pleased to know that it has at last come to fruition. It is my hope that Lehmann's reflections on the Decalogue and a human future will spark readers who are new to Lehmann's work to explore his ethics further by reading *Ethics in a Christian Context* and *The Transfiguration of Politics,* as well as his numerous and insightful essays. Over the years Lehmann's work has influenced a great number of scholars and pastors. It is hoped that this work will be welcomed by those already familiar with him as well as by those who have not read his work before.

It is to my great sorrow that Paul Lehmann died before seeing this book in print.[23] He did, however, know that the manuscript had made it to the publisher and that it would appear in print within the year. He was enormously grateful for William B. Eerdmans's patient support and assurance that the project would be published. He would also have been grateful for the careful and painstaking work of Jennifer Hoffman in editing the manuscript.

Paul's life began on September 10, 1906, and ended on February 27, 1994. During his career he studied and taught with some of the great theologians of our time: Dietrich Bonhoeffer, Karl Barth, Paul Tillich, and Reinhold Niebuhr, to name a few. His influence on today's scholars and preachers around the world is immeasurable. It is with great reluctance and sorrow that we bid him farewell. I offer the introduction of this book to the memory of Paul Lehmann and in honor of Marion Lehmann, his wife of sixty-four years.

NANCY J. DUFF
PRINCETON THEOLOGICAL SEMINARY
SEPTEMBER 1994

23. For a transcript of the memorial sermon preached at Paul Lehmann's funeral at Nassau Presbyterian Church in Princeton, New Jersey, on March 2, 1994, see Fleming Rutledge, "A Tribute to Paul Louis Lehmann," *Princeton Seminary Bulletin* 15, 2 (1994): 165-69. Fleming Rutledge, senior associate at Grace Church in New York City, was one of Lehmann's students at Union Theological Seminary. Wallace Alston, pastor at Nassau Presbyterian Church and Lehmann's longtime friend, also officiated at his funeral.

PART I

Disregard, Disarray, and Discovery

CHAPTER ONE

On Not Keeping the Commandments

Gospel as Law vs. Law as Gospel

Praxis

Although its roots lie far back in classical Greek culture and usage, the word *praxis* is a relatively new word in theological reflection and interpretation. It has been introduced and given wide currency by theological scholars and teachers in the so-called Third World. From Latin America, it has traveled to Asia and to Africa and become an identifying keyword of liberation theology. Unlike the word *practice,* more widely used by the so-called First World of Europe and North America, the word *praxis* tries to bring and keep together what the word *practice* distinguishes and too often separates. The word *practice* means putting into action a particular idea or previously arrived at understanding of what is to be done. The word *praxis,* on the other hand, means that thinking and acting are distinguishable but inseparable components of understanding-in-action or action-directed-understanding.

The church, as the community of faith and life to whom both gospel and law have been entrusted, can only be grateful to the theologians of liberation for reminding and recovering for the church its ancient Old Testament perception that thought and action, idea and practice, interpretation and behavior belong and go together when thinking and speaking about God. Otherwise, theology is at the service of some other god than the God of the Bible and of Jesus Christ.

Scripture, Praxis, and Law

When we look at the connection that the Reformers saw between Scripture and praxis, we find there a movement from a world of origin and destiny, of purpose, possibility, and promise (Scripture), toward and within a world that is the environment provided for, made fit for, and being kept fit for being human in. The move is centrifugal — that is, outward from its originating and centered purpose toward its purposed fulfillment in this world. This connection between the biblical story and the human story defines Christian praxis and provides evidence for the fact that life at a human level is always and at the same time life in two worlds; it is always on the move from the world of origin and destiny toward and within the world of human story; and from the world of human story it moves under and toward the destiny purposed at and by its origin.

Our attention in this present project will focus on the role and purpose of biblical laws (specifically those found in the Decalogue) in relation to both the world of origin and destiny (the biblical story) and the world of human story. It seems that a basic distinction can be made between the interpretation of those who find in Scripture a law that operates as fate, and thus as the nemesis of human freedom and fulfillment, and those who find in Scripture a law that operates as a sign of promise, and thus as the harbinger of human freedom and fulfillment. In both cases the world of experience is understood to be at radical odds with the world of origin. In the first case (when law is understood to operate as fate), the world of experience is understood to be so radically at odds with the world of origin and destiny as to require a radical *denial* of reality to the world of experience as the touchstone of responsibility. In the second case (when law is understood to operate as promise), the world of experience is understood to be so radically at odds with the world of origin and destiny *as to have been given a second chance* at the taking of responsibility for the shaping of that world for the destiny promised in and with its origin.

In the first case (when law is seen as fate), law is the *negative* sign of the connection between Scripture and praxis and converts the centrifugal move from transcendent claim to responsible response into a centripetal one. In the second case (when law is understood as promise), law is the *positive* bond between Scripture and praxis and indicates the limits and the possibilities, the directions and the reciprocities, among those who are being claimed by a world of origin and destiny for the responsibilities that shape a rebellious world in freedom for fulfillment.

Law and Gospel

There is, as Karl Barth has taught us, a world of difference between the praxis of the gospel as law and the praxis of law as gospel.[1] The praxis of the gospel as law is the theonomous statement in word and sign that "the law is the *form* of the gospel." The praxis of the law as gospel, on the contrary, is the heteronomous insistence upon law as the *norm* of the gospel, definable by the literal and propositional reciprocity of word and sign.[2]

On the positive side, the praxis of the gospel as law is a response to the freedom for which Christ has set us free (Gal. 5:1). On the negative side, the praxis of the law as gospel exhibits, at the very least, a failure of nerve that prefers the alleged security of the letter to risking "the wind [that] blows where it chooses" (John 3:8). Indeed, it mistakes the letter that kills for the spirit that gives life (2 Cor. 3:6) and espouses the dubious consolation of seeking the living among the dead (Luke 24:5).

The praxis of the gospel as law, on the one hand, is rooted in the radical conviction that the God who has preferred not to be God by himself has taken the risk of creating a world fit for being human in, together with the risk of purposed fulfillment, in spite of his own best-kept secret that things could go awry. The praxis of the law as gospel, on the other hand, is rooted in the convenient conviction that, for reasons best known to himself, God has retroactively given to some the keys to the kingdom of heaven (Matt. 16:19), with singular indifference to his rainbow covenant and to the perceptions of his only-begotten, self-identifying interpreter

---

1. As the distinction between "gospel as law" and "law as gospel" is made, it may be helpful to keep in mind that the former is proposed as the proper relationship between gospel and law.

2. Karl Barth, *Die kirchliche Dogmatik*, II/2 (Zurich: Evangelischer Verlag, 1942), par. 36, Leitsatz, p. 564; my translation. See also the English translation, *Church Dogmatics*, II/2 (Edinburgh: T. & T. Clark, 1957), p. 509. In describing the positive designation of "gospel as law," Barth uses this phrase: *"das Gesetz als die Gestalt des Evangeliums"* ("the law as the form of the gospel"). The force of the German word *Gestalt* is stronger than the English word *form*, for in German *Gestalt* includes form and structure. The significance of the nuance can be indicated by the difference between saying "the law is the structure of the gospel" (this would constitute the law as gospel) and saying "the gospel is structured in the law" (which would constitute the gospel as law).

that the Creator and Fulfiller of the heavens and the earth makes his sun to shine and his rain to fall upon the just and the unjust (Gen. 9:8-17; Matt. 5:45).

The praxis of the gospel as law, on the one hand, discerns that the crucifixion and resurrection of Jesus Messiah are the center and circumference of a divine initiative, priority, and fulfillment that are invulnerable to impotence, futility, fatality, or defeat. The praxis of the law as gospel, on the other hand, subverts this discernment in and through a serpentine persuasion that the *eritis sicut deus* ("you will be like gods," Gen. 3:5) can be converted from promise to reality and, in consequence, those who know without risk have been granted reserved seats in advance at the messianic banquet, and they are empowered to occupy the chief seats in the kingdom of heaven and to be baptized with the baptism with which he who is the gospel has been baptized (Mark 10:35-45 and parallels).

On the positive side, the praxis of the gospel as law is the nurture of the obedience of faith, "either by the preaching of the gospel or by the administration of the sacraments . . . [as the principal exercise of] the power of the keys, which the Lord has conferred upon the society of believers."[3] The fruits of this preaching are "complete joy in God through Christ and a strong desire to live according to the will of God in all good works," good works being "only those which are done out of true faith, in accordance with the Law of God, and for his glory, and not those based on our own opinion or on the traditions of men."[4] The praxis of the law as gospel, on the other hand, is the programing of the obedience of faith as the behavioral proof of the literal linkage of faith and life and the validation of our own opinions and of the traditions of men and women.

The praxis of the gospel as law is the commitment to the pathways and patterns of the human as the signals of the obedience of faith in a world made and redeemed for being human in — in the sure and certain hope that we are justified by faith but saved by hope (Rom. 5:1; 8:24), and that, in consequence, we are to rejoice, not that demons are subject

---

3. John Calvin, *Institutes of the Christian Religion,* ed. John T. McNeill, Library of Christian Classics, vol. 21 (Philadelphia: Westminster Press, 1967), 4.1.22, p. 1036.

4. Heidelberg Catechism, questions 90 and 91. For a convenient text of the catechism, see *The Proposed Book of Confessions, with Related Documents* (Atlanta: The Presbyterian Church in the United States [PCUS], 1976), p. 70.

to us, but that our names are written in heaven (Luke 10:20). The praxis of the law as gospel, on the other hand, is the commitment to the tithing of mint and dill and cumin while neglecting the weightier matters of the law: justice and mercy and faith (Matt. 23:23; Luke 11:42). It is to rejoice in belonging to and furthering a moral majority, blissfully and blasphemously ignorant of the fact that the strident confidence that "we are on the Lord's side" is no guarantee that the Lord is on our side.

It does indeed make a world of difference if one is engaged in the praxis of the gospel as law, wherein the law is the *form* of the gospel, or if one proposes a praxis of the law as gospel, wherein the law is the *norm* of the gospel.

Rediscovering Luther

The present exploration of the Decalogue, with the aid of certain newly discovered pioneering perceptions of Martin Luther, seeks to identify the pathways and patterns of a human future to which they point. The thesis of this book is that the Decalogue is at once the sum of the gospel and the pathfinder toward motivations, structures, and concreteness of responsible behavior in a world being shattered and shaped, in Norbert Wiener's phrase, for "the human use of human beings." What is going on is a transfiguration of the political and socio-psychological dynamics of what it means to be human in this world. In the course of the displacement of possibilities, patterns, and powers that have played themselves out by possibilities, patterns, and powers that are coming to be, a liberating and fulfilling congruence may be discerned between Luther's pioneering perceptions and certain basic and baffling human questions, upon the responsible resolution of which may well depend, not only a human future, but any future at all.

Between the publication of Luther's *Large Catechism* in 1529 and the complex and perplexing times in which we live, the catechetical story has gone awry. It has turned in upon itself and succumbed to irrelevance and disregard, widely evident both in the church and in the culture. The nurture of humane apperception, for which a catechetical appropriation and implementation of the Commandments were and are remarkably suited, has steadily atrophied. Such apperception being moribund, the political, social, and cultural upheaval signaled by the Reformation has steadily fallen into disarray in the critical arena of human motivation and interrelation, individuality and community, freedom and order, justice and law, authority and responsibility — in short, in the praxis of the self-evidence of what it takes to be and to stay human in the world.[5]

The proponents of the Decalogue have been so preoccupied with drawing lines between keeping and not keeping the Commandments that their contemporaries have taken them at their word and in increasing numbers have decided that the Commandments are indeed not worth keeping. Not keeping the Commandments has become the order of our day because there has been no clear and persuasive human way of obeying them. Faith and doubt have come increasingly to paralyze each other. And in so doing, a paralysis has overtaken the generative power of each to blaze trails along which patterns of human responsibility might emerge in areas where being human is at risk.

We set out for a discovery of the Decalogue beyond the disregard and disarray to which not keeping the Commandments has inevitably led. The Commandments are, indeed, not to be "kept"; they are to be obeyed! They are to be obeyed by pursuing the pathways and patterns of human behavior that the Commandments identify, and by pursuing the prospect of a human future to which the Commandments point.

For twelve years (1516-28), Luther had been preaching the principal parts of what was sent in full to Zwickau on 23 April 1529 as *Der Grosse Katechismus*. During February, May, September, and December of 1528, Luther addressed himself seriatim to the Ten Commandments, the Apostles' Creed, the Lord's Prayer, baptism, and the Lord's Supper. He took these occasions to expand upon his growing concern over the proper confessional preparation for attendance upon the Sacrament: *"zum Sakrament gehen,"* as he liked to say. There seemed to him to be a marked neglect of catechetical instruction by the church, both Roman and Lutheran. There was, Luther wrote,

> no Doctor in the whole world who knew the whole Catechism, that is, the Lord's Prayer, the Ten Commandments, the Creed, that they should understand and teach them, as they are now, praise God, taught and learned, even by young children. For this state of affairs, I call to witness their books, both theologians and lawyers. Should there be any one who

5. For a fuller discussion of this disarray as it surfaced in the twentieth century, and of a biblical alternative, see my book *The Transfiguration of Politics* (New York: Harper & Row, 1975).

can learn correctly a single bit of the Catechism from these books, I shall let myself be drawn and quartered [*so will ich mich raedern und aedern lassen*].[6]

There is very little more risk now than there was in Luther's day. Then, as now, the church was preoccupied with other than catechetical matters: notably, in Luther's time, the church's own magisterium, and in our day, the relevance and organizational effectiveness of the church. Then, there were doctrinal controversies, which kept tradition alive at the cost of expanding routinization. Now, there is the debilitating spectre of the church at cross-purposes between the platitudinal and the latitudinal. Then, there was a neat adjudication of powers and things between "the spiritual and the secular arms," as the tidy and touching phrase went, guaranteed by established institutionalization. Now, disestablishment, official or unofficial, is the order of the day; *cuius regio, eius religio* has been gradually phased into *cuius communio, eius passio (sive libido)*, so that pastors and teachers, as well as trustees and councils of congregations and sessions and/or synods, are perforce exercised by what it takes to tend the store more than by what the store that is being tended actually is.

As for the Commandments, the significance of Luther's catechetical order, both to Luther and for the importance of the Commandments to the prospect for a human future, has been severely overtaken by events. Luther was persuaded, and sought tirelessly to persuade his contemporaries, that the Decalogue provided, both substantively and educationally, "the true and lively" way of the praxis of the gospel as law. He insisted that the Commandments be first in order, in both preaching and teaching, before the creed, the Lord's Prayer, and the sacraments. It is misleading to assume that this order was simply an accommodation to the young, who could more readily memorize and recite the Decalogue than the creed and Jesus' Prayer. In fact, it was Luther's firm conviction that the Decalogue preeminently puts the questions: "Whose world is this?" and "What are the concreteness and the structures of responsibility?" It makes a world of difference whether the world is God's or the devil's and whether it belongs to the boom or to the bust. At least it did for Luther.

6. See Johann Christian Wilhelm Augustus, *Versuch einer historischkritischen Einleitung in die beyden Haupt-Katechismen der Evangelischen Kirche* (Elberfeld: Bueschler'sche Verlagshandlung und Druckerei, 1824), pp. 124-25. My translation.

Prescriptive vs. Descriptive Interpretation
of the Commandments

At this point, the root of a fateful distortion begins to show itself. The distortion is that the catechetical order prescribes the Commandments as a *preparatio fidei et sacramentorum* (a preparation for faith and the sacraments). For Luther, however, the Decalogue expresses another agenda altogether. The Commandments are an apperceptive description of what the gospel affirms about life in this world and of what a realistic assessment of life in this world involves. In short, the Commandments are not *prescriptive* statements of duties toward God and one's neighbor in a world that God has created, redeemed, and will make new. They are, on the contrary, *descriptive* statements of what happens behaviorally in a world that God has made for being human in — given, in Jesus Christ, a second chance for the experience and the fulfillment of what it means to be human — and promises to bring to the fullness of desire, memory, and hope, in a new heaven and a new earth.

Luther's vision and conviction, however, did not carry the day. Apperception nurtured by proclamation gave way to memorization achieved by repetition. Description gave way to prescription; obedience — that is, responsiveness toward and responsibility for the humanness of life in God's world — gave way to a calculus of permissions and prohibitions. Heteronomy displaced theonomy as the generative and regenerative reason for living by the Commandments at all. The imposition from without of limits upon desires and dynamics of the will (heteronomy) effectively obscured the freedom for God and one's neighbor that nurtures a steady and enlarging sensitivity and commitment to what the human thing to do simply is (theonomy).

In Luther's own day, and steadily since, those inside the household of faith have been brought up to "keep" the Commandments rather than to obey them, while those who are increasingly disenchanted both with the treadmill of keeping the Commandments and with the tedium of disregarding them have been driven to the principled rejection of heteronomy and toward the pursuit of autonomous possibilities of human fulfillment in a world without God.[7]

---

7. For a fuller discussion of the distinction between "heteronomy" and "theonomy" and their relationship to "autonomy," see my book *Ethics in a Christian Context* (New York: Harper & Row, 1963), pp. 344-67.

Apperception

The line between keeping the Commandments and obeying them is drawn by apperception. Apperception is the uniquely human capacity to know something without knowing how one has come to know it, and to bring what one knows in this way to what one has come to know in other ways, and, in so doing, to discern what is humanly true or false. In distinction from learning — a process of bringing perception, conception, and practical application behaviorally together — apperception is the experience of self-evident self-discovery through which one is drawn into the heritage and the reality of what it takes to be and to stay human in the world. Apperception is the experience of retrospective and prospective immediacy — whatever may be its biological and psychological vectors — which shapes and is shaped by the dynamics of human responsiveness to God, world, and society. Apperception belies John Locke's persuasion that the mind is a tabula rasa; it evidences instead that human feeling, willing, and thinking — or judging, as Hannah Arendt calls it[8] — occur in a matrix of humane sensibility that is always there and at hand beforehand. Thus, Socrates went about as a midwife, as he used to say, discovering with and to people that they already knew that justice was the foundation of the *politeia,* even though they had never seen a just person. Similarly, Jesus draws upon the formative power of apperception in reminding us that "no one can, by taking thought, add one cubit to his stature" (Matt. 6:27, AV), and that "the eye is the lamp of the body. So, if your eye is sound, your whole body shall be full of light" (Matt. 6:22, RSV).

Similarly, Immanuel Kant can proceed to the "transcendental deduction of the categories" from an early observation of human experience in the world. In exploring the possibilities as well as the limits of human reason, Kant comes to the conclusion, toward the close of the *Critique of Pure Reason,* that every person knows, without knowing how they know, that there are three critical questions which point reason beyond experience to certain ideas ("speculative," Kant calls them), which in turn point back to experience, thereby making sense of it. The question "What can I

---

8. Hannah Arendt, *The Life of the Mind:* volume 1, *Thinking;* volume 2, *Willing* (New York: Harcourt Brace, 1978). The third volume of this Gifford Lectures trilogy was to be called *Judging.* Arendt was at work upon it when death interrupted her.

know?" Kant declares is a purely speculative question. The question "What ought I to do?" is a purely practical question. Whereas the question "What may I hope for?" is at once theoretical and practical, "for all hope is directed towards happiness" and "happiness is the satisfaction of all our inclinations."[9] Or perhaps it goes full circle, the other way around, as Julius Polyaenus of Sardis puts it with grim but moving eloquence:

> Hope is forever stealing the little
> time life allots us, and our last dawn
> overtakes us with so many dreams
> unfulfilled.[10]

From Socrates and Jesus, we come via Kant and Julius Polyaenus to Hannah Arendt, who tells us that the thinker is a truth-teller, whose vocational duty is to preserve "the factual truth" against "the deceptions practiced by contemporary politicians." The storyteller teaches us the acceptance of things as they are — factual truths. "Out of this acceptance, which can also be called truthfulness, arises the faculty of judgment."[11] So the fulcrum of what it takes to be and to stay human in the world of time and space and things is the nurture of apperception, of the uniquely human capacity to know without knowing how one has come to know

9. Immanuel Kant, *Critique of Pure Reason*, 2.2.2: "Concerning the Highest Good, as a basis for determining the ultimate Purpose of Pure Reason," in *Werke*, ed. Hartenstein, vol. 3, pp. 531-32; my translation. See also the clear and instructive discussion of the matter in John Baillie, *The Interpretation of Religion* (New York: Charles Scribner's Sons, 1933), chap. 5; and further, the discussion of Kant in my book *Ethics in a Christian Context*, chap. 6, sec. 2, pp. 172-89.

10. See the translation by I. F. Stone, according to *The New York Times*, 31 January 1979, C-14. See further *The New York Review of Books*, vol. 27, nos. 25-26 (22 February 1979).

11. Hannah Arendt, *Truth and Politics*, prepared for delivery at the 1966 Annual Meeting of the American Political Science Association, New York City, September 6-10 (n.p.: American Political Science Association, 1966), p. 23. See further the debate on apperception and ideology (for this is what it really comes to) in "Exchange on Hannah Arendt" between Elizabeth Young-Bruehl and Sheldon Wolin in *The New York Review of Books*, vol. 25, nos. 21 and 22 (25 January 1979): 46-47. One is reminded of Frantz Fanon's account of the role of the storyteller in *The Wretched of the Earth* (New York: Grove Press, 1963), p. 241. On the significance of Fanon's account of the role of the storyteller in the struggle of black people in Africa and in the United States to achieve an apperceptive identity, and on the relation between story and violence, see my *Transfiguration of Politics*, pp. 162-80.

it, and to bring what one knows in this way to what one knows in other ways, and in so doing, to discern what is humanly true or false.

Catching Up with Brother Martin

Martin Luther — whatever else may be the matter with him — is a master of the nurture of apperception. It could be of no small importance to the human condition to consider that, as regards the thrust, dynamics, and directions of what it takes to be and to stay human in the world, it is not Luther who has fallen behind us. It is rather we who have to catch up with "Brother Martin" (as his contemporaries called him), who has left us far behind.

It must, of course, be admitted that Luther himself bears some responsibility for obscuring his own catechetical achievement. For reasons that may be left to the historians to sort out, Luther's epochal apperceptive discernment was deprived of its revolutionary impact upon Luther's own contemporaries, and upon those who have called themselves "Lutherans" ever since. Owing to Luther's own preoccupation with an appropriate confessional preparation for receiving the sacraments, particularly the Lord's Supper, the *lex orandi* came to take priority over the *lex credendi*, the nurture of prayer and the liturgical healing of the soul over the nurture of the obedience of faith for the healing of human alienation and enmity. After all, Luther had been heavily involved in what Roland Bainton has called "the struggle of Lutheranism for recognition." This struggle engrossed him from the time he entered Worms, on 16 April 1521, to attend the Diet there, until 25 June 1530, when the Augsburg Confession was publicly read in the city whose name it bears, a day which might be regarded "as the death day of the Holy Roman Empire."[12]

As things turned out, the struggle proved more than sufficient to shift the focus of attention from the Commandments to the sacraments. An "in-house" controversy was going on that exposed the Catholic Church Reformed not only as sharply divided from the Catholic Church centered in Rome but also as a house divided against itself. The Second Diet of Speyer (April 1529) and the Marburg Colloquy in October of the same year not only bracketed the publication of *The Large Catechism* but virtually obscured

12. Roland Bainton, *Here I Stand* (New York: Abingdon-Cokesbury, 1950), pp. 315, 325.

its author's stated original purpose. The issue there and then was a sacramental one, too, with penance and indulgences and priestly absolution on the one side, and word and faith and the real presence and absence of God in the sacraments on the other. In the end of the day, Luther's catechetical apperception and purpose were put significantly out of joint. Indeed, between a confessional-sacramental fury, on the one hand, and, on the other, a law-gospel sequence, as the superficial distillate of Luther's earliest exegetical lectures on the Psalms, Romans, and Galatians, the catechetical order and point have been caught in a holding pattern from that day to this, a kind of "deer park" for which no control tower has yet cleared a runway safe for landing. The law continues to be regarded as the schoolmaster which brings us to Christ (Gal. 3:24); the chief end of humankind continues to be the privatized salvation of the soul; the world continues to be a place for testimony rather than for transfiguration; the Commandments go on being kept in the breach but not in the observance. Consequently, the foundational pertinence of the Decalogue to a human future has been left stranded by the side of the road without so much as a Samaritan's attention. Even Professor Bainton's winsome and inspiring biography of Brother Martin reserves scarcely three pages for his catechisms, without even an index notice of the Commandments.

Thus, the thesis we are endeavoring to explore seems weirdly set against the stream. The record seems solidly to exclude it. Indeed, except for the circumstance of another look at the *Catechismus maior,* there would seem to be neither zest for nor sense in asking whether *quasi in latebris* ("as it were in hiding places") there could be a "sleeper on the play." It lies concealed beneath the social and cultural shift that has carried our times beyond Christian and Enlightenment orthodoxy into a world more critically come of age than we have been wont to recognize. The thematic concern of these pages is to show that Luther's innovative stress upon apperception in the nurture both of humane sensibility and of the obedience of faith combines with a dynamic relational sociology of the human condition in identifying concrete pathways and structures of human interaction in the obedience of faith. As the apperceptive core and thrust of Luther's catechetical perception and purpose have been surrendered in Christian preaching and teaching to routinization and to heteronomy, so the dynamics of human motivation and interaction have been surrendered to an increasing preoccupation, both inside and outside the church, with an egalitarian displacement of hierarchy as the necessary precondition of the freedom to be human in the world. Shaped as we all have been by the changing relations between faith and doubt, on the one side, and by the increasingly ideological appropriations of the Enlightenment and the French Revolution, on the other, we find ourselves beset behind and before by a haunting search for a hermeneutics of humanization, and a *tertium quid* beyond hierarchy and equality.

No document of Brother Martin's is more eloquent in testimony to the prospect of a human future than is the Large Catechism. Already in the brief preface to the first edition of 1529, based upon a catechetical sermon of 15 May 1528, Luther wrote:

> This sermon has been undertaken for the instruction of children and uneducated people. Hence from ancient times it has been called, in Greek, a "catechism" — that is, instruction for children. Its contents represent the minimum of knowledge required of a Christian. Whoever does not possess it should not be reckoned among Christians nor admitted to a sacrament, just as a craftsman who does not know the rules and practices of his craft is rejected and considered incompetent. . . .
>
> Therefore, it is the duty of every head of a household to examine his children and servants at least once a week and ascertain what they have learned of it, and if they do not know it, to keep them faithfully at it. . . . As for the common people, however, we should be satisfied if they learned the three parts which have been the heritage of Christendom *[Christenheit]* from ancient times, though they were rarely taught and treated correctly. [This one should do as long as necessary, until one has himself become practiced and fluent in them, both young and old; whosoever wishes to be called, and to be, "Christian."][13]

A year later, Luther added a longer preface that can scarcely be ignored because it so vividly exhibits his mastery of apperception, as well as the catechetical situation of his day, echoes of which still whisper loudly in our own times. Luther wrote,

> It is not for trivial reasons that we constantly treat the Catechism and strongly urge others to do the same. For we see to our sorrow that many pastors and preachers are very negligent in this respect and despise both

---

13. Martin Luther, preface to the Large Catechism, in *The Book of Concord*, trans. and ed. Theodore G. Tappert (Philadelphia: Fortress Press, 1959), p. 362. Where Tappert's translation has seemed to me to be less faithful to Luther's vivid and pointed language, I have ventured to undertake my own translation of the text as given by George Buchwald, *D. Martin Luther's "Grosser Katechismus"* (Leipzig: Verlag von Bernhard Liebisch, 1912), p. 6. My own translations are indicated by brackets.

their office and this teaching itself. Some because of their great and lofty learning, others because of sheer laziness and gluttony *[Bauchsorge]* behave in this matter as if they were pastors or preachers for their bellies' sake and had nothing to do but live off the fat of the land all their days, as they used to do under the papacy. . . .

Besides, a shameful and insidious plague of security and boredom has overtaken us. Many regard the Catechism as a simple, silly teaching which they can absorb and master at one reading. After reading it once they toss the book into a corner as if they are ashamed to read it again. Indeed, even among the nobility there are some louts and skinflints *[Ruelze* and *Filze]* who declare that we can do without pastors and preachers from now on because we have everything in books and can learn it all by ourselves. . . . This is what one can expect of crazy Germans *[den tollen Deutschen]*. We Germans have such disgraceful people among us and must put up with them.

As for myself, let me say that I, too, am a doctor and a preacher — yes, and as learned and experienced as any of those who act so high and mighty. Yet I do as a child who is being taught the Catechism. Every morning, and whenever else I have time, I read and recite word for word the Lord's Prayer, the Ten Commandments, the Creed, the Psalms, etc. I must still read and study the Catechism daily, yet I cannot master it as I wish, but must remain a child and pupil of the Catechism, and I do it gladly. . . .

This much is certain: anyone who knows the Ten Commandments perfectly knows the entire Scriptures. In all affairs and circumstances he can counsel, help, comfort, judge, and make decisions in both spiritual and temporal matters. He is qualified to sit in judgment upon all doctrines, estates, persons, laws, and everything else in the world. . . .

Therefore, I once again implore all Christians, especially pastors and preachers, not to try to be doctors prematurely and to imagine that they know everything. Vain imaginations, like new cloth, suffer shrinkage! Let all Christians exercise themselves in the Catechism daily, and constantly put it into practice, guarding themselves with the greatest care and diligence against the poisonous infection of such security or vanity. Let them continue to read and teach, to learn and meditate and ponder. Let them never stop until they have proved by experience that they have taught the devil to death *[dass sie den Teufel tot gelehrt haben]* and have become wiser than God himself and all his saints.[14]

14. Tappert, pp. 358-59, 361. See Buchwald, pp. 1-2, 5.

Religiously, culturally, and pedagogically, we are indeed where Brother Martin found himself four hundred and fifty years ago. Catechetically speaking, we have come full circle. Between us and the sixteenth century, there is, however, a distinction without a difference. The contemporaries of Brother Martin kept the Commandments at a safe distance, under benign and not so benign neglect. We have been nurtured in the keeping of the Commandments by supposing either that we are obeying them or that we have displaced them by more enlightened counsels of prudence and virtue. Common to Brother Martin and ourselves is a past of trivial, even frivolous disregard of the Commandments as a liberating apperceptive resource for the obedience of faith and for humane sensibility. In view of that past, keeping the Commandments does no little injury and injustice to the common life. The Commandments are thereby deprived of their basic and sustaining significance for a human future. It could be that, by *not* "keeping" the Commandments, an apperceptive regeneration could befall us and direct us in our doings by retrieving the light that the community of faith has been called to be in the world from under the bushel where it has been lodged, and by setting it upon a stand where it belongs (Matt. 5:15-16).

CHAPTER TWO

Beyond Hierarchy and Equality

The "Age of Reason" in a "World Come of Age"

Catching up with Brother Martin brings us to the discovery of the structural realism of the Decalogue. This realism expresses and exposes the concrete purposes, directions, patterns, and boundaries of human relations and interrelations, action and interaction, in a world called into being and being shaped by God's freedom. Hence the Decalogue is at once parabolic and paradigmatic of what God is doing in the world to make room for the freedom and fulfillment that being human takes.

In focusing on these patterns and boundaries of human relations, it is noteworthy that in our day the privileged stratification of a hierarchical society has properly come under a long overdue egalitarian rebuke. Clearly, hierarchical society has manifestly been unable to bring personal and social relations and mobility under a creative and liberating tension. But what has also become increasingly apparent is that the passions and goals of the French Revolution that are represented in egalitarianism have been widely translatable into operational terms as regards *liberté*, more narrowly as regards *fraternité*, but only marginally, if at all, as regards *égalité*. On every hand, we are witnessing the transformation of the egalitarian vision into the fractious frenzy of an ideological egalitarianism that converts hard-won extensions of equal justice under law into a protracted and proliferating struggle for the extension of the rights of all as the harbinger of the rights of each. In short, since Luther's Large Catechism was prepared, published, and distributed, it has become ominously evident that neither hierarchical *nor* egalitarian social, economic, cultural, and political structures are capable of furthering the freedom that being human in this world requires. Neither a hierarchical nor an egalitarian structure alone is able to bring personal caring and social reciprocity under the discipline of a foundational justice, indispensable to what Jefferson called "a civil body politick."

Hence a cultural and political question of momentous significance for a human future arises. The question is this: Is it possible to relate the facts of differentiation and variation in social interaction (to which the experience of hierarchy refers) to the facts of shared identity, commonality, and need in social interaction (to which the experience of equality refers)? If so, can this relation be identified and described as evidence of the fact that the structural reality of social existence can express and further a creative and fulfilling reciprocity between apperception and responsibility in the human life of each through the human life of all?

Such a possibility is political because the facts of social interaction are rooted in social reality. They are exhibited and focalized in the dynamics of power and structure. Accordingly, reciprocity between and among the hierarchical and egalitarian facts of social interaction is indispensable to their ordination to order against the dynamics of chaos to which they are otherwise vulnerable. Politics is at once the science and the art of human community, as Aristotle, following Plato and Socrates, discerned and explored. The chief aim and agenda of politics are making room for community as the chief end of social interaction as human interaction. Toward the achievement of these purposes, appropriate "virtues" (as the "age of reason," faithful to its classical heritage, preferred to say) or "values" (as "a world come of age" finds it more natural and concrete to say) are the principal guides and aids. In a strong and succinct phrase of Sheldon Wolin's, "a sense of institutions must be combined with a sense of community."[1] This is what politics is fundamentally and really about.

Professor Wolin's phrase occurs in the context of his perceptive and instructive discussion of John Calvin, and with special reference to Calvin's kinship with and difference from Luther. Over against Luther's inclination toward political "simplicity" (pp. 162ff.), Calvin "discovered political complexity" (p. 189). In contrast to Luther's encouragement by word and example of the "flight from civility," Calvin struggled to set forth and to achieve a "Christian image of civility" (p. 175). For Luther, "the political relationship, like the religious, was a personalized rather than an institu-

---

1. Sheldon Wolin, *Politics and Vision* (Boston: Little, Brown, 1960), p. 190. Subsequent references will be given parenthetically in the text.

tionalized one" (p. 163). For Calvin, there was a fundamental relation between power and order, which led him to stress the importance of discipline, through which both church and civil government shared responsibility for shaping "a context of restraints and controls" designed to reshape believers and citizens into creatures of order (p. 174).

On the other hand, Calvin shared with Luther the liberating stress upon the church as primarily a fellowship for salvation, not an institutional guarantor of salvation. Consequently, a certain priority accrued to "a 'social' form over a 'political' form, . . . a voluntary fusion over a society subjected to externally enforced norms" (p. 166). He shared with Luther, too, the commitment to the "priesthood of all believers," which "was marvelously successful in arousing the enmity of the followers against all forms of religious status; . . . and yet it also supplied a sense of elevated equality among the believers, an undifferentiated mass status" (p. 193). Insofar as Luther "vehemently rejected hierarchical distinctions among Christian believers, yet . . . assumed that a social hierarchy was natural and necessary . . . his thought represented a striking combination of revolt and passivity" (p. 164). Hierarchy could never be the same again. Luther, with Calvin, Zwingli, and others, in contrast both to Machiavelli and Hobbes, was "among the first to catalyze the masses for the purpose of social action" (p. 193).

Neoconservative Resistance to Equality

In the context of this background and development, the question of the relations between hierarchy and equality in social interaction is plainly on a different course from that evident from the sound and fury of neoconservatism, blustering its way to recognition and power as the twentieth century gives way to its successor. Neoconservatism is essentially elitist, not humanist. Its passionate antiegalitarianism, according to Peter Steinfels, is fueled by "the fear of equality."[2] Blind to its own ideological commitment to the bond between privilege and power as the surest guarantee of the minimal order

2. Peter Steinfels, "Neo-conservatism and the Fear of Equality," in *Dissent,* Spring 1979. This article is part of a book entitled *The Neo-conservatives: The Men Who Are Changing America's Politics* (New York: Simon and Schuster, 1979). Citations are from the article in *Dissent.* Subsequent references will be given parenthetically in the text. Among the more vocal and formative shapers of neoconservatism to whom attention is drawn are Nathan Glazer, Martin Diamond, Daniel Bell, Robert Nisbet, Charles Frankel, Normal Podhoretz (the editor of *Commentary*), and Irving Kristol.

indispensable to a human society, neoconservatism unremittingly rebukes and repudiates the egalitarian movement of these days for what these conservatives regard as "a vast inflation of the idea of equality, a conversion of the idea of equal political liberty into an ideology of equality . . . a demand for equality in every aspect of human life" (p. 169). Alike indifferent to one of the surest signs of ideological possession, and to the inviolable bond between justice and humanness in the political community, these neoconservatives persist in seeing the beam in the eye of the egalitarians and not noticing the mote that is in their own eyes (Matt. 7:3-5; Luke 6:41-42). As a case in point, Irving Kristol criticizes those who "prize equality more than liberty" and is convinced that "the kind of liberal egalitarianism so casually popular today will, if permitted to gather momentum, surely destroy the liberal society" (cited in Steinfels, p. 169). Likewise, Daniel Bell inveighs against what he calls "contemporary populism," which, "in its desire for wholesale egalitarianism, insists in the end on complete leveling. . . . Its impulse is not justice but resentment. What the populists resent is not power but authority — the authority represented in the superior competence of individuals" (cited in Steinfels, p. 169). The end of this process for Robert Nisbet is "a new despotism," in the arrival of which what Nisbet calls "the New Equality . . . has the widest possible appeal, and . . . undoubtedly represents the greatest single threat to liberty and social initiative" (cited in Steinfels, pp. 169-70).

The arrogant ease with which equality is opposed to merit, equality of condition is juxtaposed to equality of opportunity, and privilege combined with power is intertwined with competence and authority unmasks the neoconservative disregard for the political complexity of relating the social facts of hierarchy and equality in a creative and fulfilling human reciprocity. Neoconservatism is at once inimical to and obstructive of the search for a *tertium quid* beyond hierarchy and egalitarianism to which the Decalogue points the way, as the chapters following will try to show.

"The Willful Acquisition of Vulnerability"

There is, however, a cultural as well as a political aspect of this quest that compounds the disingenuousness of the neoconservatives. We may succinctly and briefly understand what culture is fundamentally and really about through a perceptive and provocative formulation of the Italian novelist Niccolò Tucci. Writing about the need for redefinition of courage,

Tucci says: "In fact, culture is nothing but the willful acquisition of vulnerability."[3] What Tucci means by that sentence is not necessarily interchangeable with what his words have suggested to me. Nevertheless, if culture be defined as "the willful acquisition of vulnerability," important facets of human experience and activity are being identified and emphasized. At least two such facets are central to the present exploration of the relations between hierarchy and equality. The first has to do with the distinction between political and cultural social activity; the second with our understanding of "willful vulnerability."

First, as regards cultural in distinction from political social activity, it is significant that social interaction includes not only structural and institutional factors but also voluntary and participatory factors. A distinction and distance are recognizable in human behavior between determinate and indeterminate constituents of this behavior. People behave not only according to and within the relations, possibilities, and limits that are given in, with, and under their behavior. They also behave in relation and response to powers and possibilities resident within and among themselves, which give shape to the way people are what they do, and do what they are. In a word, social reality and cultural reality are distinct and reciprocal.[4]

The definition of culture as "the willful acquisition of vulnerability" underlies the critical correlation between reciprocity and responsibility in social interaction as human interaction. Unless reciprocity is willed as well as given, culture can only be regarded as epiphenomenal — that is, without foundational human reality and significance. As such, it may occasion immediate, and even pleasurable, gratification, but it has no ultimate point

3. Niccolò Tucci, "The Whole Problem of Courage Needs a Re-definition," in *The New York Times,* 31 May 1982, op. ed. page.

4. This distinction and reciprocity underlie the perennial debate in the social sciences between the structural and the cultural determinists. The issue under consideration here belongs also to that debate, but its focus is not upon the resolution of the debate. It is rather upon the implications of political and cultural social and human reality for a *tertium quid* beyond hierarchy and equality. I have been instructed in the broader issues of this debate, as well as in its application to the specific relations of "Power and Authority in Organized Religion," through a draft paper on that theme by Professor Richard A. Schoenherr of the Department of Sociology at the University of Wisconsin in Madison. The paper was prepared for presentation at the annual meetings of the Society for the Scientific Study of Religion and the Association for the Sociology of Religion, at Providence, Rhode Island, 22-24 August 1982. I wish here to acknowledge my indebtedness to Professor Schoenherr for his work and for sending me a copy of his presentation.

and purpose. Unless reciprocity thus willed is willed responsibility, it is difficult to see what other ultimate point and purpose culture could express except the human compulsion to

> Exaggerate to exist, possessed by hope, . . .
> With power to place, to explain every
> What in [our] world but why [we are] neither
> God nor good, . . .
> As [we bumble] by from birth to death
> Menaced by madness.[5]

The *bellum omnium contra omnes* would then be the order of the day. "Authority not wisdom" would "make the law," and the elitist passion of the neoconservatives and the passion for power of the ideological egalitarians would have come upon a common and socially destructive point.[6]

The second facet central to the present exploration of the relations between hierarchy and equality has to do with "willful vulnerability." The bearer of the wisdom of culture in Tucci's definition is the word *vulnerability*. "The willful acquisition of vulnerability" underlies the priority of weakness over strength, of humility over pride in the possession of capacities, opportunities, achievements, according to "nature's lottery."[7] "The willful acquisition of vulnerability" gives priority to the common life over individual advancement — in short, to "the love of glory for the sake of justice" over "the love of justice for the sake of glory"[8] in political and cultural existence and activity. According to this priority, intrinsic to

---

5. W. H. Auden, *The Age of Anxiety* (New York: Random House, 1947), pp. 23-24. The sequence of the lines has been altered slightly in accord with the present context.

6. "The war of all against all," from Thomas Hobbes, *Elementa philosophiae de cive, Praefatio ad lectores* (Amsterdam, 1668), pp. 12-13. Compare further, Plato, *Laws*, bk. I, 625e, 626a. As regards the phrase concerning authority, wisdom, and law, see my book *The Transfiguration of Politics* (New York: Harper & Row, 1975), pp. 343-44 n. 35.

7. John Rawls, *A Theory of Justice* (Cambridge: Harvard University Press, 1971), e.g., p. 96: "the arbitrariness of natural contingency and social fortune." Further to the matter, see Rawls's discussion of "Democratic Equality and the Difference Principle," pt. 1, chap. 13; and of "Relevant Social Positions," pt. 1, chap. 16. The phrase "natural lottery" appears in a critique of Rawls by Charles Frankel in *Commentary*; see Steinfels, pp. 175, 177.

8. Augustine, *The City of God*, trans. Marcus Dods, Modern Library (New York: Random House, 1959), bk. 5, chap. 22.

culture is the risk of capacities, interests, achievements, and expectations centered in the self for the sake of those others with whom selves are socially bound together in hierarchical and egalitarian relations and structures. The priority claimed for the risk of self for the sake of self, so that the other may possibly benefit, too, is the primary anticultural and antisocial act.[9] If ideological egalitarianism courts this anticultural and antisocial priority in its antihierarchical passion, it risks vulnerability for the sake of invulnerability. In turn, the antiegalitarian passion of the ideological elitism of neoconservatism pursues the priority of order over freedom, law over justice, individual achievement over human need, in order that the invulnerability may dispose of the risk of vulnerability altogether. The litmus test of "the willful acquisition of vulnerability" is the priority of need over greed, of responsibility over rights, of justice over power in human affairs. The critical question is not whether hierarchical social structures are inimical to egalitarian social structures, or whether egalitarian social structures require the elimination of hierarchical ones. The critical question is the question of the responsible reciprocity between hierarchical and egalitarian facts of social and cultural reality. To this question the Decalogue is specifically addressed. The pertinence of the Decalogue to a human future depends directly on the pertinence of the Decalogue to this question.

A Fresh Assessment

Thus it would seem that the time has come for a fresh assessment of hierarchical and egalitarian concerns and claims. Is it, for instance, the case that the failure of hierarchical social, cultural, and political structures to overcome, or even check significantly, the injustices of human inequality is a sufficient warrant for an egalitarian rejection of a hierarchical factor as intrinsic to social interaction? Contrariwise, is it the case that the failure of an egalitarian social, cultural, and political reconstruction of the "civil body politick" to overcome, despite important checks, the injustices of human inequality is a sufficient warrant for a hierarchical rejection of an egalitarian factor as intrinsic to social interaction? Before these questions are dismissed as rhetorical instances of the fallacy of the excluded middle,

9. See Rawls, "Democratic Equality and the Difference Principle," pp. 75ff. in *A Theory of Justice.*

let it be recalled that the "time of troubles" (Toynbee) of a social order compounded of hierarchy and equality has been effectively relegated to the margins of political and cultural formation and development without being eradicated as a fact of social interaction. Let it be further recalled that the "time of troubles" of a social order compounded of equality and inequality is increasingly becoming a central preoccupation of political and cultural formation and development — "planning" is the current codeword for it — unable to overcome the stubborn facticity of hierarchy and inequality in social interaction. More than seventy years ago, Ernst Troeltsch remarked at the close of his monumental account of *The Social Teaching of the Christian Churches:* "Every idea is still faced by brutal facts, and all upward movement is checked and hindered by interior and exterior difficulties."[10]

Accordingly, we are summoned "to recognize the significant in the factual." That, says Bonhoeffer, "is wisdom. The wise man is aware of the limited receptiveness of reality for principles, for he knows that reality is not built upon principles but that it rests upon the living and creating God."[11] To be sure, this wisdom is not reserved for Christians only. It belongs to whosoever is single-hearted, not a person of two souls, an *anēr dipsuchos,* as the author of the Letter of James puts it (1:8). Perhaps this is a major reason for the inclusion of the Wisdom Literature in the canon of the Old Testament,[12] and what Jesus had mainly on his mind when he declared that the pure in heart are blessed, "for they will see God" (Matt. 5:8). The way lies neither to the left, toward Gnostic mysteries or Montanist enthusiasms, nor to the right, toward technocratic-bureaucratic expertise or the computerization of human life. It lies along the way of single-minded discernment of the Commandments, designed for making the crooked straight and the rough places a plain (Isa. 40:4; Luke 3:5). To

---

10. Ernst Troeltsch, *The Social Teaching of the Christian Churches,* trans. Olive Wyon (London: George Allen & Unwin, 1949), p. 1013.

11. Dietrich Bonhoeffer, *Ethics,* ed. Eberhard Bethge, trans. Neville Horton Smith (New York: Macmillan, 1965), p. 69.

12. Particular mention may be made of Prov. 1:1-7; 14; 16. Bonhoeffer's use of the words *simplicity* and *simple* is the opposite of the use of *simple* in Proverbs. In Proverbs, *simple* is interchangeable with *folly,* and *simplicity* is interchangeable with *foolishness.* Bonhoeffer appropriates these words to denote the "single-mindedness" or "single-heartedness" required for the knowledge of God and thus also of reality. What is involved in the pursuit of wisdom, however, is identical in Proverbs and in Bonhoeffer's *Ethics.*

this messianic purpose and responsibility for life in this world Christians are called to bear witness and to be faithful, and with no monopoly whatever of these messianic perceptions, resources, and achievements.

> For since, in the wisdom of God, the world did not know God through wisdom, God decided, through the foolishness of our proclamation, to save those who believe. For Jews demand signs and Greeks desire wisdom, but we proclaim Christ crucified, a stumbling block to Jews and foolishness to Gentiles, but to those who are called, both Jews and Greeks, Christ the power of God and the wisdom of God. For God's foolishness is wiser than human wisdom, and God's weakness is stronger than human strength. (1 Cor. 1:21-25)

So "our business now," as Bonhoeffer remarks,

> is to replace our rusty swords with sharp ones. A man can hold his own here only if he can combine simplicity with wisdom. . . . To be simple is to fix one's eye solely on the simple truth of God at a time when all concepts are being confused, distorted and turned upside- down. . . . Because the simple man knows God, because God is his, he clings to the commandments, the judgements and the mercies which come from God's mouth every day afresh. . . . It is precisely because he looks only to God, without any sidelong glance at the world, that he is able to look at the reality of the world freely and without prejudice. And that is how simplicity becomes wisdom. . . . That is why only that man is wise who sees reality in God. To understand reality is not the same as to know about outward events. It is to [discern — *Erschauen*] the [really real in the] nature of things [*des Wesens der Dinge*]. The best-informed man is not necessarily the wisest. Indeed there is a danger that precisely in the multiplicity of his knowledge he will lose sight of what is [really real]. But on the other hand knowledge of an apparently trivial detail quite often makes it possible to see into the depths of things. And so the wise man will seek to acquire the best possible knowledge about events, but always without becoming dependent upon this knowledge.[13]

Bonhoeffer clearly echoes "the law and the prophets," especially the Book of Deuteronomy. But one would have paid less than careful attention to the passage from the preface to Luther's Large Catechism, already referred to,

---

13. Bonhoeffer, pp. 68-69. I have occasionally departed from the published translation, as indicated by brackets.

should one overlook Luther's formative influence upon Bonhoeffer's own nurture as a Christian. By the same sign, it may be noted that the Decalogue expresses in concrete terms of reciprocal personal and social relationality the divine-human wisdom that "sees reality as it is" and "into the depths of things." Indeed, Luther and Calvin are entirely in accord, and Bonhoeffer, too, in the conviction that "true and substantial wisdom consists principally in this, the knowledge of God and of ourselves."[14] With the Commandments before us, and before turning more specifically to their bearing upon a human future, let us try "to acquire the best possible knowledge about events, but always without becoming dependent upon this knowledge."

Sharp Swords for Rusty Ones

Second only to the Large Catechism as a hiding place for God's wonderful preservation of the church is contemporary macrosociological theory, as a source for "the best possible knowledge about events." As with the catechism, it would scarcely have occurred to me to look there for the regeneration of the obedience of faith. Roman, Anglican, and process theologians continue to nurse their predilections for philosophy; and they are being joined by theologians of Reformation lineage who find it in accord with their own mediocrity to celebrate the alleged dénouement of the theology of Karl Barth. Indeed, except for certain strident neo-scholastic omnisciences that emanate from New College, Edinburgh, and from Protestant eminences in Munich, one has learned the hard way that Kant was more nearly on target than offside when he found himself under the necessity, as he said, "to abolish knowledge in order to make room for faith."[15] A Copernican revolution in

14. John Calvin, *Institutes of the Christian Religion,* ed. John T. McNeill, trans. Ford Lewis Battles (Philadelphia: Westminster Press, 1960), 1.1.1, p. 35. If Calvinists had been more hospitable to the Large Catechism than they seem to have been, they might have been more alert to the perception of Calvin that led him to the consideration of the Decalogue in the context of the mediatorship of Jesus Christ. Calvin's discussion of the Decalogue — though briefer and tidier than Luther's — closely parallels Luther's exploration, which gives priority to the human parameters of the Commandments over their apparently legalistic form. If Calvinists have indeed noticed this kinship, they have been singularly adept at concealing their discernment.

15. Immanuel Kant, *Kritik der reinen Vernunft* (Riga: Johann Friedrich Hart-knoch, 1781), Vorwort zur zweiten Auflage, p. 26: "Ich musste also das Wissen aufheben, um zum Glauben Platz zu bekommen. . . ."

astronomy and physics, to say nothing of the Bible, requires a Copernican revolution (as Kant called his philosophical undertaking)[16] in the analysis of the relation between what is really real and what we can claim to know about it. Hence, where faith and ethics are concerned, music is more pertinent than metaphysics, and poetry than mathematics. The point is that the description of a discernment is more pertinent to the purpose and sense of human life in this world than is a statistical readout on the cybernetics of social organization and control.

The frontier between conceptualization and computation in the investigation and interpretation of social interaction, processes, and structures has been difficult to identify, and more difficult to hold. Apart from conspicuous exceptions (Ferdinand Toennies and Georg Simmel, Max Weber and R. H. Tawney, Talcott Parsons and Robert Merton), sociological theory has been atomized and quantified with such zeal and trivialization as to anesthetize, if not obliterate, the distinction between data and knowledge. Add to this development the explosion of information, especially in the behavioral sciences, and one can readily identify with the confession of a certain cracker-barrel philosopher, introduced to me not long ago by a postcard from a friend. Seated in a corner of a country store, corncob pipe in mouth, he announced: "There has been an alarming increase in the number of things I know nothing about." The predicament does not mean that data are disreputable. It means rather that the evidence of things seen is neither the warrant for disregarding nor the demonstrated evidence of the things that are not seen (2 Cor. 4:18). It is an unintended signal of a discovery beginning to dawn, hard upon asking, and asking on and on. Robert Penn Warren describes it as the "Code Book Lost":

> What does the veery say, at dusk in shad-thicket?
> There must be some meaning, or why should your heart stop,
>
> As though, in the dark depth of water, Time held its breath,
> While the message spins on like a pool of silk thread fallen?
>
> When white breakers lunge at the black basalt cliff, what
> Does the heart hear, gale lifting, the last star long gone now,
>
> Or what in the mother's voice calling her boy from the orchard,
> In a twilight moth-white with the apple blossom's dispersal?

16. Kant, pp. 14-19.

Yes, what is that undeclared timbre, and why
Do your eyes go moist, and a pain of unworthiness strike?

What does the woman dying, or supine and penetrated, stare at?
Fly on ceiling, or gold mote afloat in a sun-slit of curtains?

Some message comes thus from a world that screams, far off,
Will she understand before what will happen, will happen?

What meaning, when at the unexpected street corner,
You meet some hope long forgotten, and your old heart

Like neon in shore-fog, or distance, glows dimly again?
Will you waver, or clench stoic teeth and move on?

*

Have you thought as you walk, late, late, the streets of a town
Of all dreams being dreamed in dark houses? What do they signify?

Yes, message on message, like wind or water, in light or in dark
The whole world pours at us. But the code book, somehow, is lost.[17]

"The whole world pours at us. But the code book, somehow, is lost." The
circumstances are different. But a not dissimilar situation could be noted "in
the eighteenth year of King Josiah," when "the king sent Shaphan . . . , the
secretary, to the house of the LORD. . . . The high priest Hilkiah said to
Shaphan the secretary, 'I have found the book of the law in the house of the
LORD'" (2 Kings 22:3, 8). So the codebook is once again unexpectedly at
hand. It surprisingly illuminates and is confirmed by certain reinforcements
that have taken positions on the frontier between conceptualization and
computation in the investigation and interpretation of the dynamics and
structures "manifest in observable patterns of social associations."[18]

---

17. Robert Penn Warren, "The Code Book Lost," in *Now and Then* (New York:
Random House, 1978), pp. 43-44.

18. Peter Blau, *Inequality and Heterogeneity: A Primitive Theory of Social Structure*
(New York: Free Press, 1977), p. 1. Subsequent references will be given parenthetically
in the text using the abbreviation IH.

Although Blau hesitates to dissociate himself from "his belief in the importance
of the quantitative dimension of social life" (p. 17), he does acknowledge the primacy
of "conceptual clarification of this dimension before it can receive mathematical

Role vs. Calling

"The fundamental fact of social life," writes Peter Blau, "is precisely that it is social — that human beings do not live in isolation but associate with other human beings. The associations of people — their recurrent social interaction and communication — exhibit regularities that differentiate their role relations and social positions" (IH, p. 1). Luther would have said *"Amt,"* rather than "role positions," and it should be noted that there is a world of difference between Luther's time and ours. The word *Amt* (i.e., place and office as calling) denotes responsibility with function. The word *role,* on the other hand, denotes function as situationally and/or occupationally rather than vocationally determined, without identifying reference to responsibility. For a teacher, for example, the role accent falls functionally upon credentials and performance, established by transcripts, references, previous conditions of servitude, and student-faculty opinion polls. The accent does not fall upon calling and commitment, upon caring about the connection between who people are and what they can show that they know (whether or not they do know), upon the excitement rather than the mere transmission of a cultural tradition, upon the pursuit and resonance of learning, rather than upon how much or how little of what one knows can be "verified," upon the music in the scores rather than upon the scores that have been amusingly computed and catalogued. For a father or mother, for example, the role accent falls functionally upon whether one has been synsomatically present both at conception and in the delivery room, upon pal potential as the sign of trust potential, upon adaptability to role interchangeability (with or without the benefit of Princeton family seminars), rather than upon the awesome mystery and gift of birth and kinship, of the calling to be worthy of and competent for the entrustment to parenthood that every human fetus brought to birth brings into the world into which it has been born.

These are not tendentiously rhetorical alternatives. They are deadly serious options in a subcatechetical, statistically oriented world. Although I do not have Peter Blau's permission to co-opt him for Martin Luther, neither do I have Martin Luther's permission to co-opt Peter Blau for him. What is

---

treatment." As one whose mathematical competence is so low as to approach nullity and thus is not even to be compared with Blau's, I venture, nevertheless, to concur in the order of priority that Blau has affirmed and to suggest that Luther would be pleased.

being suggested is that in our subcatechetical, statistically oriented world, there is "light at the end of the tunnel," which offers a significant confirmation of Luther's catechetical resource for discerning "the significant in the factual." "Can anything good come out of Nazareth? . . . Come and see" (John 1:46).

An Assist from Macrosociology

What there is to see may not be "the best possible knowledge about events." There are, however, three macrosociological analyses of human life as social life of singular perceptiveness, precision, and depth; and they signal a conceptuality beyond hierarchy and equality for a human future in a world come of age. Peter Blau's book *Inequality and Heterogeneity: A Primitive Theory of Social Structure* has been hailed as "a significant advance in the Theory of Social Structure [which] will become a classic in sociology."[19] Two further volumes are by Louis Dumont; the first is entitled *Homo Hierarchicus: The Caste System and Its Implications,* and the second bears the title *From Mandeville to Marx: The Genesis and Triumph of Economic Ideology.*[20] We shall turn first to *Homo Hierarchicus;* then, in the following section, we shall consider Professor Dumont's later volume and venture upon an interpretation of the conceptuality of Professor Blau.

A conceptuality beyond hierarchy and equality cannot exclude either social fact (i.e., hierarchy or equality) in its relation to the other. Nor can such a conceptuality seek a neatly balanced equilibrium between the two.

19. Rose L. Coser, professor of sociology at the State University of New York at Stony Brook, on the jacket of the book. Peter Blau is Quetelet Professor of Sociology at Columbia University and a past president of the American Sociological Society. His book came to me as a gift from the author in furtherance of conversations over a quarter century about the interrelations between sociological and theological assessments of the human condition. For this, as well as for his informative and enriching work, I wish to express my great gratitude.

20. Dumont, *Homo Hierarchicus,* trans. George Weidenfeld (Chicago: University of Chicago Press, 1970); *From Mandeville to Marx* (Chicago: University of Chicago Press, 1977). Subsequent references to both works will be given parenthetically in the text using the abbreviations HH and MM. Louis Dumont is Director d'Études at the École Practique des Hautes Études in Paris.

I wish to express particular gratitude to Professor Mark Juergensmeyer of the Center for Ethics and Social Policy of the Graduate Theological Union at Berkeley, California, for directing me to Professor Dumont's work.

"Equality and hierarchy," Dumont writes, "are not in fact opposed to each other in a mechanical way which the exclusive consideration of values might lead one to suppose; . . . each implies the other and is supported by it" (HH, p. 257). Talcott Parsons, for example, has pointed out that distinction of status carries with it and presupposes equality within each status. On the other hand, where equality is affirmed, it is within a group that is hierarchically related to others, as in the Greek cities, or, in the modern world, in the relations between the super powers and the industrially developed and developing nations.[21] In the modern world, however, the egalitarian ideal has become so intensely ideological as to be incapable of acknowledging hierarchy as a social fact. On the record, according to Dumont, hierarchical societies include equality, whereas egalitarian societies reject hierarchy.

> It is this structural relation [i.e., between hierarchy and equality] that the egalitarian ideal tends to destroy. . . . In the first place, the relation is inverted: equality contains inequalities instead of being contained in hierarchy. In the second place . . . hierarchy is repressed, made non-conscious: it is replaced by a manifold network of inequalities, matters of fact instead of right, of quantity and gradualness instead of quality and discontinuity. (HH, p. 257)

A fateful and far-reaching consequence of this inversion and repression is the egalitarian confusion of fact with right, and, as a corollary, the confusion of quantity with quality, and of the gradual extension of rights, factually regarded, with an amelioration of the radical discontinuity between equality and inequality in social life.

At the methodological level this confusion of fact with right is implicit in the current debate among sociologists over what they refer to as "social stratification." The trick is to facilitate passage from the principle of the equality of all participants in social interaction, whatsoever their roles and functions may be — whether as citizens or governors, as managers or employees, as males or females, parents or children, teachers or students — to the notion that all human beings are identical. This is done by compounding one statistical study upon another (one foundational or federal grant after another), cataloging and classifying the various strata and levels and diversifications of social groups. The meth-

21. Talcott Parsons, "A Revised Theoretical Approach to the Theory of Social Stratification," in *Class, Status and Power: A Reader in Social Stratification,* ed. Reinhard Bendix and Seymour Martin Lipset (London, 1954); cited by Dumont in HH, p. 257.

odological presupposition is that from such minutiae, exhaustively collected, "a system of social stratification" may be extrapolated, characterized by features taken exclusively from the morphology of groups, in disregard of the formative significance of the ideology, that is, the social set of ideas and values that underlie behavior (HH, pp. 214, 263).

There is, however, a substantive level on which the consequences of the egalitarian inversion and repression of hierarchy are evident. Since we shall be returning to this level as we proceed, one case in point may be noted here. Some readers may remember the shock and dismay, and even self-justifying anger, which greeted the publication of Gunnar Myrdal's *An American Dilemma: The Negro Problem and Modern Democracy*.[22] The furor focused upon the close connection that Myrdal claimed to have discovered between egalitarianism and racism. In America, according to Myrdal, "the essentially moral doctrine of the 'natural rights' of man rests on a biological egalitarianism: all men are 'created equal.'" During the period 1830 to 1860, the debate over slavery raged over equality and inequality of races. The opponents of slavery argued in the name of natural equality. Says Myrdal:

> The dogma of racial equality may, in a sense, be regarded as a strange fruit of the Enlightenment. . . . The race dogma is nearly the only way out for a people so moralistically egalitarian, if it is not prepared to live up to its faith. A nation less fervently committed to democracy could probably live happily in a caste system. . . . Race prejudice is, in a sense, a function (a perversion) of egalitarianism. (Cited in HH, p. 256; parentheses Myrdal's)

Dumont's comment on Myrdal's conclusions is that

> It is permissible to doubt whether, in the fight against racism in general, the mere recall of the egalitarian ideal, however solemn it may be, and even though accompanied by a scientific criticism of racist prejudices, will be really efficient. It would be better to prevent the passage from the moral principle of equality to the notion that all men are identical. One feels sure that equality can in our day be combined with the recognition of differences, so long as such differences are morally neutral. People must be provided with the means for conceptualizing differences. The diffusion of the pluralistic notions of culture, society, etc., affording

22. Gunnar Myrdal, *An American Dilemma: The Negro Problem and Modern Democracy* (New York, 1944), p. 89; referred to by Dumont in HH, pp. 256ff., 342.

a counter-weight and setting bounds to individualism, is the obvious
thing. (HH, pp. 256-57)

The obvious thing! Yes. But there's the rub. Differences, regarded as morally
neutral, are in effect regarded as variants of a common human identity. What
counts are all the ways in which others are like ourselves, not the claims of
others upon ourselves to take responsibility for differences. Since Myrdal, the
egalitarian ideal has passed from "mere recall" to an intense ideological
conjunction of status with power. Sexism has been joined with racism as the
phalanx of a struggle for the rights of all minorities. Yet, again and again, it
has become apparent that the rights of African Americans turn out to be less
than coequal with reductions in discrimination, minimal as they have been,
achieved by the women's movement.

The hierarchical ideal, about which the Large Catechism makes no
attempt to dissemble, did not adequately generate the responsibility for
difference. But it did recognize difference as the occasion for the reciprocity
that being human in the world requires. The means for conceptualizing
differences were at least rudimentarily available. The egalitarian ideal,
however, is rooted in an individualism that regards difference as exigenous
rather than as indigenous to the human condition. Hence the *modus
vivendi* according to which everybody is accorded the right to pursue his
or her own rights, so long as such pursuit does not interfere with the rights
of others. As the prophet Habakkuk put it at the turn of the seventh into
the sixth century B.C.E. — so incisively as virtually to have foreseen it:

> Why do you make me see wrong-doing
>   and look at trouble?
> Destruction and violence are before me;
>   strife and contention arise.
> So the law becomes slack
>   and justice never prevails.
> The wicked surround the righteous —
>   therefore justice comes forth perverted.
>
>   (1:3-4)

So this question arises: Is human society a hive, as Mandeville's celebrated
Fable of the Bees satirically asserts?[23] Or is society an anthill, as Dostoevsky's

23. Bernard Mandeville, *The Fable of the Bees,* 2 vols., ed. F. B. Kaye (Oxford:
Oxford University Press, 1924). See Dumont, MM, chap. 5, esp. pp. 62-72.
   In this satirical fable, a hive is presented as a mirror of human society. The hive

grim anticipation of the Marxist vision of a classless society fears?[24] Or is there a human prospect for a society now in transition from the "Age of Reason" in a "world come of age" toward a human future coming our way? Such a prospect awaits the fusion of a humane apperception nurtured in the way of the Commandments with the structural realism of the Decalogue.

Hive, Anthill, or Human Community

An initial step toward the fusion just alluded to is at our disposal, owing to a macrosociological clarification of hierarchy and equality as social realities. It has already been noted that the experience of hierarchy refers to the facts of differentiation and variation in social interaction, and that the experience of equality refers to the facts of shared identity, commonality, and need in social interaction. Turning now more precisely to the

---

lives in corruption and prosperity, yet it possesses sufficient nostalgia for virtue to pray for it. When the prayer is granted, a transformation occurs; with vice gone, activity and prosperity disappear and are replaced by sloth, poverty, and boredom in a much-reduced population.

The work was an attack upon Anthony Ashley Cooper, the Earl of Shaftesbury, a disciple of John Locke. Shaftesbury held that humankind is made for society, society thus being the goal of the individual and the warrant for virtue. Mandeville, in opposition, notes that self-interest, not self-denial, is the solid basis of life, though regarded as the source of all evil. The fable shows how completely the hierarchical order of society had fallen into disarray and how vigorously the place of the individual in society had become a matter of debate.

24. The image of the anthill is the theme of Fyodor Dostoevsky's powerful social and political novel *The Possessed*. See the Modern Library edition, with foreword by Avraham Yarmolinsky (New York, 1936). *The Possessed* is a vigorous attack upon the nihilism of the Russia of the last quarter of the nineteenth century and is often regarded as a prophetic anticipation of the events of 1917. Dostoevsky's fear was that "the individual whose needs . . . are of a spiritual and irrational order, must be degraded in a Socialist Society organized according to a reasoned scheme in the interest of the group" (p. vii).

The anthill is a picture of the great leveling of society that occurs when individuals are alienated from society and are submerged beneath and dominated by bureaucratic structures, and when individuals and society are devoid of the vision indispensable to human freedom and a humane order of life. Thus the anthill joins the hive in symbolizing a deep and destructive cleavage between the individual and society; in short, the ultimate displacement of the vision of a human community by barbarism.

analysis of Louis Dumont, hierarchy and equality are fundamentally to be understood as social ideals that give rise to and shape social structures and cultural values and patterns. For Peter Blau, the structural evidences of hierarchy and equality are more determinative of social interaction than are cultural values and patterns, although the cultural values and patterns are not less significant.

Dumont has put it this way: hierarchy is "the principle by which the elements of a whole are ranked in relation to the whole" (HH, p. 66). Equality is the principle by which "the human individual . . . is conceived as presenting, in spite of and over and above his particularity, the essence of humanity" (HH, p. 4). Each is the equal of each, and thus all are the sum of all. The "equal of each" means that each is the same as, no more and no less than, the other, in relation to each other and to the whole. Consequently, the identity of each is the essence of the humanity of each, and of all. Equality and individualism thus stand or fall together; so also do hierarchy and holism — that is, society taken as a whole.

From Peter Blau we have at hand a conceptuality that complements Dumont's sociocultural investigations of holistic patterns and values. Blau's analysis offers a conceptual revision of the interpretation of hierarchy and equality as social ideals and structures of far-reaching significance for interpreting social interaction and behavior. For Blau, there are "observable patterns of social associations" (IH, p. 1). The fact that social associations exhibit patterns of social interaction rather more than random contacts of proximity or distance makes it possible to extrapolate from these patterns certain "structures of differentiated social positions and role relations" (IH, p. 1). The recognition and identification of such structures mean that society, as humanly experienced and lived in, is not a fortuitous aggregate of otherwise isolated components but is instead an ordered configuration of relations, roles, and functions. Or better, as the Commandments show us, an ordered configuration of relations, responses, and responsibilities. This semantic alteration is more than an intrusion of one universe of discourse upon another. It is a major indicator of the bearing of biblical and theological perspectives upon social analyses. Biblical and theological perspectives protect the human factor in such analyses from reductionist quantification.[25]

---

25. Dumont's critique of social stratification — made, as we have seen, in the name of comparative sociology — implies such a recognition of the irreducibility of the human factor from the sociological side. Such an implication suggests the possi-

More specifically, then, "a social structure," according to Professor Blau, "can be defined as a multidimensional space of different social positions among which a population is distributed" (IH, p. 4). Such a structure, moreover, "is delineated by its parameters" (IH, p. 6). The term *parameter* is borrowed from mathematics, more specifically from conics. A parameter denotes "an arbitrary constant characterizing . . . some particular member of a system of expressions, curves, surfaces, functions, etc."[26] Applied to social structures, Blau distinguishes between "nominal parameters" and "graduated parameters" (IH, p. 7). "A nominal parameter divides the population into subgroups with distinct boundaries. . . . [But] there is no inherent rank-order among these groups." Examples of such nominal parameters are sex, religion, race, and occupation. "A graduated parameter," on the other hand, "differentiates people in terms of a status rank-order. . . . Income, wealth, education, and power are graduated parameters." So also are age and intelligence. "In principle," says Blau, "the status gradation is continuous, which means that the parameter itself does not draw boundaries between strata. But the empirical distribution may reveal discontinuities that indicate class boundaries" (IH, p. 7). Income, wealth, power, education, and age, for example, differentiate between less and more, older and younger, stronger and weaker. Within the same status or rank-order group empirical discontinuities may occur. But these differences do not significantly affect the role relations. Tenured and nontenured members of faculties, for instance, may live and work together with something less than optimum felicity. But they have more in common with each other than either does with the maintenance crews of the schools to which both groups happen to be attached.

As graduated parameters identify status associations, relations, and rank-order, nominal parameters identify group associations, relations, and roles in which one or more attributes influence people in ways that make in-group relations more prevalent than out-group relations. People who speak the same language are drawn together more readily than people who

---

bility of a fruitful conversation between sociologists and theologians toward the clarification of language referents and also of the question whether two different contexts of discourse are, in fact, referring to the same "observable patterns of social associations" (IH, p. 1).

26. See Webster's. A secondary but related meaning is: "an independent variable through functions of which may be expressed other variables as the co-ordinates of a locus."

speak different languages. For example, before the 1977 national conference of the National Organization of Women (NOW) in Houston, Texas, at a dinner party, unless subverted by host and/or hostess, males tended to drift toward males and females toward females. Since Houston, the subversion is more deliberately contrived, and conversational roles are beginning to show signs of equalization. The Decalogue, as Luther explores it, exhibits not only these parameters but also critical attention to the relations and responsibilities intrinsic to equality and inequality in and among social structures.

This description of social parameters underscores two considerations of crucial pertinence to social reality and to the bearing of the Commandments upon it. The first consideration has to do with the primacy of structures over ideology in human society. The second is that, with Peter Blau's help, we may have come in sight of that *tertium quid* beyond hierarchy and equality in our relations and associations with one another in a world made for being human in.

As to the first consideration, Peter Blau turns out to be a Calvinist in disguise. Or perhaps it would be more precise to call him a secular Calvinist; that is, a person who shares Calvin's humanism, but is unable to embrace the faith which informed that humanism. When Blau declares: "I am a structural determinist, who believes that the structures of objective social positions among which people are distributed exert more fundamental influences on social life than do cultural values and norms, including ultimately the prevailing values and norms" (IH, p. x), he is making exactly Calvin's point. Calvin got it, of course, from the Bible. But we need not insist upon a biblical byline — which Calvin would readily supply, but which Blau as a humanist finds superfluous. The common point is that the world in which people live and associate as human beings is already there and fit for being human in. The ultimately prevailing values and norms, howsoever diverse these may be, are under the criterion of what Freud called "the reality principle" and Calvin called "the secret counsel of God." Where human association is concerned — *tertium non datur!*

This does not mean that cultural values and norms are — either for Freud or for Calvin — human contrivances superimposed upon reality and designed either to repress or to adorn it. Thus to regard and practice them is the very core of heteronomy. Owing to this heteronomy, the structure and dynamics of the self are involved for Freud in "the psychopathology of every day life" and for Calvin in "a long and inextricable labyrinth" of the conscience from the snares of futility before the law and of the fear of liberty.[27] Freud's discovery of the unconscious, as Ann and Barry Ulanov have shown, has identified and liberated us from "the devices and desires of our own hearts,"[28] which project or reject values as checks upon reality or as escapes from it. "We have come to recognize," the Ulanovs write, "that our actions are inextricably intertwined with value systems that live far beneath the human surface, gathered around clusters of images and energy charges that deeply influence what we do and how we evaluate what we do."[29] As Calvin saw it, long before the Ulanovs and Freud, the human mind "is a perpetual factory of idols"[30] — not because it seeks ends and fashions values, but because it pursues this creativity in alienation from the Creator whose purpose and will and action set limits to chaos, that is, the power and bewitchment of unreality. Creation means that the world is "a spectacle of God's glory"[31] and the context within which values come to be, and become signs of the truth that sets us free (John 8:32). The tensions between the *mysterium electionis* and the *mysterium iniquitatis* are older in their persistence and in their discernment of reality than the debates between the structural and the cultural determinists seem to take account of. This insufficiency among "the wise and the intelligent" (Matt. 11:25; Luke 10:21) suggests that Calvin was nearer to Freud and Freud nearer to Calvin than any of their disciples first believed. From this potential "chicken and egg" cul-de-sac Luther's robust sense of the immediacy, depth, and ambiguity of human motivation and interaction happily delivers us. It is idle and diversionary speculation, as his strictures against human reason extravagantly but unmistakably note, to be preoccupied with determining which is first — structure or value, apperception or structure — or which are more important to the reality and prospect of a human future. For Luther — anticipating both Calvin and Freud — apperception and structure belong together. They are at once depth-derived and reciprocally related, and in their fusion responsible behavior takes shape.

The second consideration, significantly implicit in Peter Blau's de-

27. Calvin, *Institutes,* 3.19.6-7, pp. 838-39.

28. From the General Confession according to the Order for Morning Prayer, in *Book of Common Prayer* (New York: Thomas Nelson and Sons, 1929), p. 6.

29. Ann and Barry Ulanov, *Religion and the Unconscious* (Philadelphia: Westminster Press, 1975), p. 141. See the whole of chapter 8: "Ethics after the Unconscious."

30. Calvin, *Institutes,* 1.11.8, p. 108.

31. Calvin, *Institutes,* 1.5.5, p. 58.

scription of social parameters, leads us to a conceptuality beyond hierarchy and equality. The conceptuality takes account of the fundamental structural polarity that comparative sociological inquiry has been able to identify in terms of hierarchy and equality. What has happened in the course of Blau's analysis is that the dimensions have been exchanged, and in the exchange the terms of reference have been inverted. According to Blau,

> The two generic forms of [social] differentiation, under which the variety of its specific forms can be subsumed, are heterogeneity and inequality. Heterogeneity or horizontal differentiation refers to the distribution of a population among groups in terms of a nominal parameter [i.e., sex, race, religion, occupation, etc.]. Inequality or vertical differentiation refers to the status distribution in terms of a graduated parameter [i.e., income, wealth, education, power, age, etc.]. (IH, pp. 8-9)

Thus equality has been de-ideologized and become heterogeneity, and hierarchy has been radicalized as inequality. Since heterogeneity and inequality are the two basic structural forms of social differentiation, the critical question becomes: What is the humanizing relation between heterogeneity and inequality? It is precisely to this question that the relational sociology of Luther's exploration of the Decalogue offers the congruent reply.

CHAPTER THREE

The Structural Realism
of the Decalogue

Secular Individualism and Social Responsibility

The attempt to identify the humanizing relation between heterogeneity and inequality presupposes a fundamental and far-reaching conceptual move beyond hierarchy and equality. The critical issue is no longer the elimination of hierarchy so that inequality can be converted into equality. That course stands unmasked as the denial of structure by ideology. Nor is the critical issue the dissolution of inequality by the proliferation of heterogeneity. That course stands unmasked as the denial of structure by quantification. The Commandments have displaced the quantification of the common life by identifying the context and direction of *reciprocal responsibility.* "There is too much inequality," Blau declares, "but there cannot be too much heterogeneity."[1]

The move toward a conceptuality beyond hierarchy and equality involves a shift of perspective upon and valuation of the dynamics and direction of social interaction and mobility. The shift is as basic as that which marked the cleavage between a hierarchical and an egalitarian society during the last three centuries. It cannot be too strongly stressed, as Dumont has pointed out, that "among the great civilizations the world has known, the holistic type of society has been overwhelmingly predominant; indeed, it looks as if it had been the rule, the only excep-

---

1. Peter Blau, *Inequality and Heterogeneity* (New York: Free Press, 1977), p. x. Subsequent references will use the abbreviation IH.

tion being our modern civilization and its individualistic type of society."[2]

This curiously transitional society of modern civilization is characterized by the rejection of hierarchy in the name of equality, the rejection of subordinationism in the name of individualism, and the rejection of a vertically structured authority in the name of democratic constitutionalism and centralism (from Locke to Lenin). In this society, authority has been derived horizontally, either from a doctrine of the general will (Rousseau) or from a historical determinism (Marx). "Democracy breaks the chain," wrote Alexis de Tocqueville, "and severs every link."[3]

That the egalitarian individualism of the Western world should find its place in the social history of humankind as an episode and not as an epoch does not diminish its significant achievements. Among these achievements are the pursuit of "liberty and justice for all," the mastery of nature for human well-being, and the technological unification of the world. Yet these achievements must not blind us to the limitations of our socioethnicity. Among these are the priority that we assign to liberty over justice, to rights over responsibility, to privilege over poverty, to power over freedom, and, not least, to solitariness over society. The failures of a holistic society, hierarchically structured, to express its religious foundations and perspectives in the forging of adequately humanizing bonds between privilege and need, inequality and justice, liberty and responsibility, and, not least, authority and freedom are conspicuous. But these failures provide no warrant for persisting in the polarization of hierarchy and equality, of rights and responsibility, of authority and freedom, of the individual and society.

From Religion to Secularism

Such polarization diverts attention from the sobering consequences of the shift from hierarchical to egalitarian, from holistic to individualistic social structures. A revolution in values separates the modern world from tradi-

2. Louis Dumont, *From Mandeville to Marx* (Chicago: University of Chicago Press, 1977), p. 4. Subsequent references will use the abbreviation MM.

3. Alexis de Tocqueville, *Democracy in America*, trans. Henry Reeve (London, 1875), vol. 1, pp. 40-41; quoted in Louis Dumont, *Homo Hierarchicus* (Chicago: University of Chicago Press, 1970), p. 14. Subsequent references to *Homo Hierarchicus* will use the abbreviation HH.

tional societies (MM, p. 7). This revolution has meant a transition from the religious orientation of traditional societies to the secular orientation of modern society. According to Dumont, we can learn from a serious consideration of the caste system in India that a hierarchical society presupposes a relation to the whole that is religious in the most basic and persistent sense. This sense is the refusal to take itself for granted as given, and in thinking of itself, instead, as sustained and ordered in accordance with a transcendent ideal, upon which the society as a whole is dependent. In India, this ideal happens to pivot upon the distinction between the pure and impure, a distinction that functions as a cohesive social force, at once inviolable and flexible. Variants of this Brahmanic distinction in other societies are, for example, light and darkness in ancient Persia; eternity and temporality, soul and sense, in the Periclean Age; Creator and creation in the ancient Near East. The latter has, of course, been formatively transmitted to Western society through the piety and culture of ancient Israel and the history of Christianity.

The secular individualism of the modern world, by contrast, has been unable to find a sustaining matrix for the contractual nature of the bond between the individual and society. "Man will now draw from himself an order which is sure to satisfy him" (HH, p. 253). The order, however, has been, and still is, a house divided against itself: between Locke and Hobbes, between *The Wealth of Nations* and *Das Kapital*. This antinomy is both seed and fruit of another basic shift in the transition from hierarchical to egalitarian, from holistic to individualistic social structure. In the "traditional societies," Dumont writes, "the relations between men are more important, more highly valued, than the relations between things. This primacy is reversed in the modern type of society, in which the relations between men are subordinated to the relations between men and things" (MM, p. 5).

From Community to Individualism

For us, in the United States, there are awkward, even grievous echoes of this shift in our own history. When we recall that in Jefferson's first draft of the Declaration of Independence there stood the Lockian phrase: "life, liberty, and property," and that this phrase was altered in the debate in the Continental Congress to "life, liberty, and the pursuit of happiness," we can scarcely help being reminded of Tocqueville's report of his observation that "in the United States there was an alliance between the spirit of religion and the spirit of liberty."[4] Reflecting further upon this alliance, Tocqueville concludes: "For my own part I doubt whether man can support at the same time complete religious independence and entire public freedom. And I am inclined to think, that if faith be wanting in him, he must serve, and if he be free, he must believe."[5]

In the United States, as elsewhere in the Western world, it has turned out that the hierarchical assessment of wealth as immovable (i.e., land) was not only sharply distinguished from movable wealth (i.e., money and chattels), but actually subordinated to it. This is the case, despite John Locke's insistence that

> subordination goes overboard and with it the link it maintained between relationships among men and relations between men and inferior creatures. A split between the two is established, one could say, institutionalized. Between men and beasts, it is a matter of property or ownership: God has given the earth to the human species for appropriation — and homologously, man is . . . God's word and property. As for men, there is among them no inherent difference, no *hierarchy:* they are all free and equal in God's eyes, the more so since any difference in status would, in this system, tend to be coterminous with ownership. (MM, pp. 48-49; emphasis added)

In Locke's own words: "there cannot be supposed to be any such *Subordination* among us, that may Authorize us to destroy one another, as if we were made for another's uses, as the inferior ranks of Creatures are for ours."[6]

Let it be noted that Tocqueville's discernment of the link between faith and freedom is nearer to Luther's catechetical explanation of the responsibility for creation that freely follows from a humanizing faith in the Creator than it is to the weak Deism of Locke's ultimate reference to the Creator as the support for his curiously structured universe of equality and property without subordination. Patently, as Dumont remarks, "some kind of subordination is empirically necessary in political society, [but] such subordination can be built only on the unanimous consent of the

4. Tocqueville, vol. 1, pp. 40-41.

5. Tocqueville, vol. 2, p. 19; quoted in Dumont, HH, p. 19.

6. John Locke, *Two Treatises of Government,* rev. ed., ed. Peter Laslett (Cambridge: University of Cambridge Press, 1963), II, § 6, 11.16-19. Quoted in Dumont, MM, p. 49.

constituting members" (MM, p. 49). This requirement signals a remarkable abstractness, especially in the light of Luther's remarkably concrete account of social interaction. Similarly, Locke's account of the world is remarkably neat, as well as abstract, when compared to Luther's concrete and vivid account of the relations between Creator and creatures in explaining the first commandment.

According to Locke, the world is essentially a three-tier affair. The three tiers are (1) God, (2) humankind, and (3) inferior creatures (nature). Equality characterizes the human tier, while the relation between human beings and nature is one of "property," a subordination according to an order arranged by the Creator. For Locke, of course, human equality was entirely compatible with a minimal hierarchical structure of property. No contradiction obtained between equality and ownership.

But during the century and three-quarters that separated Locke from Marx, a remarkable inversion occurred, severing another link in the chain that democracy had cut. Human beings, as owners of private property, were subordinated both to social classes and to nature, regarded as the source of the primacy of production. Co-relatively, human beings as individuals were subordinated to a historical determinism of humanity as, and in, society.

Dumont recalls some pertinent passages from the *Grundrisse,* a work of Marx's later years. There Marx wrote:

> The point is rather that private interest is itself already a socially determined interest, which can only be achieved within the conditions established by society and through the means that society affords, and that it is thus linked to the reproduction of these conditions and means.[7]

These conditions and means are determined, according to Marx, by "a definite form of production [which] thus determines the forms of consumption, distribution, exchange, and *also the mutual relations between these various elements.* Of course, production *in its one-sided form* is in turn influenced by the other factors."[8] Furthermore, these conditions achieve the ultimate development and final emancipation of the individual, not *from* society (as with Mandeville, Locke, Adam Smith, and other eighteenth-century pioneers of the emerging correlation of economics and politics), but *in* and *through* society.

7. Karl Marx, *Grundrisse* (basic extracts), ed. and trans. David McLellan (New York: Harper Torchbooks, 1971), pp. 65-66. Quoted in Dumont, MM, p. 159.
8. Marx, p. 33. Quoted in Dumont, MM, p. 160.

The *Grundrisse* makes available to us the precision of the German language, which enables us to penetrate the force and subtlety of what is going on from Mandeville to Marx. The biological, empirical individual *(das Individuum)*, recognized as such by all the opponents of hierarchy in the name of equality, turns out to have been equipped with a very short life span. As the *Grundrisse* notes:

> The eighteenth century individuals, constituting the joint product of the dissolution of the feudal forms of society and of the new forces of production that had developed since the sixteenth century . . . is in the most literal sense a *zoon politikon*, not only a social animal, but an animal which can develop into an individual *(sich vereinzeln)* only in society. . . . All production is appropriation of nature by the individual within and through a definite form of society.[9]

In line with a startling passage early in *Das Kapital*, these brief excerpts let us in on the semantic secret of the whole story. Referring to primitive cooperation, Marx observes: "The individual *(das einzelne Individuum)* is yet as little detached from the umbilical cord of the tribe or community as the individual bee from a swarm of bees."[10]

Clearly, this passage surprisingly echoes Mandeville's *Fable*. Surprising also is the comparative linguistic illumination of a comparative sociological finding concerning the egalitarian rejection of subordination-ism.[11] The secret of egalitarian individualism, shared by the shapers of the modern world from Mandeville to Marx, from Locke to Lenin, lies hidden in the semantic subtlety that informs a German play on words. *Das Individuum* — that is, the biological, empirical individual — be-

9. Marx, pp. 17, 21. Quoted in Dumont, MM, pp. 163-65.

10. Karl Marx, *Das Kapital,* I, chap. 11, trans. from the German, 3rd ed. (Hamburg, 1883), p. 333; quoted in Dumont, MM, p. 164, and in Dumont, *Religion, Politics and History in India* (Paris: Mouton, 1920), pp. 134-35.

11. "Comparative sociological," in distinction from those ideological, ethical, sociopolitical analysts whose ill-concealed hostility to Marx's trenchant critique of the exploitation and class conflict of industrial society fueled the self-conceit that claimed the self-righteous clairvoyance that saw it all coming and thus immunized itself against what Ernst Troeltsch — himself contemporary with these soothsay-ers — had prophetically identified as "nichts Geringeres als das Problem des so-gennaen Historismus überhaupt" ("nothing less than the problem of Historism as such"). See *Der Historismus und seine Probleme* (n.p.: Scientia Aalen, 1961). Translation mine.

comes at the human level *der Mensch als Einzelner* or *der einzelne Mensch,* that is, the human being as one-of-a-kind, the single or solitary individual. This human individual is a creator of value, since he or she is at once a participator in and a representative of humanity as a whole. The *objective* individual thus becomes the *subjective* individual. The discrete individual becomes the single or solitary individual: *das Individuum* becomes *der einzelne Mensch.* Of this individual, Locke says that

> he and . . . Mankind are one Community. . . . And were it not for the corruption and viciousness of degenerate Men, there would be no need . . . that Men should separate from this great and natural Community and . . . combine into smaller and divided associations.[12]

By contrast, Adam Smith is positively ecstatic. For him, as Dumont summarizes it:

> Man is the creator of wealth, of value: man, and no longer nature. . . . This active man who creates value is the individual man in his living relation to nature, or the material world. Moreover, this natural relation between the individual and things gets somehow reflected in the egoistic exchange of things between men. And this exchange, in turn, albeit a substitute for labor, imposes its law on labor and allows the progress of labor. As with property in Locke, we see here the elevation of the individual subject, of man as "self-loving," laboring-and-exchanging, who through his toil, his interest, and his gain works for the common good, for the wealth of nations. (MM, p. 97)

"Somehow," indeed! Locke's bow to the Creator has now become an "Invisible Hand." The Deism that replaced the agnosticism of the *Philosophes* is on the way to atheism. To be sure, even in Smith, Deism lingers on in *The Theory of Moral Sentiments.* It does not matter that *The Wealth of Nations* takes a markedly different fork in the road. There, the creator of wealth, whom Locke had already shifted from God to the individual participant in the essence of humanity, becomes the creator of more wealth, of the "substance of value," as Marx said of Smith more than once. This "Luther of political economy," as Marx calls Adam Smith,[13] had identified

---

12. Locke, II, par. 128. Quoted in Dumont, MM, p. 58.
13. Marx, *Grundrisse,* pp. 37ff.; and earlier in the 1844 manuscripts, published as Karl Marx, *Early Texts,* ed. David McLellan (Oxford: Oxford University Press,

increase of wealth, or surplus value through exchange. It was indeed "surplus value" — or *Mehrwert*, in Marx's language. Marx found *The Wealth of Nations* epoch making, not so much in its categorial precision and thoroughgoing analysis, but especially in its analysis of the dynamics and components of production. He made *Mehrwert* the copestone of his radical criticism of Smith's account of the production relations of human society. In the end of the day, these relations in their capitalistic context effectively deprived labor of its rightful compensation for the wealth it had created. Labor had become "surplus value," the inescapable corollary of the "value surplus" (profit) to which the increase of wealth inevitably led.[14] The "Invisible Hand" has been unmasked and replaced by historical materialism and its dialectical development. As a result, the individual has found the way back into society. The hierarchical order relating the original status to the exchange status of the human creators of increase of wealth has been replaced by the priority that Marx assigned to society over the individual, to history over nature, as the human dimension of nature.

But just as the egalitarian rejection of subordinationism had been unable to dispose of its *bête noire* altogether, so the biological, empirical individual *(das Individuum)* — which at the human level becomes the solitary individual, the creator of value *(der einzelne Mensch)* — now becomes, along the way and at the end of the road, the isolated individual *(der vereinzelte Einzelne)*. The German nuance, differentiating between *Einzel* and *vereinzelt*, between the single or solitary and the isolated individual, suggests an individual not only separated in solitariness from the human community, as that community has been separated from nature. The German nuance penetrates more deeply and subtly into the bone and marrow of egalitarian individualism and finds there an individual so encapsulated in solitariness, so turned inward upon the self, as to be not only isolated from the human community and from nature but also isolated in the self from the self. The world that the egalitarian individual set out to conquer, to make new, and to dominate now binds that individual in a prison of his or her own making. *Faust* has become *The Sorcerer's Apprentice*.

1961), pp. 119-20. Quoted in Dumont, MM, p. 84. According to Dumont, Marx borrowed the phrase from Engels.

14. Dumont's account of this development, and of the relation between Smith and Marx, is particularly instructive. It has altered my previous understanding of the relations between Smith and Marx by providing a fresh perception of their kinship and divergence. See esp. MM, chap. 6; and the appendix on "Value and Labor in Adam Smith," MM, pp. 189-204.

Reciprocal Responsibility and the Decalogue

The road from Mandeville to Marx thus leaves us with the discovery that the distinction between the hive and the anthill is a distinction without a difference. Along that route, the two basic structural forms of social differentiation — whether as hierarchy and equality or as inequality and heterogeneity — are unable to express and sustain human community. Missing is a matrix of meaning and value, of individual motivation and social interaction, within which private and public differentiation and reciprocity are generative of the commitment, responsibility, and trust required for being and staying human in the world. At the center, where, in Yeats's phrase, "the best lack all conviction, while the worst / are full of passionate intensity," there is a deepening and widening chasm between apperception and structure.[15] In the void, a disjunction is increasingly discernible between the self-evidence of the meaning and value of being human and the pathways and patterns of social interrelations and inter-actions, through which the experience of being human takes persuasive and fulfilling shape.

How *do* apperception of the human and the humanity of human structures reciprocally intersect, so that meaning and value and exchange and power[16] give human shape to human life? With this question, the road from Mandeville to Marx approaches the intersection of another road along which the Decalogue has been traveling from disarray and disregard toward the unlikeliest of discoveries. The discovery is that, at the very center of that intersection, the disjunction between humane apperception and humanizing structures is overtaken by the prospect of a formative conjunction between conceptuality beyond hierarchy and equality and a liberating dynamic of reciprocal responsibility. It could be that at that intersection *Pluto's Republic*[17] reenters the orbit of *Plato's Republic,* and a human future may be glimpsed in a fresh commingling of "the two cities,

---

15. W. B. Yeats, "The Second Coming," in *The Collected Poems of W. B. Yeats* (New York: Macmillan, 1951), pp. 184-85. See also my book *The Transfiguration of Politics* (New York: Harper & Row, 1975), p. xi.

16. The phrase "exchange and power" comes from the title of an earlier book by Peter Blau, which in retrospect is preparatory and intrinsic to inequality and heterogeneity, and further confirms the analysis being attempted in these pages. See Peter Blau, *Exchange and Power in Social Life* (New York: Wiley, 1964).

17. Peter Medawar, *Pluto's Republic* (New York: Oxford University Press, 1982).

the earthly and the heavenly,"[18] and "from the time of Abraham to the end of the world."[19]

Meanwhile, the road from Mandeville to Marx has brought us under an ultimately unbearable tension between two coordinates. One is the modern innovation of politics and economics; the other is religion and society, representing "the continuity with the traditional universe that remains in the modern universe" (MM, p. 22).

We are on the threshold of a breakthrough beyond hierarchy and equality. Two brief passages from *Homo Hierarchicus* underline with particular persuasiveness and clarity the focus and prospect opening before us. The task and opportunity bequeathed to us by "traditional societies" are to take due and creative account of

> hierarchy and complementarity: one ranks rather than excludes, and complementarity permits both, the loosest and broadest integration of extraneous elements. In fact the process takes various forms which must be distinguished. But all tend to ensure a certain permanence of form by integration of the extraneous element. (HH, p. 193)

At the same time, this task and opportunity must be taken up with due and creative attention to "the modern revolution."

> As against the societies which believed themselves to be natural, here is the society which wants to be rational. Whilst the "natural" society was hierarchized, finding its rationality in setting itself as a whole within a vaster whole, and was unaware of the "individual," the "rational" society on the other hand, recognizing only the individual, i.e. seeing universality, or reason, only in the particular [person], places itself under the standard of equality and is unaware of itself as a hierarchized whole. In a sense, the "leap from history into freedom" has already been made, and we live in a realized Utopia. (HH, p. 253)

As these passages suggest, the threshold on which we stand is the possibility of a fresh consideration of hierarchy as a liberating structure coordinate with inequality; and of equality — as the inescapable structural opposite of hierarchy — as a liberating structure coordinate with heterogeneity.

18. Augustine, *The City of God*, trans. Marcus Dods (New York: Random House, 1950), bk. 11, chap. 1.

19. Augustine, bk. 18, chap. 1.

These coordinates mean the transfiguration of hierarchy as inequality and of equality as heterogeneity. In consequence, inequality and heterogeneity are the determinate structures that — in their concreteness and flexibility, their order and reciprocal adaptability — exhibit a functional congruity with the reciprocal responsibility, exhibited and explored in Brother Martin's account of the concrete human possibility and sense of the "two tablets of Moses." At issue is a society lived in and experienced as human, and being made fit for being human in.

If we today can detach ourselves sufficiently from the ideological sound and fury that obscure the prospect of a humanizing relation between inequality and heterogeneity, it may be given to us to discover that in Luther's account of what the Commandments state and involve there is indeed a middle term between inequality and heterogeneity upon which the accent falls. That middle term may be identified as *reciprocal responsibility*. Luther's catechetical exploration of the Decalogue offers us a description of the way along which the human meaning of human life is to be discerned and practiced. The Catechism refers, in Peter Blau's terms, "to a structure of *social* relations among subunits in a society," not to "a structure of *logical* relations of propositions in a theoretical model" (IH, p. 2). Heteronomy and individualism are intrinsically simply unreal. Prescriptive laws for living by rules are banished both from religion and from society. The Commandments are neither *directives for* nor *norms of* living on God's terms in a world that God has purposed for human wholeness and fulfillment. In such a world, the Commandments are indicators of pathways and patterns along which the ultimate and the penultimate dimensions of human existence (in Bonhoeffer's phrase) concretely intersect, and through which the freedom to be human simply happens.[20] Once again we are reminded that "the law is the form of the Gospel."[21]

20. See the exploratory and groundbreaking discussion of "The Last Things and the Things Before Last," in Dietrich Bonhoeffer, *Ethics,* ed. Eberhard Bethge, trans. Neville Horton Smith (New York: Macmillan, 1965), pp. 120-42.

21. In Barth's own words: "Ethics as the doctrine of God's command explains the law as the form of the gospel, i.e., as the human experience of being made whole through God's election which has come upon humankind"and further to the point: "The command of God sets humankind free" (*Die Kirchliche Dogmatik,* II/2 [Zurich: Evangelischer Verlag, A.G., 1942], par. 36, 1, p. 564, and par. 37, 3, p. 650, my translation; see also the English translation of the *Church Dogmatics* by G. W. Bromiley, II/2 [Edinburgh: T. & T. Clark, 1957], pp. 509, 586).

Apperception, Structure, and Responsibility

The threshold of possibility at which we have arrived returns us to this question: How *do* an apperception of the human and the concrete structures of social interaction reciprocally and responsibly intersect? Given Brother Martin's participation in and perspectives beyond the ideological findings of an instructive comparative macrosociological analysis, the answer to this question may be drawn from the structural realism of the Decalogue. This realism illuminates a reciprocal pressure of apperception upon structure and of structure upon apperception in human experience and action. This pressure also generates and intensifies the question of responsibility for what being and staying human in the world elementally require. It is to this reciprocal pressure that Luther's exploration of the Decalogue chiefly addresses itself. In so doing, it points us toward the ways and patterns through which the future coming our way shapes the reality of every human present. Indeed, the discovery, with Luther, of the structural realism of the Decalogue could well be the "zero-option" to George Orwell's apocalyptic vision of 1984.[22]

The Orwellian vision invites a reprise of Shakespeare's *Troilus and Cressida*. The immediate contexts of each are vastly different. Nor is any causal connection between Orwell and Shakespeare implied. It is the office of seers, however, to point to the perils and the prospects of a human future, according to their appointed times and seasons; and through the faithfulness of each to the office to which they have been summoned, a kinship of discernment emerges. In this sense, Shelley has correctly discerned that "the poets are the unacknowledged legislators of the world."[23] It is in this sense that an extended recollection of what Odysseus said to Agamemnon may unfold to us certain perennial reciprocities of the structural realism of the Decalogue, which acquire particular urgency and force in the social and cultural transition under way, owing to the transfiguration of hierarchy and equality as inequality and heterogeneity.

These perennial reciprocities exhibit (1) the pressure of apperception upon structure, which gives rise to the question of freedom; (2) the pressure of structure upon apperception, which gives rise to the question of power; and (3) responsibility, as the nexus of freedom and power, which

22. George Orwell, *Nineteen Eighty-four* (New York: Harcourt Brace Jovanovich, 1949).

23. The concluding sentence of Percy Bysshe Shelley, *A Defense of Poetry.*

gives rise to the question of justice. Freedom, power, and justice are — as it were — underwritten by the Decalogue and bear witness to the indispensability of the Decalogue to the possibility and the prospect of a human future. A brief consideration of each of these questions must suffice to carry the present discovery of the Decalogue sufficiently beyond the disregard and disarray that have deprived the present time of access to it, and to open the way for another look at "the Two Tablets of Moses" themselves.

A Reprise from Troilus and Cressida

Regarding our present discussion, a close consideration of the text of Shakespeare's play *The History of Troilus and Cressida* leads us to take note of three substantive and crucial matters that Shakespeare has to teach us.

The first is that there is an order in the cosmos — alike to nature and to human community — which signals a covenantal design according to which part and whole, in reciprocal interaction, express place and function, dependency and difference, identity and integrity. Degree is a sign that order neither controls nor governs the design; the design shapes and governs order. It is the office of order to facilitate the motions and the movements through which the parts reciprocally further the whole, and the whole reciprocally steadies and frees the parts for their appointed purposes.

> The heavens themselves, the planets, and this center
> Observe degree, priority, and place,
> Insisture, course, proportion, season, form,
> Office, and custom, in all line of order.
> And therefore is the glorious planet Sol
> In noble eminence enthron'd and spher'd
> Amidst the other; whose med'cinable eye
> Corrects the ill aspects of planets evil,
> . . . .
>
> . . . . . But when the planets
> In evil mixture to disorder wander,
> What plagues and what portents, what mutiny,
> What raging of the sea, shaking of earth,
> Commotion in the winds, frights, changes, horrors,
> Divert and crack, rend and deracinate

> The unity and married calm of states
> Quite from their fixture!
>
> (Act 1, sc. 3, ll. 85-101)[24]

These purposes transfigure reciprocity as responsibility, so that the order of freedom for fulfillment becomes from each according to ability to each according to need.

The second crucial matter concerns the specialty of rule. This specialty is responsibility, not power; more precisely, it is power at the service of responsibility. When rule *subverts* its specialty by aims and ends other than responsibility, degree usurps its appointed purpose, takes control of order, and sows the seeds of its own captivity to disorder and to dissolution. Power has violated responsibility, and communities are converted into hives.

> How could communities,
> Degrees in schools, and brotherhoods in cities,
> Peaceful commerce from dividable shores,
> The primogenity and due of birth,
> Prerogative of age, crowns, scepters, laurels,
> But by degree stand in authentic place?
>
> (ll. 103-8)

When rule *ignores* its specialty by abdicating its responsibility for power, degree dissolves in discord, and discord oscillates between apathy toward and frenzy for power.

> Take but degree away, untune that string,
> And hark what discord follows. Each thing meets
> In mere oppugnancy. The bounded waters
> Should lift their bosoms higher than the shores
> And make a sop of all this solid globe.
>
> (ll. 109-13)

Power has refused responsibility, and communities are converted into anthills.

> Strength should be lord of imbecility,
> And the rude son should strike his father dead;

---

24. Quotations from *Troilus and Cressida* are taken from *The Complete Works of Shakespeare*, 3rd ed., ed. David Bevington (Glenview, IL: Scott, Foresman, 1980).

> Force should be right, or rather, right and wrong,
> Between whose endless jar justice resides,
> Should lose their names, and so should justice too.
>
> (ll. 114-18)

The third substantive and crucial matter has to do with justice. The disjunction of power from responsibility and of responsibility from power exposes justice as the talisman of both degree and order, and as the criterion of power purposed for responsibility. Thus justice is at once the concrete starting point for doing what is right and the decisive boundary dividing right from wrong and wrong from right. As such, justice is the warrant for the ultimate indispensability and the immediate expendability of the distinction between right and wrong to the human meaning of individual and social interaction. In turn, the distinction between right and wrong in its indispensability and expendability is the warrant for the ultimate and the immediate inviolability of justice in human action, both private and public. In short, justice is the ultimate and the immediate clue to and criterion of the responsible use of power. The range and depth and urgency of this bond between power and justice, in its bearing upon "the unity and married calm of states," as also upon that "peace" which "is the tranquility of order,"[25] are eloquently focused in the penultimate lines of Ulysses' address. In them, the bond between responsibility for power and the power of responsibility is movingly discerned as engraved in humane apperception. If that bond is violated or ignored, or just plain absent,

> Then every thing includes itself in power,
> Power into will, will into appetite;
> And appetite, an universal wolf,
> So doubly seconded with will and power,
> Must make perforce an universal prey,
> And last eat up himself.
>
> (ll. 119-24)

These lines carry us almost headlong into the orbit of the cosmic and social perceptions and forebodings of the Orwellian vision. The kinship seems to say that the disjunction of power and responsibility has reached the catastrophic edge of dehumanization. The subordination of persons to things and of things to management and control has converted the

25. Augustine, bk. 19, chap. 13.

primeval Garden into an animal farm. The mystery of language has become the cacophany of speech. The brain, once the receptacle and vessel of the discovery and communication of the primacy of soul, has become the model of the cybernetic technocratization of life. Knowledge is being transmuted into information, and information is computerized into power.

The speed, range, magnetism, and boundless expectations from — if not confidence in — these developments is soberingly signaled by a cover article in *Harvard Magazine.* Referring to Dr. Anthony Oettinger, professor of applied mathematics and of informative resources policy at Harvard, the cover title reads: "He's got the whole wired world in his hand."[26] What is sobering about this signal is not its unclear and present danger as a revolutionary extension of the industrial revolution. A revolution can be the future's way of breaking in upon the present so as to shape the past for human freedom and fulfillment. The sobriety of the signal is occasioned rather by the ambiguity of its promise and peril. One way of identifying this ambiguity is to note that, together with his colleagues and students, the one who has "got the whole wired world in his hand" is "out to improve the information available about the information age, and by so doing, reduce the casualties and damage of the post-industrial revolution" (p. 36). Another way is to note the fresh and fundamental exploration of the ageless question of the relation between knowledge and power. "To this day we don't know how the human brain takes an utterance like 'Fruit flies like a banana' to determine it must mean this or that, and certainly nobody has figured out how to get a computer to *disambiguate* things like that" (p. 39; emphasis added). The extension of the frontiers of knowledge is intrinsic to the curiosity that is basic to human apperception. The fascination of knowledge is irresistible. But the companion of this fascination is the twin temptation to manipulate knowledge for and by power and to disregard the question of limit that is intrinsic to the reciprocity between knowledge and power. In a surprising modernization of the *Zweireichenlehre,* the experts are quoted as saying: "Writing legislation is not the knowledge business, it's the power business." Almost straight out of Luther, the assessment continues: "We think those businesses are kind of mutually exclusive. If we had too much influence, we'd lose our impartiality and be useless as suppliers of information" (p. 41).

Perhaps the most sobering identification of the ambiguity of the promise and peril of the information age is to note the ambiguity of its vision.

---

26. *Harvard Magazine* 84, 5 (May-June 1982): 36-42. Subsequent references will be given parenthetically in the text.

"We're talking about areas in which there is a great deal of controversy and obscurity," Professor Oettinger says. "That's why the insane-seeming breadth of the program. If you focus on one narrow area, you lose track of the fact that all of the action is *between* the classical areas. We've seen a lot of folks make terrible errors by failing to have peripheral vision" (p. 38; emphasis in the original). Agreed! But suppose the peripheral vision is detached from, or tangential to, or astigmatic of the central vision! It could be that to have "the whole wired world" in one's hand is the likeliest and safest guarantee of keeping peripheral vision peripheral to the center, which is indispensable for identifying the light in the darkness. But in face of the "growing importance [of] the long term implications of a major shift in our notion of literacy" (p. 42), the vividly clever shift from "the whole *wide* world in his hand" to "the whole *wired* world in his hand" is more than a journalistic transmutation of reverence into function. An ominous Freudian slip has occurred, unmasking the cultural and social extension of the dehumanizing alliance between *Faust* and *The Sorcerer's Apprentice*.

The Pressure of Apperception upon Structure: The Question of Freedom

The slip means that the unintended disclosure is not unintentional. Beneath the threshold of intentionality, there is an apperceptive awareness of selfhood that precedes and preempts the passion for the power of knowledge through the passionate claim to knowledge as power. The Promethean myth is often simplistically understood and espoused as the usurpation of the power of knowledge, rooted in the passion for knowledge as power. But this reading overlooks a more fundamental passion of Prometheus. Unlike the Tower of Babel (Gen. 11:1-9), attempted and constructed as a usurpation of the power of knowledge for the sake of a shift in the control of knowledge as power from divine to human jurisdiction, Prometheus's passion was directed toward the availability and accessibility of fire for human need and fulfillment. In short, the rash pride of Prometheus seized power for the sake of freedom and justice; the "Babelites" seized power for the sake of domination and control.

The mythological record of the human story thus points to an unyielding pressure of apperception upon structure. The dynamics of selfhood are insistently in pursuit of the congruence of identity and integrity that brings recognition and reliability liberatingly together. Self-awareness and self-acceptance converge upon a common point: the discovery of who one is through what one says and does. To arrive at this discovery is to find oneself called to be — and to receive and relate to a world of persons, places, and things — as and where one is, and as one is coming to be, wherever one is. Around this discovery cluster the ineluctable, sometimes fascinating and sometimes frightening, sometimes bewildering and sometimes beguiling questions of origin and destiny, of point and purpose, of promise and threat, of desire and default, of limit and limitlessness, of responsibility and guilt. Why here and not there? Why now and not then? Why me, just as I am, and not some other whom I would have preferred to be?

This is the stuff of apperception, the mystery of being and belonging, of going from somewhere to somewhere, which the discovery and acceptance of who we are as we are confirms. This confirmation is the height and length and breadth and depth of what we have always known, without knowing how we know it, and of what we bring to the being and doing of who we are in a world that shapes us for giving shape to it.

The two most telling indicators of the mystery of dynamics of selfhood are liturgy and language, in that order. *Liturgy* signals the Creator's celebrative peroration of creation as the prelude to the creature's receiving with thankfulness and praise what is there beforehand. Liturgy gives to sounds and acts the power to point to the ultimate in the immediate, the unique in the common, the memorable in the forgettable, the trustworthy in the transient, the ties that bind amid the singularities that separate. *Language* gives the shape of words to sounds and meaning to acts in the power of self-identifying giving and receiving self-communication. In and through the shared similarities and diversities of discovering and doing who and what we are, liturgy and language are the chief tutors and nourishers of human apperception.

Perhaps the most vivid and concrete instance of the conjunction of liturgy and language in the expression and nurture of apperception is the experience of children at play and learning to speak and to understand language. Indeed, they understand language before they speak it. In play, children relate to each other in unself-conscious spontaneity. Imagination and eagerness involve them in a game with an abandon that signals a conjunction of freedom and order, of apperception and structure, unique to childhood. The pressure of freedom upon order, of apperception upon structure, exhibits, on the one hand, the priority of freedom over order, of apperception over structure, and on the other hand, the instrumentality of order to freedom, of structure to apperception. Indeed, children at play exhibit in a basic and unambiguous way the reality and centrality of freedom in the formation of human identity and integrity through participation and interaction. Even the terrifying cruelty of children at their play is but the grim companion of the unself-conscious abandon that spells out freedom in the give-and-take of discovering who one is in what one does. More terrifying than the hurt inflicted by such cruelty is the vulnerability of cruelty to transmutation into power as childhood moves toward maturity.

More awesome and wondrous than children at play is the mystery of identity through otherness signaled by the phenomenon of language. The transmutation of sound into speech, of speech into names, of names into the recognition of otherness in things and persons, and, suddenly or gradually, the liberating move from the "otherness" to the "who-ness" of the self is surely an awesome experience of the depth and range of the pressure of apperception upon structure rooted in freedom. Of course, the world, with all its multiplicities and diversities, its boundaries and arrangements, is always there beforehand. But the pronominal sequence from identification to identity — from "that-me" to "you-me," to "me-you," to "me-I" — is the cuneiform of freedom designed to guard and to extend the priority and place of being human in and for the sake of a nonhuman world, and to keep the reciprocities at the service of responsibility. This is why "unless you turn round and become like children, you will never enter the kingdom of Heaven" (Matt. 18:3, NEB), and why "it would be better for [one] to be thrown into the sea with a millstone round his neck than to cause one of these little ones to stumble" (Luke 17:2, NEB).

By these criteria, Lewis Carroll would certainly have entered the kingdom of heaven long since, and would never have been endangered by a long sea mile by a millstone around his neck. In *Alice's Adventures in Wonderland,* the wonder of the discovery of identity and integrity born of apperception comes out this way:

> Alice . . . went on talking: "Dear, dear! How queer everything is to-day! And yesterday things went on just as usual. I wonder if I've been changed in the night? Let me think: was I the same when I got up this morning? I almost think I can remember feeling a little different. But if I'm not the same, the next question is, Who in the world am I? Ah, *that's* the great puzzle!" . . .

> Alice was more and more puzzled, but she thought there was no use in saying anything more till the Pigeon had finished.
> "As if it wasn't trouble enough hatching the eggs," said the Pigeon; "but I must be on the look-out for serpents night and day! . . ."

"But I'm *not* a serpent, I tell you!" said Alice. "I'm a — I'm a — "

"Well! *What* are you?" said the Pigeon. "I can see you're trying to invent something!"

"I — I'm a little girl," said Alice, rather doubtfully, as she remembered the number of changes she had gone through. . . .

It was so long since she had been anything near the right size, that it felt quite strange at first; but she got used to it in a few minutes, and began talking to herself, as usual: " . . . How puzzling all these changes are! I'm never sure what I'm going to be, from one minute to another! However, I've got back to my right size: the next thing is, to get into that beautiful garden — how *is* that to be done, I wonder?"[27]

Much later, in a report on happenings that occurred much earlier but that continue "for the time being" to raise the question of freedom through notations on the pressure of apperception upon structure, W. H. Auden describes it this way:

For the garden is the only place there is, but you will not find it
Until you have looked for it everywhere and found nowhere
        that is not a desert;
The miracle is the only thing that happens, but to you it will
        not be apparent,
Until all events have been studied and nothing happens
        that you cannot explain;
And life is the destiny you are bound to refuse until you
        have consented to die. . . .

Therefore, see without looking, hear without listening,
        breathe without asking:
The Inevitable is what will seem to happen to you purely by chance;
The Real is what will strike you as really absurd;
Unless you are certain you are dreaming, it is certainly a dream
        of your own;
Unless you exclaim — 'There must be some mistake' — you
        must be mistaken.[28]

27. Lewis Carroll, *Alice's Adventures in Wonderland* and *Through the Looking Glass* (Harmondsworth, Middlesex, England: Puffin Books, 1976), pp. 36, 74-76.

28. W. H. Auden, "For the Time Being: A Christmas Oratorio," in *The Collected Poems of W. H. Auden* (New York: Random House, 1945), p. 412.

The Pressure of Structure upon Apperception: The Question of Power

In Wonderland — which is the garden — the priorities are straight, howsoever topsy-turvy and out of shape they seem. It is when the pressure of structure upon apperception obscures the mystery, meaning, and promise of freedom that a sobering reversal shows itself. The priority of freedom over power begins to give way before the priority of power over freedom. Among the persistent symptoms of the shift are the importance assigned to measure over myth, to causality over mystery, to becoming over being, to control over surprise, and to the tested and the repeatable over the unexpected and the unique, in the determination of what is really going on, and, therefore, worth it.

A particularly vivid case in point unveiled itself to my surprise and consternation in the course of a conversation with a recognized authority on data processing and the communications revolution currently permeating and pervading our lives as human beings. The chairperson of the department of electronics and computer engineering at Rensselaer Polytechnic Institute was virtuostically knowledgeable and forceful in his command of the field and in his capacity for persuasive presentation. By his own admission, he was so passionately involved in and committed to the significance of his research, teaching, discoveries, and verifications that he invited his listeners to interrupt his remarks for clarification if the velocity and voluminosity of his description and analysis should momentarily have transformed him into a computer himself. Expressing admiration for his competence and persuasiveness, I ventured to ask whether he was in any wise disquieted by the vision of the future that he had unfolded. Instantly, and unhesitatingly, a credo of confidence and conviction took the shape of three crisply stated grounds for the denial of any disquiet whatsoever. "No!" came the reply. "It's here! It's progress! It's good!"[29] As a verbal symphony of the complexity and contrapuntality of the human condition, the three articles of the Nicene Creed seemed at more than a little remove from the computorial creed just expressed. Howsoever regrettable their distance may be, the Nicene articles have at least nurtured across the years the wisdom of resistance to simplistic demystification. Meanwhile, the

29. This conversation took place in the course of a conference on faith and science, under the auspices of the Synod of the Northeast of the United Presbyterian Church (U.S.A.), 15 July 1981, at the Stony Point Conference Center, Stony Point, New York, following a lecture by Dr. Lester Gerhardt.

professor of electronics and computer engineering deserves a memorable place in the human story as a pioneer in the wiring of us all in a proleptically wholly wired world. The descendants of Esau are ever with us, prepared to barter away our human birthright (see Gen. 25:29-34). Or could it be that wired lentils can and will satisfy the famished?

Primordially, however, power is intrinsic to the structures that define the possibilities and the limits of apperception. Power is at once the catalyst and the nemesis of the freedom intrinsic to the apperceptive awareness of the identity and integrity of selfhood. Power is the *catalyst* of freedom because it sets the limits in response to which and within which the time and space for the discovery of "who-ness" in differentiation from "what-ness" are made room for. To put it another way, power is the way otherness comes through to selfhood as the bearer of its human identity and integrity. Power is the *nemesis* of the freedom intrinsic to the apperception of being and doing what is human because power is possessed of a mysterious dynamic. This dynamic converts the limits that evoke and make room for apperceptive selfhood into the limitlessness that mistakes the domination, control, and manipulation by the self of what is other than the self for the freedom of the self to be itself. The paradox is that the discovery and the destruction of selfhood are apperceptively linked in the mysterious conjunction of freedom and power. *Eritis sicut deus!* (Gen. 3:5). Apart from power, the apperceptive discovery of freedom for human identity, integrity, and fulfillment would dissolve in anonymity, apathy, and anarchy. Conjoined with power, the apperceptive discovery of the freedom to be and to do what is human in the world is vulnerable to the overextension of narcissism or the tyrannical manipulation and domination of all that is other than the self. *Peer Gynt* will have homoousially joined the alliance of *Faust* and *The Sorcerer's Apprentice.* The pressure of apperception upon structure and of structure upon apperception brings the question of freedom and power to a liberating point. What, it may now be asked, is the humanizing point of the intersection between freedom and power in the experience of being and doing what is human in the world?

Responsibility as the Nexus of Freedom and Power: The Question of Justice

The answer to the question just raised is *responsibility.* Responsibility is the nexus of freedom and power in the experience of being and doing what is human in the world.

Responsibility is rooted in humane apperception — that is, in what persons, without knowing how or why they know, simply bring to the world on their own initiative, elicited by the pressure of what is there. Liturgy and language both signal this primordial response to the givenness of the world. Paleoanthropologically considered, the finding is that selves — as primitive animism makes plain — in differentiation from inanimate and other animate others in the world as experienced, do not merely react, they respond. In the course of responding, a discovery is made that selves are at once involved in and called to account for the response that is being or has been made. Involvement and accountability are thus the twin components of the freedom that is intrinsic to the identity and integrity of being human in the world. Theologically considered, in a world experienced as creation, the world and the freedom and room to be human in it are received as gifts from the Creator whose will and purposes shape the involvement and accountability of human creatures. These creatures are called into existence as "little less than God," crowned "with glory and honor," and given "dominion over the works of [God's] hands" (Ps. 8:5-6, RSV).

The freedom to respond to and take responsibility for the identity and integrity of being human is companioned by power. Power is the gift of the possibility, energy, and ability to respond to and take responsibility for the freedom to be human in the world. The power to be involved and to be both accountable and held to account is thus the corollary of the freedom to be human. The critical conjunction, or nexus, of freedom and power in being and doing what is human in the world is the recognition, acceptance, and praxis of responsibility. The conjunction is indispensable to the experience, identity, integrity, involvement, and accountability that are intrinsic to humane apperception. The conjunction is critical because, apart from or in disregard of responsibility, the dynamics of self and otherness in reciprocal interaction overrun and overrule the limits that freedom sets to power and power sets to freedom. Apart from or in disregard of responsibility, involvement is sundered from accountability, accountability becomes its own law, power assumes priority and precedence over freedom, human apperception and humanizing structures are deprived of their liberating congruence, and dehumanization becomes the disorder of the day. Then "the earth endures," but "seedtime and harvest, cold and heat, summer and winter, day and night" not only "shall not cease" (Gen. 8:22), but they succeed one another with meaningless fatality and dehumanizing circularity.

Responsibility, thus catapulted out of the orbit of freedom and into the orbit of self-destructive power, is poised upon the nearer edge of the descent into irresponsibility. The question of setting right what is not right in the world is on the move from penultimate options to the immediacy of ultimate decisiveness. The moment of truth has reached the point of no return as the humanization or dehumanization of the future coming our way can no longer be delayed or deferred. The question of setting right what is not right in the world is the question of justice. The maxim of *suum cuique* (Cicero) and the winsome reasonableness of justice as fairness (Rawls) have been overtaken by events.[30] Apperception has become the prisoner of structure; freedom is captive to the power to co-opt. Beyond the hive and the anthill, the prospect of a human future has been seduced and reduced by the tedium and terror of a society serviced by corporate management and control. As Augustine tellingly and eloquently sums up the shattering experience,

> Justice being taken away, then, what are kingdoms but great robberies? For what are the robberies themselves but little kingdoms? The band itself is made up of men; it is ruled by the authority of a prince; it is knit together by the pact of the confederacy; the booty is divided by the law agreed upon. If, by the admittance of abandoned men, this evil increases to such a degree that it holds places, fixes abodes, takes possession of cities, and subdues peoples, it assumes the more plainly the name of a kingdom, because the reality is now manifestly conferred on it, not by the removal of covetousness, but by the addition of impunity.[31]

This is, of course, the praxis of atheism — whatever the theoretical and rhetorical state of the matter may be. The sign is the effective absence of justice, which signifies both the effective absence of "the one true God" and the effective disjunction of faith from obedience and of obedience from faith. With comparable impunity, the effective absence of justice penetrates the Kremlin and Foggy Bottom. It erupts in Angola and Afghanistan, in Nicaragua and El Salvador, in Iran and Iraq, in Judaea and Samaria, in South Africa and Argentina. "For he cannot be free from infelicity who worships Felicity as a goddess, and forsakes God, the giver

---

30. The Ciceronian maxim *suum cuique* ("to each his due") may be found in *De legibus* 1.6.18. See John Rawls, *A Theory of Justice* (Cambridge: Harvard University Press, 1971). See also my book *The Transfiguration of Politics*, pp. 250-59.

31. Augustine, bk. 6, chap. 4.

of felicity; just as he cannot be free from hunger who licks a painted loaf of bread, and does not buy it of the man who has a real one."[32]

On the other hand, justice being present, then the possibility, patterns, and prospects of the regeneration of responsibility are available on every hand. For justice is the sign and signal of the responsibility of freedom for power and of power for freedom. The setting right of what is not right in the world is the liberating resource that human apperception brings to the structural reshaping of inequality toward the enlargement of heterogeneity. Conversely, the setting right of what is not right in the world is the clue both to the *inviolability* of apperception by structure and to the *viability* of structures permeated by human apperception. On this "tight-rope" (Nietzsche), the humanization of inequality through the enlargement of heterogeneity happens, as the future coming our way gives human shape to our present, lest it be in the way.

The Structural Realism of the Decalogue

The structural realism of the Decalogue is its power to bring rubric and reality together in the nurture of humane apperception. The reality is a world created, purposed, covenanted, and structured for human fulfillment. The rubric identifies the reciprocity between God's humanizing will, purpose, and action in and for the world and a macrosociological perception of "the relations among various parts of entire societies in terms of the differentiation of these parts. [The] focus is on differentiation and its implications for the interrelations of parts in a social structure, which is conceptualized in terms of differentiation" (IH, p. 2). In line with Luther's innovative stress upon apperception, combined with a dynamic relational sociology of the common life, a hermeneutics of humanization and the parameters of the Decalogue intersect. Beyond hierarchy and equality, *reciprocal responsibility* emerges as the necessary condition of the freedom to be human in the world. As such, reciprocal responsibility functions as the operational criterion of the mobility requisite to inequality and heterogeneity as humanizing coordinates of a structurally ordered society.

"You always have the poor with you," said Jesus, "and whenever you will, you can do good to them; but you will not always have me" (Mark 14:7, RSV). Jesus had, of course, picked up this clue to reality from the

---

32. Augustine, bk. 6, chap. 23; see further bk. 5, chap. 9.

codebook discovered by Josiah. There it is written: "Since there will never cease to be some in need on the earth, I therefore command you, 'Open your hand to the poor and needy neighbor in your land'" (Deut. 15:11). It is no accident that, just as justice is the test case of the responsible use of the relation between freedom and power, so the poor are the test case of justice, of setting right what is not right in a world of inequality and heterogeneity.

As regards the rubric of the Decalogue, the text conspicuously makes no mention of justice.[33] The reason for this omission, however, lies not in the irrelevance of justice to the Decalogue or the indifference of the Decalogue to justice. Nor can it be ascribed to the indifference of Brother Martin. On the contrary! The reason is that justice underlies and underlines the reality of the human relations and interrelations concretely de-

33. On this crucial point, two interpretations of the Decalogue by Old Testament scholars widely recognized as authoritative may be noted. One interpretation, that of Walter Harrelson in *The Ten Commandments and Human Rights* (Philadelphia: Fortress Press, 1980), seeks to explore the meaning and significance of the Ten Commandments to a crucial issue of contemporary culture and society. The second interpretation, that of Gerhard von Rad (*Die Theologie des Alten Testamentes*, vol. 1 [Munich: Chris. Kaiser Verlag, 1962]), explores, inter alia, the central place of the Decalogue in relation to the development and content of law in ancient Israel, and in the context of religion and civilization of the ancient Near East.

Concerning the centrality of justice to the Decalogue and of the Decalogue to contemporary culture and society, Harrelson notes that "we have let slip from us the biblical picture of a God who cares fiercely about justice on earth and will not forever permit injustice to continue" (p. 9).

Concerning the Decalogue as the pivotal indicator of responsibility in a covenantally purposed world, von Rad underlines the righteousness of God as the criterion and clue to the wholeness and happiness of Israel and of humanity. Von Rad writes:

> Under all circumstances, the intimate connection between the Commandments and the covenant must be kept in mind. . . . The critical question thus became the question of the form and structure *(Gestaltung)* of the life of those who found themselves in this new situation. Accordingly, the Decalogue could never have meant for Israel an absolute moral law *(ein absolut moralisches Sittengesetz)*. Rather more, and instead *(Vielmehr)*, Israel regarded the Decalogue as the disclosure of the will of Jahweh in a particular moment of her history through which the healing and wholeness of life *(das Heilsgut des Lebens)* were offered to her. . . . The claims of the Commandments and the promise of life *(Zuspruch des Lebens)* were obviously interchangeable from time immemorial *(waren einander sichtlich seit alters)*. (p. 207; my translation)

scribed and parabolically proposed by the text as the context and course of reciprocal responsibility in a world created and covenanted for "the human use of human beings." In such a world, the poor are the bearers of inequality as a righteousness not their own. They are the human reminders of that vertical dimension of life in this world apart from which the freedom to be and to stay human cannot generate the discernment and the mobility necessary to the increase of a heterogeneity that humanizes. "The whole world pours at us" (as Robert Penn Warren put it), and will do so continually. There is no doubt about that. But the codebook has been found again and is at hand!

According to the rediscovery, it is precisely the responsibility for justice that brings apperception and structure together in the discernment and implementation of what is required of any present by any future as a human future. The codebook includes its own classic summation — succinct, operational, and unforgettable — of the dynamics of apperception and structure in the praxis of reciprocal responsibility:

> You shall therefore lay up these words . . . in your heart and in your soul; and you shall bind them as a sign upon your hand, and they shall be as frontlets between your eyes. And you shall teach them to your children, talking of them when you are sitting in your house, and when you are walking by the way, and when you lie down, and when you rise. And you shall write them upon the doorposts of your house and upon your gates, that your days and the days of your children may be multiplied in the land which the LORD swore to your fathers to give them, as long as the heavens are above the earth. (Deut. 11:18-21, RSV)

Of this praxis of reciprocal responsibility the Decalogue is the pivotal and critical instance. With the help of Brother Martin, we proceed now to explore the Commandments and certain pivotal and critical pathways and patterns of a human future to which they point.

PART II

Pathways and Patterns
of Reciprocal Responsibility

Prologue

In borrowing Robert Penn Warren's term *codebook* to refer to the Decalogue, we are dealing not with Hammurabi but, as the Reformers insisted, with the Sermon on the Mount. We are drawn not under the rules but into parables. The word *code* denotes not a repository of regulations but the clue to responsibilities. The Decalogue underlines the *indicative*, in distinction from the *legalistic*, the *descriptive* as opposed to the *prescriptive* relation of the Commandments to the human living of human life. The tone of the Decalogue is not: "This is what you had better do, or else!" On the contrary, the tone is rather: "Seeing that you are who you are, where you are, and as you are, this is the way ahead, the way of being and living in the truth, the way of freedom!"

It could be that discerning and taking responsibility for what it takes to be human in the world could become common again. The Decalogue is the "codebook" that signals an apperceptive preparation for living by pathways and patterns of reciprocal responsibility in a world that has been made fit for being human in. In this world, the Decalogue is at hand as a primer for learning to spell, and especially to spell out freedom.

"The Two Tablets of Moses"

Turning now directly to Luther's discussion of the Decalogue in the Large Catechism, we discover what Luther himself prepared for us to read and hear and follow. In the "Shorter Preface" to the Catechism, this is what Luther's contemporaries heard him say:

The Ten Commandments of God

1. You shall have no other gods [besides] me.

2. You shall not [go about with the name of God as though it made no difference].

3. You shall [make a day for celebration] holy.

4. You shall honor father and mother.

5. You shall not kill.

6. You shall not [break a marriage].

7. You shall not steal.

8. You shall not [speak falsely] against your neighbor.

9. You shall not covet your neighbor's house.

10. You shall not covet his wife, [servant, maid, livestock, or anything that belongs to him].[1]

Luther's ordering of the Commandments differs from the order followed by Calvin, who adheres to the ancient Hebrew order as given in Exodus 20:2-17. At least three considerations seem to have guided Luther's arrangement. The first is his apperceptive purpose; the second is his nearer adherence to the catechetical tradition of the church; and the third, a corollary of the second, concerns the use of the catechism in confessional preparation. Particularly striking are the variants that show up at the beginning and at the end of the list.

Calvin, in line with the emphasis both of Exodus 20:1-17 and of

---

1. Martin Luther, Large Catechism, in *The Book of Concord,* ed. and trans. Theodore Tappert (Philadelphia: Fortress Press, 1959), pp. 362-63. Subsequent references to this work will be given parenthetically in the text, using the abbreviation LCT. I have ventured my own translation in a few places, indicated by brackets. For the German text, see *Grosser Katechismus,* ed. D. Johannes Meyer (Leipzig, 1914), pp. 36-37.

Deuteronomy 5:6-21, finds it necessary to supplement the strong mono-theism of the first commandment with an explicit prohibition against graven images in the second commandment. The legal mind seems singularly adept at making assurance doubly sure, so that other lawyers can double the search for loopholes. The pastoral and pedagogical preoccupation of Luther, on the other hand, is informed by the shrewd perception that the nub of the nexus between monotheism and idolatry is the fascination with the more promising options that always seem to be lurking around. "No other gods besides me" thus seems precisely designed to kill more than two birds with the same stone.

At the other end of the spectrum there is the tricky matter of covetousness. Calvin appears to have regarded one notice as sufficient. Luther, on the other hand, unlike Calvin — who, if the Westminster Catechisms are to be taken at their word, was better at defining sin than at eliminating it — had a lively alertness to the resourcefulness of the devil. Accordingly, he deemed covetousness worthy of a double billing, and in the ascending order of greed. Shrewdly, Luther declares: "You shall not covet your neighbor's house." The wife, and the staff, and the movable goods come next. Owing to the egalitarian preference for things first, people second, which has come between Luther and us, covetousness as often proceeds in the same order.[2]

In the *Short Form of the Ten Commandments* (1520),[3] Luther explains that the first three commandments occupy the "first and right-hand tablet" given to Moses *(die rechte Tafel Mosi)*. They have to do with what it means "to have a God" *(einen Gott haben)* and with how we should be related to him. The left tablet of Moses *(die linke Tafel Mosi)* refers to the tablet held in Moses' left hand as he descended from the mountain of God. As the "right

2. But then, as Luther said, he was up against *tolle Deutsche*. Calvin, on the other hand, was predisposed to the astigmatism of the Swiss, who have never been very adept at seeing through or around things, since, as Heine pointed out, in Switzerland, every time one really wants to see something there is a mountain in the way. (According to Dr. Walter M. Mosse, this was the explanation Heine gave when his friends chided him for taking his holidays in the Netherlands rather than in Switzerland.)

3. Martin Luther, *Kurze Form der Zehen Gebote, des Glaubens und des Vater Unsers* (1520), in *Dr. Martin Luther's sämmtliche Werke*, ed. Johann Konrad Irmischer (Carl Heyder, 1833), vol. 22, pp. 5, 6. Subsequent references to this edition will use the abbreviation EA (Erlangen Ausgabe). My translation.

tablet" directs us in the pathways and patterns of responsibility toward God, so the "left tablet" directs us in the patterns and pathways of reciprocal responsibility toward our neighbor. As the "right tablet" tells what is involved in a realistic, liberating, and fulfilling commitment between God and human beings, so the "left tablet" tells us what is involved in a realistic, liberating, and fulfilling commitment between and among persons as neighbors. In Luther's words, we are directed toward "what a person owes to another person and his neighbor to refrain from and to do" *(was er den Menschen und seinem Nähsten schuldig ist zu lassen und zu thun).*[4]

The sequence of reciprocal responsibilities concerns boundaries and behavior. It begins with father and mother, as bearers of an authority that means freedom — the fourth commandment. Next in importance is the inviolability of one's neighbor as a person like oneself — the fifth commandment. In the third place *(das dritt lehret),* there is the relation to one's neighbor's highest good, which, next to his own person, is his wife *(ehlich Gemahl),* child, or friend. These are all to be held in high esteem and are not harmed — the sixth commandment. The fourth set of relations involves the neighbor's temporal goods, which not only are not to be taken for oneself but are to be furthered and not hindered *(nit nehme noch hindere, sondern fordere)* — the seventh commandment. The fifth set of relations has to do with one's neighbor's temporal integrity and reputation *(zeitlich Ehre und gut Gerucht),* which are not to be weakened but increased *(nit schwaeche, sondern mehre),* protected and sustained *(schutze und erhalte)* — the eighth commandment. The last two commandments underline the evil in our natures *(wie boes die Natur sei)* and the perils of unlimited desire for sensual satisfaction and for material things *(wie rein wir von allen Begierden des Fleisches und Guter sein sollen),* which begin with the neighbor's property and end with his wife, his household, and his livestock — the ninth and tenth commandments.

According to Luther, we have only to look squarely at the facts of these human relations to discern the significant in the factual — namely, "how cost-less and alike *[billig und gleich]* all these Commandments are, since they command nothing relating to God and the neighbor which any one would not wish for himself were he in God's and his neighbor's place *[an Gottis und seines Nähsten statt wäre].*"[5]

4. Luther, *Kurze Form,* p. 6.
5. Luther, *Kurze Form,* pp. 6, 7.

Luther and the Bible

The *Short Form of the Ten Commandments, the Creed, and the Lord's Prayer,* early in 1520, was followed later in the same year by the powerful tract entitled *The Freedom of a Christian (Die Freiheit eines Christenmenschen).* As the former signaled Luther's linkage with and high estimation of the tradition of the Middle Ages in the nurture of human apperception, the latter call to Christian freedom signaled Luther's pioneering move toward a new and fulfilling human linkage between freedom and responsibility. At least textually, this move warrants the claim that the Decalogue is the primer for learning to spell and to spell out freedom. Lost amid the sound and fury of the time, however, and owing not a little to the heteronomous literalism of Luther's own successors (as has been noted) was the fact that Luther's further move from *Die Freiheit eines Christenmenschen* (1520) to *Der Grosse Katechismus* (1529) was a direct and inspired replay of the move from the covenant to the law in ancient Israel.[6]

In confirmation of this assessment, we turn briefly to Gerhard von Rad's masterful account of *The Theology of the Old Testament.*[7] In the course of a discussion of the general significance of the Commandments, von Rad tells us that in Israel, early echoes of "legal interpretation" of the commands of Jahweh were at variance with the thrust and ethos of the covenantal commitment of Jahweh to Israel, and of Israel to Jahweh. "Israel's ear," he writes,

> began to be more sensitive; one started to sense behind the negative demand a totally other meaning in the making. The need emerged to fill in positively, and in the sense of the prohibition, the space which had been freed by the prohibition. In the case of the commandments of the Decalogue concerning father and mother and concerning the Sabbath . . . the negative and original understanding only has carried the day. (TAT, vol. 1, p. 212)

Furthermore, according to von Rad,

---

6. Luther, EA, vol. 27, p. 173. Luther sent his text *De libertate christiana (On Christian Freedom)* to Pope Leo X, with an accompanying communication in which he declared, "This writing contains a complete summation of a Christian life."

7. Gerhard von Rad, *Die Theologie des Alten Testamentes,* 2 vols. (Munich: Christian Kaiser, 1962, 1965). Subsequent references will be given parenthetically in the text. My translation.

> The laws of the Old Testament . . . presuppose the covenant of Jahweh
> with Israel; there is no law whatsoever which, as a kind of "legal foun-
> dation" *[Grundgesetz]*, constitutes, on its part, this covenantal order. . . .
>
> Furthermore, these commandments are far removed from comprising
> *[umreissen]* something like an ethos; much more do they describe in
> their negative formulation really only possibilities *[doch nur Möglich-
> keiten]* which lie on the outermost periphery of the circle of human life,
> namely practices which are absolutely displeasing to Jahweh. Whosoever
> belongs to Jahweh does not break up a marriage *[bricht nicht die Ehe]*,
> subverts no boundary *[verrueckt keine Grenze]*, and does not kill. (TAT,
> vol. 2, pp. 415, 417)

Luther adheres to the Scriptures in a similar way. This is notably evident
from his biblical prefaces in support of his reciprocal relational explanation
of the Decalogue. In the Preface to the New Testament, for example,
Luther writes:

> Just as the Old Testament is a book in which are written God's law and
> commandments, together with the history of those who kept and of
> those who did not keep them, so also the New Testament is a book in
> which are written the gospel and the promises of God, together with
> the history of those who believe and of those who do not believe them.[8]

That was sixteen years after the Large Catechism — that is, in 1545. But
seven years before the Catechism — that is, in 1522 — Luther apologizes
for writing a preface at all. The reason he gives for doing so nonetheless
has a curiously contemporary ring. "It would be right and proper," Luther
wrote,

> for this book to go forth without any prefaces or extraneous names
> attached and simply have its own say under its own name. However
> many unfounded *[wilde]* interpretations and prefaces have scattered the
> thought of Christians to a point where no one any longer knows what
> is gospel or law, New Testament or Old. Necessity demands, therefore,
> that there should be a notice or preface, by which the ordinary man
> can be rescued from his former delusions, set on the right track, and
> taught what he is to look for in this book, so that he may not seek laws

---

8. In *Luther's Works*, vol. 35, *Word and Sacrament*, ed. E. Theodore Bachmann
(Philadelphia: Muhlenberg Press, 1960), p. 358. See von Rad, TAT, vol. 2, p. 414, n. 1.

and commandments where he ought to be seeking the gospel and promises of God."⁹

The same fate, however, overtook Luther's "codebook" that had overtaken Josiah's, and with the same result. The thrust, sense, and purpose of the book were inverted and subverted. Of Deuteronomy, von Rad notes that the fact that

> its promulgation under King Josiah signified a turning-point has often been emphasized. Nevertheless, the manner of its impact upon later times and its own understanding *[Auffassung]* of the revelation of Jahweh's will for Israel must be distinguished. In the latter case, it still lay completely beyond every legalization, indeed, it became a particularly impressive proclamation of Jahweh's prevenient and saving will *[Jahwehs zuvorkommenden Heilswillen]*. (TAT, vol. 2, pp. 420-21)

Luther's sermonic preparation and purpose for the catechism likewise carry his commentary upon the Commandments beyond every legalization of responsibility before God and for human life.

Yet believers and unbelievers alike have missed this central Scriptural and catechetical point. Thus both believers and unbelievers have been vulnerable to a certain confusion in face of Heinrich Heine's rhapsodical praise of Luther. Believers have repudiated Heine's ironic lyricism as a blasphemous caricature of Christian faith and history. Unbelievers have been sometimes delighted and sometimes puzzled by the same caricature, converting the caricature into contempt, the irony into satire. But Heine was nothing if not his own man. His prose masterpiece is an attempt to explain to the French — whose passion for the ideals of the Revolution had reached a point of insufficient self-criticism, and whose experience of the Germans had reinforced a persuasion that the Germans were obviously devoid of both freedom and culture — that the Germans had in fact gone on record on behalf of both. Of this fact Heine calls Luther and the Bible to witness. In a passage at once eloquent and fascinating, Heine writes:

> I have already shown how through him we attained the widest liberty of thought. For Martin Luther gave us not only freedom of movement,

9. *Luther's Works*, vol. 35, p. 357. This passage was deleted from the Preface to the New Testament of 1545.

but also the means of movement. To the spirit he gave a body; he gave word to the thought; he created the German language.

This he did by translating the Bible.

The Divine Author of this book seems to have known as well as we do that the choice of a translator is by no means a matter of indifference. He himself chose His translator, and endowed him with the marvelous faculty of translating out of a dead and already buried language, into a tongue that had not as yet come into existence. . . .

Every expression and every idiom to be found in Luther's Bible is essentially German; an author may unhesitatingly employ it; and as this book is in the hands of the poorest classes, they have no need of any special learned instruction to enable them to express themselves in a literary style. This circumstance will, when the political revolution takes place in Germany, result in strange phenomena. Liberty will everywhere be able to speak, and its speech will be Biblical.[10]

What Heine shows us is that believers who know that "God means freedom" (to paraphrase Ernst Käsemann)[11] — and unbelievers who

---

10. Heinrich Heine, *De l'Allemagne depuis Luther,* translated and published in German under the title: *Zur Geschichte der Religion und Philosophie in Deutschland* (1834); English translation by John Snodgrass, with a new introduction by Ludwig Marcuse, entitled *Religion and Philosophy in Germany* (Boston: Beacon Press, 1959), pp. 53-54, 56.

Two addenda may be noted. First, as these pages were in preparation a German friend and colleague, Ferdinand Schlingensiepen, wrote from Düsseldorf that the town fathers there have circumvented or defeated all efforts to honor Heine in his home town, as Goethe has been honored in Weimar. The proffered reason is Heine's reputed atheism.

Second, an American friend, the distinguished journalist I. F. Stone, once asked me what I was about. When I told him, "Luther on the Ten Commandments," he replied with characteristic probing, gentility, and quizzicality: "Have you ever read Heine on Luther?" I had not, but I set about at once to fill in the gap. In consequence, I trust that Izzy Stone will accept my thanks and be not only no longer puzzled but also able to concur.

11. The phrase has been suggested by Ernst Käsemann's book *Der Ruf in der Freiheit* (Tübingen: J. C. B. Mohr [Paul Siebeck], 1968). The English translation of this work bears the title: *Jesus Means Freedom* (London: SCM Press, 1969; Philadelphia: Fortress Press, 1970). The German edition was so widely received as to require three editions within the year of publication. The English edition is based upon the third revised German text. A fifth chapter is added in the English edition, but the notes that are invaluable in the German edition are regrettably missing. On the other hand, the English title seems a happy inspiration. The German title literally reads: "The Call

sooner or later come to suspect that freedom, later if not sooner, runs into the Bible, if not into God — have the possibility through Luther of a promising rendezvous with a human future coming their way.

---

to Freedom." This is, indeed, what Jesus' life and teaching are all about. Hence, "Jesus Means Freedom" is almost a revelatory identification both of what Jesus' life and teaching are all about and of what the perceptive insistence of the Reformers upon the interchangeability between the Decalogue and the law of love is all about. In any case, the word *God,* understood as denoting "the One who" or "the Authority who means freedom," is the crux of Luther's explanation of the "right tablet of Moses."

CHAPTER FOUR

Of God and Creation: The Right Tablet of Moses

(The First, Second, and Third Commandments)

The sense in which, and the extent to which, the "two tablets of Moses" are a primer for learning to spell and spell out freedom is readily discernible when we begin at the beginning. The beginning points to the Archimedian point for the recognition and praxis of the nurture of human apperception. The apperception of the human is not to be understood as a human psychological attribute identifiable according to the discipline of psychology, nor as a pre-learning capacity for learning, familiar and useful in educational psychology, nor even as a "pre-understanding" *(Vorverständnis)* stressed and celebrated by Rudolf Bultmann and his disciples. The word *apperception* denotes, on the contrary, a sign of the transfiguration of the mystery of experience in the experience of mystery. The apperception of the human proceeds from and is a response to a clear and distinct awareness and acknowledgment of what it means — in Luther's phrase — "to have a God." "You shall have no other gods besides me" (first commandment); "You shall not go about with the name of God as though it made no difference" (second commandment); "You shall make a day for celebration holy" (third commandment). The authority who means freedom is the Whom identified by "the right tablet of Moses."

What Does It Mean to Have a God? The Heart and Its Trust

The First Commandment:
"You Shall Have No Other Gods Besides Me"

"To have a God," Luther explains, "properly means to have something in which the heart trusts completely."[1] "Properly" makes the whole difference. The difference is between "possession of" and "being related to," and Luther wastes neither words nor breath in getting to the point. "To have a God," he declares, "does not mean to lay hands upon him, or put him into a purse, or shut him up in a chest. . . . To cling to him with all our heart is nothing else than to entrust ourselves to him completely. He wishes to turn us away from everything else, and to draw us to himself, because he is the one, eternal good" (LCT, 366:13-15).

To Luther's musical ear and intuitive perceptiveness, Gothic and Old German words sounded better and better expressed the human reality and sense of what is going on than did their Anglo-Saxon semantic variants. *Gott* and *Gut* are interchangeable and signify both the worth, without which life would not be worth it *(Gott)*, and the relation upon which we can utterly and unfailingly depend *(Gut)*.[2] To this worth and this relation the word *God* intrinsically refers. There is no time when nor space where God is not present as utterly worthy of trust and as utterly reliable to trust. Such a Presence wears authority self-evidently and indispensably. As the self-identifying gift of such a Presence, authority acquires its only true and human sense — that is, as an experience of ultimacy and intimacy, behind which, beyond which, before which, and around which one simply does not and cannot imagine going, or wishing to go. To trust and to entrust oneself to this authority is to enter into that perfect freedom which is the foretaste of the possibility and the power to be who one is, where one is, and as one is, and, in quietness and

---

1. Martin Luther's Large Catechism, in *The Book of Concord,* trans. and ed. Theodore G. Tappert (Philadelphia: Fortress Press, 1959), p. 366, par. 10. Subsequent references will use the abbreviation LCT and will give page and paragraph numbers.

2. Although the two words, both in Old German and in Gothic, are not etymologically connected, Luther asserted the interrelation more than once. See LCT, 368 n. 5. Perhaps philology is related to etymology as "the significant" is to "the factual." Or perhaps it was Luther's phonetic ear that led him to rescue the Anglo-Saxon predilection for the interchangeability between "God" and "good" from aesthetic and/or moral vacuity and to attempt to express the concrete human sense of the connection.

confidence, in all one's needs, desires, doings, to count upon and to move toward the fulfillment that is coming one's way.[3]

Luther's phonetic, etymological insight breaks fresh and far-reaching theological and ethical ground. It identifies and underscores what is involved in the primordial beginning that makes all the human difference in the world. The theological breakthrough draws the line between the human sense and nonsense of speaking about God. The ethical breakthrough draws the human sense of speaking about God and responsibility before God upon a common point. The human sense of speaking about God finds concerns about God's existence, nature, and attributes peripheral and speculative. They are irrelevant to the concrete reality of the experience of being called into question, and of being ineluctably drawn into the pursuit of the identity, purposes, and claims of the one and only Author and Finisher of the heart's complete trust. The human sense of speaking about God assigns priority to the question of *who* God is over the question of *whether* God is, and even over the affirmation *that* God is! The human sense of speaking about God is rooted in the discovery that God is experienced and known at the center, not on the edges, of our lives — as Bonhoeffer, with perceptive faithfulness to Luther, has underscored.[4]

God and Good

The ethical breakthrough achieved by Luther's phonetic, etymological correlation of worth and relation *(Gott* and/with *Gut)* is the conjunction

3. Thus is the mystery of experience upon a Lutheran course in declaring that "all theology is anthropology." And Kierkegaard was authentically Lutheran in declaring against Hegel that "truth is subjectivity." Kierkegaard's lively sense for the transfiguration of the mystery of experience in the experience of mystery led him to think and write theology maieutically. Feuerbach, although right for the wrong reasons, lacked sensitivity to the transfiguration of transcendence. See Ludwig Feuerbach, *Das Wesen der Religion,* popular ed. (Leipzig: Alfred Kroner, 1851). The book consists of thirty lectures given in Heidelberg in 1848. The phrase referred to comes at the beginning of the third Heidelberg lecture. See further the instructive essay on Feuerbach by Karl Barth in *Die Theologie und die Kirche,* Gesammelte Vorträge, vol. 2 (Munich: Chris. Kaiser, 1928). An English translation by Louise Pettibone Smith was published under the title *Theology and the Church* (New York: Harper & Row, 1962), chap. 7.

4. Dietrich Bonhoeffer, *Letters and Papers from Prison,* enl. ed., ed. Eberhard Bethge (New York: Macmillan, 1978), p. 282. Subsequent references will be made parenthetically in the text, using the abbreviation LPP.

thereby expressed between an identifiable name and an identifying claim. Involved in that primordial beginning which makes all the human difference in the world is the discovery at the center that the response to God and responsibility before God are interchangeable and inseparable. Not every name for God will do, however beguiling and beckoning the name may be. But that name alone is "properly" referred to by the word *God* which identifies that worth without which life would not be worth it. Correspondingly, not every claim before God, or in the name of God, will do, however passionately the claim may be asserted. But that claim alone is "properly" ascribed to the word *God* which expresses an utter and unfailing dependence and trust.

These perceptions of Luther's are rooted in the Bible. They make us beneficiaries of the underlying point and purpose of the Bible as the Canon of Holy Scripture, and of theology as "properly done" reflection upon and interpretation of Scripture. Not that the Canon is about Luther; but, contrariwise, it was a particular genius of Luther's to be about the Canon. Accordingly, we venture to be about the Canon in our own way, in faithfulness to Luther's perceptions of the identifiable name and identifying claim that "properly" belong to the name of God.[5]

YHWH-Adonai

The passage from the eleventh chapter of Deuteronomy (vv. 18-21, RSV) brings the identifiable name and identifying claim together at the center of the human response to God. In that passage, the name of God is "the LORD," and the response to that name is the praxis of apperceptive faithfulness. At the center — where name and claim and responsibility meet — a reciprocal covenantal commitment generates the appropriate and sustaining language. The words are to be laid up in the heart. They are to be "as frontlets between your eyes." They are to be taught to the children

5. We would want, for example, to accent Luther's focus upon the human sense of the name of God in the wider context of Scripture, before proceeding with him to the threat and the promise of the first commandment. There is some warrant for proceeding in this way, from the fact that only in the Latin version of the Large Catechism does the explicit reference to Exodus 20:5 come under a subtitle: "Explanation of the Appendix to the First Commandment" (LCT, 368 n. 6). The present attempt to explore the threat of the commandment in relation to its promise will be undertaken below, under the rubric of "Responsibility for Creation."

and talked of on the journey. They are to be written "upon the doorposts of your house and upon your gates." Accordingly, Luther says of the first commandment that its purpose is "to require true faith and confidence of the heart, and these fly straight to the one true God and cling to him alone. The meaning is: 'See to it that you let me alone be your God, and never seek another'" (LCT, 365:4).

The unique achievement of this praxis of apperceptive faithfulness in ancient Israel still echoes in Jewish liturgy today. This achievement is the conjunction of the inexpressible and the covenantal components of God's identifiable name and identifying claim. The so-called *tetragrammaton* — that is, the four consonants of the name *Yahweh* (YHWH) — came gradually and persuasively to be linked with the name *Adonai* in a vocalization of the commitment to "see to it that you let me alone be your God, and never seek another." In the absence of vowels, the four consonants prevent the name of God from being uttered above a whisper. Conjoined with the identifying "claim-word" *Lord,* the aspirate name and the unmistakable claim, taken together, acknowledge and say who the only God who makes human sense is. He is *YHWH-Adonai:* the God who is Lord and the Lord who is God. In this whispered utterance, the experience of mystery and the mystery of experience, the majesty and the commitment, the awe and the responsibility, the freedom for obedience and the obedience in freedom — all are bound together in a liberating human experience of utter dependence upon the utterly dependable. The fantasy and the folly, the bewitchment and the befuddlement, the disillusionment and the emptiness that mark the paralysis of options are radically excluded. As Luther explains: "In other words: 'Whatever good thing you lack, look to me for it and seek it from me, and whenever you suffer misfortune and distress, come and cling to me. I am the one who will satisfy you and help you out of every need. Only let your heart cling to no one else'" (LCT, 365:4).

Identifiable Name and Identifying Claim

This first commandment conjunction of an identifiable name with an identifying claim summarizes and focuses upon a pervasive theme of the Bible as a whole. One thinks of the psalms of praise,[6] which involve us

---

6. Inter alia, and especially Psalms 23–46. A more extended list is included in the brief account of the Psalter in Robert H. Pfeiffer, *Introduction to the Old Testament*

directly "in one of the most particular characteristics of Old Testament anthropology: praise is the most unique form of existence as a human being. . . . Praise belongs to the most elemental 'marks of being alive.'"[7] One thinks of the prophets' accounts of their summons to prophetic vocation and of their oracles of judgment and hope. One thinks of the "servant poems" of Deutero-Isaiah (Isa. 42ff.), and of the Apocalyptic confidence that the end time will be a confirmation of the beginning. The first commandment way of speaking and thinking about God is expressly signaled in the angelic instructions both to Joseph and to Mary concerning the name to be given to Jesus (Matt. 1:21; Luke 1:26-38). It echoes in Jesus' stern reminder that "not everyone who says to me, 'Lord, Lord,' shall enter the kingdom of heaven, but only the one who does the will of my Father in heaven" (Matt. 7:21). With surprising subtlety and centrality, the inviolable classical conjunction of an aspirate name and an unmistakable claim (YHWH-Adonai) turns up again in Jesus' sustaining instruction in apperceptive covenantal faithfulness.

> "Pray then in this way:
> Our Father in heaven,
> Hallowed be your name . . ."
>
> (Matt. 6:9; cf. Luke 11:2)

And hard upon this counsel, Jesus makes the pivotal human connection by way of the more than rhetorical question: "Is there anyone among you who, if your child asks for bread, will give a stone? Or if the child asks for a fish, will give a snake? If you then, who are evil, know how to give good gifts to your children, how much more will your Father in heaven give good things to those who ask him!" (Matt. 7:9-11; cf. Luke 11:11-13). In the practice of prayer, identities and identifications, Otherness and inwardness are at once ultimate and immediate. The aspirate becomes the intimate in a personal warrant for the dependence that means freedom. The distance becomes the unmistakable assurance of a reliability that undergirds the risk of trust.

(New York: Harper and Brothers, 1941), pp. 637-44. Pertinent to the present context is Pfeiffer's indication of the struggle to keep the identifiable name and identifying claim together, especially in the face of a widening gap between poverty and plenty within the community of faith itself.

    7. Gerhard von Rad, *Theologie des Alten Testamentes*, vol. 1 (Munich: Chris. Kaiser, 1962), p. 381; my translation. Subsequent references will be given parenthetically in the text, using the abbreviation TAT.

Behold, here you have the true honor and the true worship which please God . . . that the heart should know no other consolation or confidence than that in him, nor let itself be torn from him, but for him should disregard everything else on earth. . . . So, too, if anyone boasts of great learning, wisdom, power, prestige, family, and honor, and trusts in them, he also has a god, but not the one, true god. Notice, again, how presumptuous, secure, and proud people become because of such possessions, and how despondent when they lack or are deprived of them. Therefore, I repeat, to have a God properly means to have something in which the heart trusts completely. (LCT, 366:16, 10)

The Loss of God's Name:
The Heart Becomes Religion and Trust Becomes Process

The Second Commandment:
"YOU SHALL NOT GO ABOUT WITH THE NAME OF GOD AS THOUGH IT MADE NO DIFFERENCE"

These reflections so far have shown that our unreadiness for the human future coming our way is exposed by our distance from the first commandment. We are sure neither of the identifiable name nor of the identifying claim that are available to us for our freedom and fulfillment in the world in which we live. To adapt a once familiar hymn, the perceptive theme of which has been sentimentalized into triviality, we know neither Whom nor how to trust, nor Whom to obey and why. Pursuing other allegedly more intelligible and cogent paths and possibilities of thought and action, we find ourselves ever more remote from the way that leaves no room for any other. Therein, we exhibit once again the internal coinherence of the first three commandments in the right tablet of Moses.

The loss of God's name is so far advanced among us that we have reversed the order and come to suppose that the second commandment is the proper prelude to the proper praxis of the first commandment. "You shall not go about with the name of God as though it made no difference." So, translating Luther, the commandment reads. We have gone so zealously about the business of exploring the difference that the name of God *can* make that we have become indifferent to the difference that the name of God *does* make. "As the First Commandment has inwardly instructed the heart and taught faith, so this commandment leads us outward and directs the lips and the tongue into the right relation to God. The first things that issue and emerge from the heart are words" (LCT, 371:50).

At least at two levels, crucial to our openness to the future that is coming our way in our praxis of the first three commandments, we have lost God's name in trying to find it. The first is the level of words: "the first things that break from the heart and show themselves."[8] The second is our faltering responsibility for creation. The first level shows itself in the trivialization and in the timely inappropriateness of going about with the name of God as though it made no difference. The second shows itself in a deepening distrust dividing us as human creatures from God and from one another and in an intensifying disregard of creation through our consuming passion for ecological and military self-destruction. Reserving attention to the second level for the concluding section of the present chapter, let us pursue somewhat more carefully the first level, that of the heart and its words.

Trivialization of the Second Commandment

The trivialization of the heart and its words conceals from us our creeping loss of God's name.[9] None of the Ten Commandments (with the possible exception of the third) has been more vulnerable to trivialization than has

---

8. I have ventured my own translation here of Luther's words: "Denn das Erste, so aus dem Herzen bricht und sich erzeigt, sind die Worte." For the original text, see Georg Buchwald, *D. Martin Luther's Grosse Katechismus* (Leipzig: Verlag von Bernhard Liebisch, 1912), p. 17.

9. In general, it may be noted that for Luther "these two belong together, faith and God. That to which your heart clings and entrusts itself is, I say, really your God" (LCT, 365:3). For us, however, the center and the periphery of what it takes to be and to stay human in the world have changed places and priorities. Scripture has been yielded to literary criticism; faith to religion; revelation to reason; the one right thing to do to the doing of many right things. On a more sophisticated plane of analysis and interpretation, theism is practiced as a cosmic and aesthetic refutation of atheism; while atheism itself feeds upon the passionate and provocative but less than persuasive refutation of atheism. The good is commended and practiced according to a finely calibrated calculus of ends and means at the counsel of prudence, which keeps virtues at least one step ahead of vices in the measured commendation of responsibility. In consequence, and in short, our practical agnosticism commits us to the possible, and as "the best," in Yeats's phrase, increasingly "lack all conviction, . . . the worst are full of passionate intensity" (William Butler Yeats, "The Second Coming," in *The Collected Poems of W. B. Yeats* [New York: Macmillan, 1951], p. 185).

the second commandment. The other nine tend to be either flaunted, ignored, or deliberately violated, but the second commandment has been interpreted and commended in ways that would be innocuous, if not downright silly, were they not replete with patent self-deception. To take the most conspicuous case in point: profanity. Swearing has tended to be regarded as the focal instance of "taking the name of God in vain," as the tradition was wont to put it. Thus, profane expletives have been driven into the hush-hush corner, as though a conspiracy of silence were a prescribed form of obedience. The trouble with profanity is its vulgarity, not its blasphemy. Its indiscriminate use not only does not ennoble; it demeans the speaker and bores or frightens the listener. It is one thing to say, "Oh hell, I forgot it!" and quite another to say, "Go to hell!" It is one thing to say, "Damn it! I've done it again!" and quite another to say, "Damn you!" The trouble with the first-named instances is that they tend to become habitual and to convert carelessness into indifference, if not into exhibitionism. The trouble with the second-named instances is that they nurture the violation of limits designed to safeguard difference (heterogeneity) as a thing of beauty and a joy forever from being converted into preference and power; and especially to keep the bearers of inequality (the affluent and the strong) mindful of the fact that the poor and the weak are not on that account less human, but precisely on that account the test case of reciprocal responsibility toward the only authority who means freedom. Indeed, the familiar *extremis* outcry: "Oh, my God!" should remind us all that all of us are vulnerable to the despair that drives us, however uncontrollably, across the threshold of faith. In short, the commandment concerning the name of God does not mean "Do not swear" but, as Luther says, "Swear properly where it is necessary and required," that is, "in the service of truth and all that is good," and explicitly not "in support of falsehood and wickedness" (LCT, 373:63-64).

Understood in this way, the second commandment is not mainly about profanity but about justice. Not going about with the name of God as though it made no difference discovers in justice the difference that the name of God makes. Justice is the principal outward sign that the heart and its words have been led and directed "into the right relation with God." In underlining justice, Luther frees the second commandment from trivialization and from triviality at a single stroke. If the commandment is "so understood," he explains,

> you have easily solved the question that has tormented so many teachers: why swearing is forbidden in the Gospel, and yet Christ, St. Paul, and

other saints took oaths. The explanation is briefly this: We are not to swear in support of evil (that is, to a falsehood) or unnecessarily; but in support of the good and for the advantage of our neighbor we are to swear. This is a truly good work by which God is praised, truth and justice are established, falsehood is refuted, people are reconciled, obedience is rendered, and quarrels are settled. For here God himself intervenes and separates right from wrong, good from evil. (LCT, 373:65-66)[10]

When the heart and its words are signed by justice, the second commandment both arrests the loss of God's name and points the way to patterns of thought and life that express the promise of the praxis of the first commandment in the common life and the consequences of a failure of commitment to such praxis. "From this," Luther declares,

> everyone can readily infer when and in how many ways God's name is abused. . . . Misuse of the divine name occurs most obviously in worldly business and in matters involving money, property, and honor, whether publicly in court or in the market or elsewhere, when a person perjures himself, swearing by God's name or by his own soul. This is especially common in marriage matters when two persons secretly betroth themselves to each other and afterward deny it under oath. . . .
>
> The greatest abuse, however, occurs in spiritual matters, which pertain to the conscience, when false preachers arise and peddle their lying nonsense as the Word of God.
>
> . . . Unfortunately it is now a common calamity all over the world that there are few who do not use the name of God for lies and all kinds of wickedness, just as there are few who trust in God with their whole heart. (LCT, 371-72:53-54, 58)

False preachers continue to arise, peddling their lying nonsense. But in this instance, "the greatest abuse . . . in spiritual matters, which pertain to the conscience" has been aided by devoted and learned heirs of Luther himself. The loss of God's name has overtaken the praxis of the first commandment, owing more than a little to an unintended distortion of Luther.

---

10. Luther instances Augustine and Jerome among the "other saints," and cites Matt. 5:33-37; 26:63-64; 2 Cor. 1:23; and Gal. 1:20.

Distortion of the Second Commandment

Luther's insistence upon the praxis of the Decalogue as the sign and seal of the primordial human fact that faith and God belong together was effectively abandoned in favor of another and more domesticatable view of what was centrally on Luther's mind. The exegetical, autobiographical, and polemical resources and riches of Luther's writings and actions were appropriated in such a way as to overshadow his catechetical commitment and purpose. The *Lectures on the Psalms and on Romans,* together with the tract on *Christian Freedom,* were heard, read, and drawn upon in support of the pivotal significance of justification by faith for the truth and the life of the community of believers *(articulus stant is et candentis ecclesiae).* In consequence, faith was converted into religion and religion into the piety of the individual. Thus Kant's critical search for a more convincing maxim for the pursuit of happiness than either the Deism or the agnosticism of the Enlightenment could provide can scarcely be adequately understood in disregard of this misunderstanding of Luther.

Kant's pivotal recognition of the good will as the point of meeting between faith and God, and between the individual believer and happiness, identified the foundations in human experience both of the moral law and of moral freedom. This achievement followed from his having "to abolish knowledge in order to make room for faith," as we have seen. It also made possible the prospect of being religious "within the limits of reason alone."[11] The celebrated definition of religion as "the recognition of our duties as divine commands"[12] has a very Lutheran flavor. Luther would have said "faith in God," not "religion," and "that to which your heart clings," not "recognition of our duties." Nevertheless, Kant's stress upon faith and freedom, God and responsibility, in the endeavor to establish the reasonableness of religion carries more than a hint of Luther's stress upon what the first commandment is centrally about. "These two belong together, faith and God," he explained, and "the purpose of this Commandment, therefore, is to require true faith and confidence of the heart" (LCT, 365:3-4).

Those who drew upon Luther's perceptions, learning, and persua-

---

11. Note the "Luther-flavor" (in distinction from the "Lutheran flavor") of Kant's reply to Schiller recorded in the introduction to Immanuel Kant, *Critique of Practical Reason and Other Writings in Moral Philosophy,* trans. and ed. Lewis White Beck (Chicago: University of Chicago Press, 1949), p. 43.

12. Kant, bk. 2, chap. 2, p. 232.

sions prevailed over Luther; and the distance widened between the first commandment and the experience of religion and responsibility. In seeking to persuade "the cultured among the despisers of religion" that they were in fact deeply religious, Schleiermacher undertook to show that he shared with them what they had come to despise and shared with them also what they had come to disregard.[13] The arid rationalism, in terms of which the theologians of the seventeenth and eighteenth centuries had attempted to provide the reciprocity of belonging between faith and God with doctrinal clarification and conviction, had converted God from the Subject of trust into an object of belief and faith from a commitment of the heart in complete trust into the acceptance of certain appropriate propositions. The "enlightened" critics of religion, on the other hand, in their alternately wistful and strident rationalism, had reached a pause on their way to the point of no return, which left their adherents poised upon a desultory midpoint between a reasonable theism and a passionate positivism and/or humanism. What a beckoning and liberating sound it was — then — to hear that "religion is a sense and taste for the Infinite,"[14] or that religion is "the consciousness of absolute dependence, or, which is the same thing, of being in relation with God," and that Christianity is the highest of all religions along a scale of piety and goodness directed toward increasing depth and inclusiveness.[15] More than a century later, religion or faith came to be described as an "invitation to pilgrimage" designed to bring and to keep "the top of our minds" in tandem with the bottom of our hearts.[16]

13. Daniel Friedrich Schleiermacher, *Reden über die Religion: An den Gebildeten unter Ihre Veraechter,* vierte Auflage (Berlin, 1831). The well-known English title is *Speeches on Religion: Addressed to the Cultured among Its Despisers,* ed. Rudolf Otto, trans. John Oman (London, 1893; New York: Harper Torchbook, 1958). The original edition of 1799 uses the word *Religion;* later, the word *Piety (Froemmigkeit)* replaced the word *Religion.*

14. Schleiermacher, p. 28. The second "Speech" on "The Nature of Religion" is the crucial one for Schleiermacher's view of religion.

15. Schleiermacher, *The Christian Faith,* trans. H. R. Mackintosh (Edinburgh, 1928), pp. 12 and 31-52.

16. So John Baillie, *Invitation to Pilgrimage* (New York: Charles Scribner's Sons, 1942); and *Our Knowledge of God* (New York: Charles Scribner's Sons, 1939), chap. 2. Baillie's "invitation" involved a different pilgrimage, rooted in and shaped by the Christian story. Schleiermacher, on the other hand, extended an invitation to discover that the identity between the finite and the infinite culminates in a community of faith, in which the religion of Jesus is found to be the saving (i.e., satisfying and fulfilling) religion of every human being and the end toward which the universe (i.e.,

But in the interval, and as the nineteenth century began to give way before the twentieth, the reciprocity of belonging between faith and God could be persuasively explored through the discovery that the propositions of dogmatics could be converted into "the subjective functions of the individual" and that the meaning of "justification and reconciliation" could be drawn from "the community's faith that it stands to God in a relation of the forgiveness of sins," and that this relation could be transposed into "the consciousness of grace and the consciousness of sin and guilt."[17] During these years, "the essence of Christianity" had become "the religion of Jesus," whose clear and simple teaching was "the Fatherhood of God" and "the Brotherhood of Man."[18] "The religion of Jesus" expressed the quintessence of the reciprocity between faith and God, providing as it did the inspiration and the highest example of "the communion of the Christian with God,"[19] and the sustaining impulse and warrant for the social gospel of "the Kingdom of God in America."[20]

The pilgrimage of faith from Kant via Schleiermacher and Ritschl to Harnack and Rauschenbusch had brought faith and God together and the Enlightenment farther along in its pursuit of happiness than either believers or unbelievers initially could have expected. In the United States, Jonathan Edwards had already laid the foundations of this achievement by a brilliant tour de force bringing John Locke, Friedrich Schleiermacher, and John Calvin together as companions on the journey. The terrors that frightened "sinners in the hands of an angry God"[21] fueled the enthusiasms

---

the cosmos and culture) is purposed and guided. Baillie, by contrast, invites participation in the integrity and painstaking care of evangelical liberalism to move beyond the uncritical biblical literalism of much Protestant orthodoxy, on the one side, and the increasingly uncritical skepticism and agnosticism to which the rationalism of the Enlightenment had succumbed, on the other. In making this move, the original Reformers, Luther and Calvin, begin again to come into their own.

17. Albrecht Ritschl, *Justification and Reconciliation*, trans. H. R. Macintosh (Edinburgh, 1902), pp. 34-35; and inter alia, pp. 3, 30, 49, 54, 63-64.

18. Adolf von Harnack, *What Is Christianity?* trans. Thomas Bailey Saunders (Gloucester: Peter Smith, 1978).

19. Wilhelm Herrmann, *The Communion of the Christian with God* (New York: G. P. Putnam's Sons, 1906).

20. The phrase is the title of a small but instructive and influential book of H. Richard Niebuhr, *The Kingdom of God in America* (New York: Harper, 1959).

21. Jonathan Edwards's celebrated Enfield sermon. See Sydney E. Ahlstrom, *A Religious History of the American People* (New Haven: Yale University Press, 1972), p. 301 n. 4.

of revival along an expanding frontier without disturbing the more tranquil pursuit of "the divine benevolence" and "the religious affections."[22] Edwards never lost sight of the fact that the crucial issue besetting the perennial controversy over divine sovereignty and human freedom in the world is the issue of the loss of God's name, identified by the covenantal story with its identifying claim. "What metaphysical situation could be more exciting: the chief critic of Arminianism forging a weapon out of the very Lockean materials which 'enlightened' theologians and deists had claimed as their own. . . . Edwards insisted that this was an orderly universe" and, citing a "nice phrase" of Paul Ramsey's, "either contingency and the liberty of self-determination must be run out of this world, or God will be shut out."[23]

God was, of course, not shut out. He was domesticated in winsome and learned, sophisticated and evangelical visions, conceptualities, and descriptions that sought above all to bring faith and God, cosmic purposes and human self-determination meaningfully together. "The Varieties of Religious Experience" accorded passing well with "the primordial and consequent nature of God" — the "Beloved Community" all the while faithfully gathering its memories and hopes and implementing them in "Christian Nurture."[24] Paradoxically enough, this going about with the name of God as though it made no difference is devoutly committed to the meaningful difference above all. What is not noticed is that in going about in this way, the relations between the first and second commandments are steadily attenuated and ultimately inverted and subverted. The first commandment becomes at best an appendage of the second, and the second commandment no longer "leads us outward and directs the lips and the tongue into the right relation to God" (LCT, 371:50). Instead, it is misused in "an attempt to embellish yourself with God's name or to put up a good front and justify yourself, whether in ordinary worldly affairs or in sublime and difficult matters of faith and doctrine" (LCT, 372:55). Process philosophies spawn process theologies; psychologies of religion are deepened and effectualized as psychiatry and religion; and as the language

22. Jonathan Edwards, *A Treatise Concerning the Religious Affections,* ed. John E. Smith (New Haven: Yale University Press, 1959).

23. Ahlstrom, p. 305.

24. The allusions are to William James, Alfred North Whitehead, Josiah Royce, and Horace Bushnell, whose works do follow them in the serious, substantive, and widely influential teaching and writing of Charles Hartshorne, Norman Pittenger, the late Daniel Day Williams, and, in these days, the irrepressible John Cobb.

of Canaan pervasively transmutes the language of covenantal trust and responsibility into a cacophony of metaphorical communication, the Bible is histrionically disseminated as the treasure-script of human transformation.[25]

No Ground Under Our Feet

Meanwhile, the future coming our way is being adumbrated in the awesome beginning and the chastened expectation with which Ernst Troeltsch concludes his monumental study of the meaning of history, and in that shattering and renewing "Reckoning Made at New Year 1943" by Dietrich Bonhoeffer, as a gift at Christmas 1942 to three particularly close friends and companions in conspiracy against the governing principalities and powers.[26]

Setting out from some account of "the contemporary crisis of history," Troeltsch noted that "we no longer theorize or construct under the protection of an all-sustaining order . . . but in the midst of a storm over the shaping of the world anew *[der Neubildung der Welt]*. . . . The ground sways under our feet." Of this shaping, its diversity and complexity, difficulty and prospect, Troeltsch concludes:

> The task itself, however, with which every epoch has been confronted consciously or unconsciously, is particularly urgent at this moment of our life. The idea of building anew *[Aufbau]* means *the overcoming of history by history* and making room for new creativity *[die Plattform neues Schaffens ebnen]*.[27]

25. As this chapter was first in preparation, two unexpected confirmations were encountered. The first was provided by the Annual Meeting of the American Theological Society at Princeton in early April 1983, which occupied itself in virtuostic excursions into metaphor, more properly noted as unacknowledged polytheistic language games. The second came in the course of a vigorous conversation with Charles Hartshorne, Dean of Process Philosophers cum Theologians, over the monstrosities of St. Augustine and John Calvin in their interpretations of divine sovereignty and human freedom in creation. The conversation was occasioned by a faculty seminar at the Texas Institute of Religion of Baylor University in Houston and resumed an exchange of long standing in which Professor Hartshorne, I am certain, found me as obdurate and incorrigible as I found him.

26. Ernst Troeltsch, *Der Historismus und Seine Probleme* (n.p.: Scientia Aalen, 1961); Bonhoeffer, pp. 1-17.

27. Troeltsch, pp. 6 and 772; translation and emphasis mine.

Troeltsch looked back upon the First World War, "which had thrown all preceding epochs into the melting pot *[Schmelztiegel]*," and denied even the remotest expectations of "an effective and integrative artistic and cultural symbol *[das wirksamste waere ein grosses kuenstlerisches Symbol]*, such as was once upon a time at hand in the *Divina Comedia*, and then later on in Faust.[28]

Bonhoeffer, on the other hand, from the very center of the storm occasioned by the Second World War and the spreading virus of totalitarianism, shares his own "reckoning" less than thirty months before the laying down of his life, and in words that astonishingly echo those with which Troeltsch began. "One may ask," he wrote,

> whether there have ever before in human history been people with so little *ground under their feet* — people to whom every available alternative seemed equally intolerable . . . , who looked beyond all these existing alternatives for the source of their strength so entirely in the past or in the future, and who yet, without being dreamers, were able to await the success of their cause so quietly and confidently. Or perhaps one should rather ask whether the responsible thinking people of any generation that stood at a turning point in history did not feel much as we do, simply because something new was emerging that could not been seen in the existing alternatives. (LPP, pp. 3-4; emphasis mine)

> *A few articles of faith on the sovereignty of God in history.*

> I believe that God can and will bring good out of evil. . . . I believe that God will give us all the strength that we need to help us to resist in all times of distress. But he never gives it in advance, lest we should rely on ourselves and not on him alone. A faith such as this should allay all our fears for the future. . . . I believe that God is no timeless fate, but that he waits for and answers sincere prayers and responsible actions. (LPP, p. 11)

> There remains an experience of incomparable value. We have for once learnt to see the great events of world history from below, from the perspective of the outcast, the suspects, the maltreated, the powerless, the oppressed, the reviled — in short, from the perspective of those who suffer. (LPP, p. 17)

28. Troeltsch, p. 776.

Brother Martin has brought us up short once again. Clearly, Bon-hoeffer's "Reckoning" is a remarkable paraphrase of the point, purpose, and cogency of Luther's explanation of the Decalogue in the Large Catechism. Out of the future coming toward us, Brother Martin bears in upon us with a liberating and sustaining resource for discerning "the significant in the factual."[29] In so doing, he not only calls into question our disregard of the first commandment in going about with the name of God as though it made no difference. He also directs us, via "the right tablet of Moses," both to "the left tablet" and to the threshold on which Troeltsch's wistful hope for an effective and integrative artistic and cultural symbol might enter upon its realization. It is not being suggested that the Decalogue, with Brother Martin's help, *is* such a symbol. The suggestion is rather that, in the wilderness beyond the Jordan (cf. Mark 1:4-8 and parallels), the Decalogue, from and through the first commandment forward, offers a point of departure for "the overcoming of history by history" in readying us for a liberating and human discernment of that which belongs to our peace. As Luther put it long ago: "It is of the utmost importance for a man to have the right head. For where the head is right, the whole life must be right, and vice versa" (LCT, 369:31). What Luther actually wrote was *"Denn wo das heupt recht gehet,"* that is, "For where the head goes in the right direction."[30] Accordingly, we could say, as Luther further explains, "where the head is on straight," "we shall be on the right path using all of God's gifts exactly as a cobbler uses his needle, awl, and thread (for work, eventually to lay them aside) or as a traveler avails himself of an inn, food, and bed (only for his temporal need)" (LCT, 371:47).

The Violation and the Restoration of God's Name: The Feminist Repudiation of Patriarchal Co-optation

"Where the head is on straight . . . we shall be on the right path using all God's gifts . . . properly" (LCT, 371:47; 373:63). "For where the head is right, the whole life must be right, and vice versa" (LCT, 369:31). "To repeat very briefly [what it means to go about with the name of God as

29. It will be recalled that the phrase is Bonhoeffer's. See p. 38 above.
30. See Luther's *Grosse Katechismus,* ed. D. Johannes Meyer, in *Quellenschriften zur Geschichte des Protestantismus,* ed. D. Carl Strange, vol. 12 (Leipzig: A. Deichert'sche Verlagsbuchhandlung, Werner Scholl, 1914), p. 44. My translation.

though it makes no difference], it is either simply to lie and assert under his name something that is not so, or to curse, swear, conjure, and, in short, to practice wickedness of any sort" (LCT, 373:62). Important as this is, however, it is not enough. One must "in addition . . . also know how to use the name of God aright" (LCT, 373:63). Going about with the name of God "properly" involves a dependable commitment "in support of the good and for the advantage of our neighbor." To swear, in this sense, "is a truly good work by which God is praised, truth and justice are established, falsehood is refuted, people are reconciled, obedience is rendered, and quarrels are settled" (LCT, 373:66).

When the second commandment is improperly understood and practiced, its disjunction from the first commandment is inevitable. The heart's complete trust has been sundered from the lips and the tongue. Going about with the name of God as though it makes no difference is a sign that the heart's complete trust is being experimented with or has been identified with another and an unworthy name. The words then signify the dissolution of the unfailing conjunction of ultimacy and intimacy that the heart unfailingly requires. Its dependency is no longer the secret of its freedom but the source of its self-enslaving bondage. Then, however the support of the good for the advantage of the neighbor be alleged, or even furthered, truth is sundered from justice, falsehood masquerades as truth, people are unreconciled, obedience is disavowed, and quarrels are not only not settled but are intensified. "So from a single lie a double one results — indeed, manifold lies" (LCT, 372:56).

John Milton, whom one would scarcely reproach as a Lutheran, and Brother Martin, who can scarcely have borrowed from *Paradise Lost,* have come upon a common identification of the devil. According to Brother Martin, "the heart by faith first gives God the honor due him and then the lips do so by confession. This is a blessed and useful habit and very effective against the devil, who is ever around us, lying in wait to lure us into sin and shame, calamity and trouble. He hates to hear God's name and cannot long remain when it is uttered and invoked from the heart" (LCT, 374:70-71). According to Milton, the devil goes about saying, "Evil, be thou my good!"[31]

"It is evident that the world today is more wicked than it has ever been" (LCT, 374:69). However arguable this assessment may be, either of Luther's own time or of ours, it tends to gather increasing confirmation as one moves from the right tablet of Moses to the left tablet. In one

31. John Milton, *Paradise Lost,* 4.1.110, in *The Poetical Works of John Milton,* ed. H. C. Beeching, new ed. (London: Oxford University Press, 1944).

respect, however, a slight shift of Luther's word order points up a too long unrecognized verification of a deep and widespread disregard of the first and second commandments at Moses' right hand. "It is evident that *today* the world is more wicked than it has ever been." *Today*, it is evident as never before that the loss of God's name has been preceded, attended, and surrounded by a violation of God's name that can no longer be ignored, suppressed, repressed, or defended. At the level of the heart and its words, the God whom the first and second commandments identify as the One who alone is worthy of trust, and in trusting Whom completely the gift of freedom for fulfillment is received — this God has been and is being violated by the disobedience of patriarchal co-optation.

The patriarchal co-optation of God's name is the domestication of the God of the covenantal journey, its story, and its Scripture, in and by a culture rooted in and shaped by attitudes and values, patterns of thought and life, institutions and power structures, which identify God primarily in terms of *male* authority, preeminence, power, achievements, and ways of being in the world. It is not being implied, nor can it be claimed, that Luther himself was, or is, exempt from the patriarchal violation of God's name, or from the threat of God's watchfulness over these Commandments. Nevertheless, as John Calvin, Luther's eminent and self-acknowledged pupil, urged upon his contemporaries and urges upon us, "Though the melancholy desolation which surrounds us, seems to proclaim that there is nothing left of the Church, let us remember that the death of Christ is fruitful, and that God wonderfully preserves his Church, as it were in hiding places . . . *[quasi in latebris]*."[32] In so remembering, let it be remembered also that Calvin is not being co-opted for the feminist movement, nor is the feminist movement being co-opted for John Calvin. On the contrary, and particularly in view of Luther's sober reminder of God's watchfulness over the first commandment, the feminist movement must be recognized as just such a hiding place for the wonderful preservation of God's church. Luther explains:

> In order to show that God will not have this commandment taken lightly but will strictly watch over it, he has attached to it, first, a terrible threat and, then, a beautiful, comforting promise. . . .
> . . . Learn . . . , then, how angry God is with those who rely on anything but himself, and again, how kind and gracious he is to those who trust and believe him alone with their whole heart. His wrath does

32. Calvin, *Institutes,* 4.1.2.

not abate until the fourth generation. On the other hand, his kindness and goodness extend to many thousands, lest [persons] live . . . like brutes who think that it makes no great difference how they live. . . .

This he has witnessed in all the records of history, as Scripture amply shows and as daily experience can still teach us. From the beginning he has completely rooted out all idolatry, and . . . just so in our day he overthrows all false worship so that all who persist in it must ultimately perish. Even now there are proud, powerful, and rich pot-bellies *[reiche wenste]* who, not caring whether God frowns or smiles, boast defiantly of their mammon and believe that they can withstand his wrath. But they will not succeed. Before they know it they will be wrecked, along with all they have trusted in, just as all others have perished who thought themselves so high and mighty.

. . . As little as God will permit the heart that turns away from him to go unpunished, so little will he permit his name to be used to gloss over a lie. (LCT, 368:29; 369:32, 35-36; 372:57)

Today, *Dei providentia* and — quite literally in this instance — *hominum confusione*, the feminist movement is at hand as the catalyst of the recovery of God's name in faithfulness to the freedom and responsibility inherent in obedience to the commandments of the right tablet of Moses. A hermeneutical, a historical, and a semantic recognition are at our disposal for the suspension of the threat and furtherance of the promise of God's watchfulness over the first commandment.

In that hiding place, wondrously wrought for the preservation of God's church and of the humanness of human life, the struggle against the loss of God's name has moved beyond the angry rebuke of the patriarchal violation of God's name. A serious, knowledgeable, and thorough search of the covenantal story of God's name, and of the human future signaled by and through it, is probing anew the question: What does it mean to have a God? Two notable accounts of this search have particularly informed the present indication of the significance of the feminist discernment of the patriarchal violation of God's name and of the clarification and guidance provided by this discernment for the understanding of the Decalogue and its bearing upon a human future. Professor Phyllis Trible's application of a rhetorical method of literary interpretation to the reading and understanding of Scripture, in her book *God and the Rhetoric of Sexuality*, together with Professor Elisabeth Schüssler Fiorenza's historical exploration of feminist memory and experience of the covenantal story and its faith, in her book *In*

Memory of Her: A Feminist Theological Reconstruction of Christian Origins, provide cogent and persuasive perspective and resources for the liberation of God's name from its idolatrous and ideological sexualization, and for the renewal of its ancient and contemporary reality as the Archimedian point of human freedom and fulfillment.[33]

The Feminist Critique and the Image of God: Phyllis Trible

Turning, then, to the hermeneutical recognition at our disposal, let us begin with a somewhat extended summary statement of Trible's understanding of feminism and of her invitation to read Scripture as a pilgrimage that includes Scripture itself:

> The Bible is a pilgrim wandering through history to merge past and present. . . . *By feminism I do not mean a narrow focus upon women but rather a critique of culture in light of misogyny.* This critique affects the issues of race and class, psychology, ecology and human sexuality. For some people today the Bible supports female slavery and male dominance in culture, while for others it offers freedom from sexism. Central in this discussion are such passages as the creation accounts in Genesis, certain laws in Leviticus, the Song of Songs, the wisdom literature, various Gospel stories about Jesus and the powerless, and particular admonitions of Paul and his successors. Out of these materials a biblical hermeneutics of feminism is emerging. (p. 1; emphasis added)

> All these contemporary interactions between the Bible and the world mirror the inner dynamics of scripture itself. The interpretive clue within the text is also the clue between the text and existence. Hence, the private and public journeys of the pilgrim named scripture converge to yield the integrity of its life. As the Bible interprets itself to complement or to contradict, to confirm or to challenge, so likewise we construe these traditions for our time, recognizing an affinity between then and now. In other words, hermeneutics encompasses explication, understanding, and application from past to present. (p. 7)

33. Phyllis Trible, *God and the Rhetoric of Sexuality* (Philadelphia: Fortress Press, 1978); and Elisabeth Schüssler Fiorenza, *In Memory of Her: A Feminist Theological Reconstruction of Christian Origins* (New York: Crossroad, 1983). Subsequent references will be given parenthetically in the text.

The definition of feminism here before us is at once succinct and central to the feminist purpose and commitment to set the human record straight, especially as regards "the knowledge of God and of ourselves."[34] It cogently identifies the significance of the interrelation between feminism and the other issues of the common life today that are undeniably critical for a human future. Furthermore, in identifying misogyny as the criterion of a critical reevaluation of culture, this understanding of feminism exposes the reality and the fundamental human consequence of the violation of God's name. The disregard of the commandments of the right tablet of Moses has defaced the Creator's self-identification in the image of God. On that primordial boundary of radical Otherness in self-identification, self-giving, and differentiation, the primordial interrelation of precedence, receptivity, and reciprocity between the Creator and humankind is imaged in the radical otherness of differentiation, self-giving, and self-identification of male and female, in responsiveness, receptivity, and reciprocity toward God and toward one another. In this primordial sense, male and female, in radical differentiation, self-giving, and self-identification, in responsiveness, receptivity, and reciprocity, *are* the image of God. In this radical sense, as Karl Barth has profoundly perceived (though not always adequately amplified), human sexuality is the sign, not of the sex of God, nor of the sex of the creature, but of the image of God.[35] As the sign of the image of God, sexuality refers to the primordial fact of male and female in radical otherness and belonging, difference and similarity, separateness and togetherness. In the uniqueness of the relation between male and female, the relation of the Creator to human creatures is experienced and identified. In accordance with the uniqueness of this relation, the pronouns signify neither masculinity nor femininity but otherness, precedence, and reciprocity, according to an order that excludes all super- and subordination from and through an ordination to reciprocal responsibility.

The "pilgrimage" (to borrow Trible's apt metaphor) of the phrase "the image of God" has been diverted, however, from its dynamic scriptural sense by ontological determinations that have sought to identify and clarify the *being* of God and the *being* of human creatures in their relation to

---

34. Calvin, *Institutes,* 1.1.

35. Karl Barth, *Church Dogmatics,* III/2, *The Doctrine of Creation,* trans. Harold Knight, G. W. Bromiley, J. K. S. Reid, R. H. Fuller (Edinburgh: T. & T. Clark, 1960), par. 45:3 passim, and esp. pp. 323-24. Further to this matter, see III/1, par. 41:2, esp. p. 186; and par. 41:3, esp. pp. 288-309.

each other. Thus it is not surprising that the effort should have turned out to be less than successful in specifying precisely what the image of God really is. In the main, theologians tended to point the exegetical evidence in the direction of reason, with freedom in the fallback position. But these undertakings were unhappily beset by the less than easy passage between metaphysics and logic, and, as Karl Barth has decisively shown, they were fatefully flawed by the triumph of logic over metaphysics in the preeminence assigned to analogy.

However appropriate the analogy of being may be between God and rational human beings, including even the analogy of being in relation, the endeavor to rest the interpretive case on analogy misses the decisive scriptural point. To this point, the poets are nearer than are the logicians and the metaphysicians, and those theologians touchingly troubled and fascinated by the wisdom of this world. The poets, as one of their number has put it, have discerned the tantalizing conundrum of analogical reasoning. The conundrum is: "When is an analogy not an analogy?" and the answer is: "When it is a metaphor."[36] Exactly! The decisive scriptural point is, to appropriate with Trible "the metaphor of a Zen sutra, . . . 'like a finger pointing to the moon'" (p. 16).[37]

The significance of Trible's way of reading Scripture is its faithfulness to the inner dynamics of Scripture. To be sure, there are other ways of reading the Bible that may be properly (in Luther's sense) judged by their similar faithfulness. Nevertheless, the pertinence of rhetorical criticism to the interpretation of Scripture, in its stress upon the text itself, is the clue to its unique meaning. As form criticism has taught us to be open to the typical meaning of a text — that is, as a type of literature corresponding to typical human situations — "rhetorical criticism investigates the individual characteristics of a literary unit." In so doing, rhetorical criticism exhibits a special kinship with and indeed "resides in the realm of art" (p. 11). In that realm, it is especially illuminating when the text is a poem, owing to its perception of the structural components of a metaphor.

An instructive case in point, both as regards Trible's method and as regards the patriarchal violation of God's name, is provided by that poetic

36. Edward Lueders, "The Need for an Essential Metaphor" (unpublished paper).

37. Trible cites Philip Kapleau, *Three Pillars of Zen* (Boston: Beacon Press, 1965), pp. 107, 174. It is scarcely "merely co-incidental" that Trible also cites Karl Barth in this context. See Trible, p. 12 n. 66.

text that describes God's creation of male and female "in the image of God" (Gen. 1:27). Particularly in the light of the diversion of this metaphor from its dynamic scriptural sense to analogical interpretation, a rhetorical critical focus upon "the language of semantic motion" (p. 17) liberates the text for its central meaning and also liberates its central meaning through the text. A further extended passage from Trible's account of what is involved may be cited because it takes us most directly to the crucial meaning of the phrase "the image of God."

> As the language of semantic motion, metaphor moves from the better known to the lesser known, from the concrete to the abstract, from the standard to the figurative. Through comparison it extends meaning to express the similarity of difference. This semantic process involves the cooperation of two elements, a vehicle and a tenor. The vehicle is the base of metaphor, the better known element, while the tenor is its underlying (or overarching) subject, the lesser known element. The sense of the metaphor results from the interaction of vehicle and tenor, an interaction that varies with different metaphors. . . . Nevertheless, both are essential for the comparison. . . . Together they produce new meanings that are not available through the individual elements. . . . In Genesis 1:27 the formal parallelism between the phrases "in the image of God" and "male and female" indicates a semantic correspondence between a lesser known element and a better known element. In other words, this parallelism yields a metaphor. "Male and female" is its vehicle; "the image of God," its tenor. (p. 17)

Trible's own forceful conclusions from her metaphorical reading of this text bring us in sight of yet another instance of the indispensability of the Decalogue to a human future. As she sees it, the rhetorical critical interpretation of Genesis 1:27 underlines "the vocabulary of humanity" in the poem. This vocabulary includes three nouns, *humankind (hā-'ādām), male,* and *female,* with their corresponding pronouns, *him ('ōtô)* and *them ('otām).* "All five words are objects of the verb, *create,* with God as its subject" (p. 17). "Given the parallel usage of this vocabulary," certain "shared and particular meanings" are expressed by the "interactions among the five words" (pp. 17-18). These meanings may be summarized as follows:

(1) The shift from singular to plural pronouns "shows clearly that *hā-'ādām* [humankind] is not one single creature who is both male and

female but rather two creatures, one male and one female" (p. 18). Androgyny is disallowed!

(2) "The singular word *hā-'ādām,* with its singular pronoun, *'ōtô,* shows that male and female are not opposite but rather harmonious sexes. . . . From the beginning, the word *humankind* is synonymous with the phrase 'male and female'" (p. 18). Humankind is not an original unity subsequently split by sexual division. On the contrary, the original unity is at the same time the original differentiation.

(3) "The parallelism between *hā-'ādām* and 'male and female' shows further that sexual differentiation does not mean hierarchy but rather equality. Created simultaneously, male and female are not superior and subordinate" (p. 18). In the passage Genesis 1:26-29, the plural pronouns and verbs show that "male and female are treated equally. . . . Both are present and both have equal power over the earth. At the same time, neither is given dominion over the other" (p. 19).[38]

(4) There is an argument from silence — that is, from what is *not* said, which belongs with what *is* said — in exploring the full meaning of the passage. Of Genesis 1:27, Trible writes: "the human creation poeticized in this verse is not delineated by sexual relationships, roles, characteristics, attitudes, or emotions. To be sure, the context itself identifies two responsibilities for humankind, procreation (1:28a) and dominion over the earth (1:26, 28b), but it does not differentiate between the sexes in assigning this work" (p. 19). As for procreation, the divine command parallels that given to the fish and the birds, yet without explicit designation as male and female (1:22). Thus "the use of the phrase 'male and female' in 1:27 does not itself signify the potential for human fertility but rather indicates, along with other items, the uniqueness of humankind in creation. . . . On the other hand, a

---

38. This interpretation is confirmed by, and in turn confirms, the second account of the creation of humankind in Genesis 2:7-9, 18-24. Here, too, although the accent does not fall upon simultaneity but upon precedence, differentiation, and reciprocal responsibility, there is no indication of hierarchy; if anything, there is a heightened accent upon equality. The semantic correlation, Woman-Man *('ishah, 'ish),* of verse 23 makes it clear that "the rib and the bone" of verses 22 and 23 are in no sense intended to mean a hierarchical order of authority and dependence. Instead, an amplification of the shared responsibility for dominion of Gen. 1:26 occurs through the emphasis upon reciprocity, rooted in a shared need. How could the tradition have gone so badly awry? Clearly, owing to the co-optation of Scripture by a patriarchal culture indifferent to or evasive of the repudiation of such co-optation by the inner dynamics of Scripture itself. A comparison of these passages from Trible's book with Karl Barth, *Church Dogmatics,* III/1, p. 186, exhibits a remarkable concurrence.

definite link does exist between the phrase 'male and female' and the responsibility to have dominion over the earth, since both of these descriptions manifest the uniqueness of humankind" (p. 19). Trible recognizes that "an argument from silence is never conclusive and often dangerous." Yet its pertinence to this particular instance is its counsel of "caution against assigning 'masculine' and 'feminine' attributes to the words *male* and *female* in this poem. . . . These words eschew sexual clichés" (p. 19).

On the basis of these findings, then, Trible's summation makes available a hermeneutical possibility for the recovery of God's name from its current patriarchal violation.

> Sexual differentiation of humankind is not thereby a description of God. Indeed, the metaphorical language of Genesis 1:27 preserves with exceeding care the otherness of God. . . . God is neither male nor female, nor a combination of the two. And yet, detecting divine transcendence in human reality requires human clues. Unique among them . . . is [human] sexuality. God creates, in the image of God, male and female. To describe male and female, then, is to perceive the image of God; to perceive the image of God is to glimpse the transcendence of God. (p. 21)

> "Like a finger pointing to the moon" . . . "male and female" is the finger pointing to the "image of God." (pp. 16, 20)

A Critique of Culture in Light of Misogyny: Elisabeth Schüssler Fiorenza

We have explored this hermeneutical recognition at our disposal for the suspension of the threat and the furtherance of the promise of God's watchfulness over the first commandment because of its bearing upon the possibility of a liberating recovery of God's name. Before pursuing this possibility to its promising prospect, it will be of more than a little significance to take account of a historical recognition also at our disposal. In doing so, we turn to Elisabeth Schüssler Fiorenza's "Feminist Theological Reconstruction of Christian Origins" and its reminder of the violation of God's name through patriarchal co-optation.

Schüssler Fiorenza's recognition is an application to Christian origins of "a critique of culture in the light of misogyny." This does not mean that Trible's definition of feminism is one that Schüssler Fiorenza has adopted or would wish to adopt. It means, rather, that the present move from hermeneutical to historical recognition proceeds from a congruent understanding of what is involved in the pilgrimage, under the first commandment, from the violation to the recovery of God's name. In Schüssler Fiorenza's own words:

> The historical-theoretical insight that the New Testament is not only a source of revelatory truth but also a resource for patriarchal subordination and domination demands a new paradigm for biblical hermeneutics and theology. . . . Biblical revelation and truth are given only in those texts and interpretative models that transcend critically their patriarchal frame-works and allow for a vision of Christian women as historical and theological subjects and actors. (p. 30)

The new paradigm for biblical hermeneutics is provided by "an alternative feminist vision of the historical-cultural religious interaction between women and men within Christian community and history" (p. 30). Such a paradigm "is not just geared to the liberation of women but also toward the emancipation of the Christian community from patriarchal structures and androcentric mind-sets so that the gospel can become again a 'power for the salvation' of women as well as men" (p. 31). In Schüssler Fiorenza's view, "biblical patriarchal religion still contributes to the oppression and exploitation of all women in our society." Since

> feminist identity is not based on the experience of biological sex or essential gender differences but on the common historical experience of women as unconsciously collaborating or struggling participants in patriarchal culture and history, . . . the reconstruction of early Christian origins in a feminist perspective is not just a historical but also a feminist theological task. . . . It becomes necessary therefore to explore all the historical dimensions of androcentric biblical texts as well as of early Christian history and theology. (p. 31)

The salvific clue and key to such historical and hermeneutic reconstruction are provided by "a subversive memory."

> Christian feminists reclaim their sufferings and struggles in and through subversive power of "the remembered past." . . . Such a "subversive memory" not only keeps alive the suffering and hopes of Christian women in the past but also allows for a universal solidarity of sisterhood with all women of the past, present and future who follow the same vision. (p. 31)

The challenge of such a "subversive memory" on the part of "the victims of religious patriarchy" cannot be met "by the denial of this self-understanding and religious vision as mistaken or ideological self-deception." It calls instead for

> an engaged solidarity and remembrance of their hopes and despair. . . . It must uncover and reject those elements within *all* biblical traditions and texts that perpetuate in the name of God, violence, alienation, and patriarchal subordination, and eradicate women from historical-theological consciousness. At the same time, such a feminist critical hermeneutics must recover *all* those elements within biblical texts and traditions that articulate the liberating experiences and visions of the people of God. (pp. 31-32)

With Bonhoeffer, whom Schüssler Fiorenza does not cite, this historical, hermeneutical recognition is precisely that "experience of incomparable value" which has been given to us in these days, that is, "to see the great events of world history from below, from the perspective of the outcast, the suspects, the maltreated, the powerless, the oppressed, the reviled — in short, from the perspective of those who suffer."[39] With J. B. Metz, whom Schüssler Fiorenza does cite, in the power of subversive memory, the memory of those who suffer, the central meaning of Christian faith becomes central again.

> At the mid-point of this faith, is a specific *memoria passionis* on which is grounded the promise of future freedom for all. [Such faith] is not a complete leap into the eschatological existence of the "new human" but rather a reflection about concrete human suffering which is the point at which the proclamation of the new and essentially human way of life announced in the resurrection of Jesus can begin. . . . In this sense, the Christian *memoria [passionis, mortis, et resurrectionis Jesus Christi]* . . . insists that the history of human suffering is not merely part of the pre-history of freedom but remains an inner aspect of the history of freedom.[40]

39. Bonhoeffer, *LPP*, p. 17. See p. 110 above.

40. As quoted by Schüssler Fiorenza, pp. 31-32. The passage cited is from Johannes Baptist Metz, *Faith in History and Society: Toward a Practical Fundamental Theology* (New York: Crossroad, 1980), pp. 111-12. I have altered the sequence of the sentences without altering their meaning.

It is fruitful, indeed, as John Calvin has already reminded us, "to remember that the death of Christ is fruitful."[41]

Accordingly, and "as it were in hiding places," Schüssler Fiorenza invites us to join her in a pilgrimage of "seeing-naming-reconstituting" that begins with a remarkably instructive and succinct evaluation of the present state of feminist theological thought. The journey continues with an account of "the Jesus Movement" as a renewal movement within Judaism that focused upon liberation from patriarchal structures and the discipleship of equals. This discipleship of equals marked the Christian missionary movement throughout the first century and expressed itself in the participation and leadership of women as well as men, but it was gradually overtaken by the rise and dominance of patriarchy in ministry in the church of the second century.

> The shift which took place in the second century was not a shift from charismatic leadership to institutional consolidation, but from charismatic and communal authority to an authority vested in local officers, who — in time — absorb not only the teaching authority of the prophet and apostle but also the decision making power of the community. This shift is, at the same time, a shift from alternating leadership accessible to all the baptized to patriarchal leadership restricted to male heads of households; it is a shift from house church to church as the "household of God." (pp. 286-87)

According to Schüssler Fiorenza, this momentous shift led to two monumental consequences. The first was a threefold alteration of leadership: (1) its patriarchalization in the local church; (2) the merger of prophetic and apostolic leadership with the patriarchally defined office of bishop; and (3) the relegation of women's leadership to marginal positions and its restriction to the sphere of women (p. 288). The second consequence was the disregard, indeed, suppression of an original prophetic-apostolic practice, according to which "all members — women and men — were eligible to act as bishop, presbyter, teacher and prophet" (p. 299). The literary and historical criticism of New Testament documents and their environment has long recognized the major influence of the Pastoral Epistles and of Ignatius of Antioch in shaping these consequences. What Schüssler Fiorenza's reconstruction makes plain, however, is that the stress on patriarchal submission and order of the church engenders the genderization of Christian ministry; and that

41. Calvin, *Institutes,* 4.1.2. See above, p. 113 n. 32.

where the post-Pauline writers seek to stabilize the socially volatile situation of coequal discipleship by insisting on patriarchal dominance and submission structures, not only for the household of God but also for the church, the original Gospel writers move to the other end of the social 'balance' scale. . . . It is, therefore, significant that the first writers of Gospels articulate a very different ethos of Christian discipleship and community than that presented by the writers of injunctions to patriarchal submission, although both address Christian communities in the last third of the first century. (pp. 315-16)

Indeed, a careful reading of the first Gospel (Mark) and of the last Gospel (John) discloses the notable participation of women as disciples of Jesus and as apostolic witnesses to him.

A certain fury for righteousness' sake pervades Schüssler Fiorenza's reconstruction, which is prepared to risk overextension on behalf of its principal, proper, and long overdue correction of the record.[42] Meanwhile, such overextensions as come to mind provide no warrant for giving less than careful consideration to the correction, as they await the revisions that such consideration invites. Meanwhile, too, the fury that echoes in this reconstruction signals its own abatement, at least at one point. This point is indicated in the call for the recognition and praxis of an ecclesia of women. Schüssler Fiorenza knows very well that *ekklesia* is a Greek word for a Hebrew word denoting the "assembly of the people of Israel before God." She also knows that in the New Testament the word *ekklesia* refers to "the gathering of God's people around the table . . . in memory of Christ's passion and resurrection

---

42. Or perhaps the fury hovers between "righteous fury" and "aggrieved fury." It is difficult to accept the inference that in biblical traditions and texts, the purpose, or even the result, has been the eradication of women from historical-theological consciousness. It is also at least open to further sociohistorical and cultural inquiry whether, in the culture or in the Christian community in the last third of the first century, women as women suffered the anonymity of oppression that afflicted slaves or the impoverished masses of the cities. Similarly, in our times, it is at least problematical to imply, if not to claim, that the word *suffering* can be univocally applied to persons in Western Europe and the United States, to the middle-class membership of NOW or kindred associations, and to the struggles for justice that mark the liberation movements among black people and poor people in the Two-thirds World. The appeal to suffering for the sake of consciousness raising and the appeal to suffering for conscience' sake are scarcely interchangeable appeals. Meanwhile, however, such ambiguities and perplexities cannot be put forward in disregard or disavowal of the central focus of the feminist critique of misogyny in biblical and theological perspective.

. . . and, in so doing, proclaiming the gospel as God's alternative vision for everyone, especially for those who are poor, outcast, and battered" (p. 345). And when she writes that "it is not over against men that we gather together but in order to become *ekklesia* before God" (p. 347), she signals that in God's vision there really is no ecclesia of women, just as there is no ecclesia of men. One must therefore pause before the imminent recovery of God's name hidden in this "serious call to a devout and holy life" before pressing reservations or rejections too quickly.[43] Schüssler Fiorenza is aware of the fact that "the church of women does not share in the fullness of the church." But she is also aware that this fullness is also denied by "male hierarchical assemblies" (p. 346). She is cognizant of the danger of "reverse sexism" to which her call to an *ekklesia* of women is exposed. But she is also cognizant of the danger to which such an objection prematurely pressed is exposed: an insufficient alertness to "the issues of patriarchal oppression and power" (p. 347).

Women's Need for the Goddess: Carol Christ

These issues are at once superficially and centrally signaled by the heart and its words, as Luther has reminded us. Superficially — and diversionarily — there is the battle of the pronouns, the now frenzied, now obsequious, now servile, now Pickwickian search for inclusive language in canon, liturgy, and hymnody — not to forget the "bouillon cube" version of the Bible — as a public relations *coup de vivre* and an unprecedented fiscal bonanza to the churches, bureaucratized in concert and in council in a fortress on Morningside Heights, overlooking Henry Hudson's river and vis-à-vis the Riverside Church.[44] Never has so much been paid to so many for an ecclesial-commercial expurgation and dissemination of the canonical record of God's

43. The allusion is to an earlier invitation to Christian spirituality by Archbishop William Law, *A Serious Call to a Devout and Holy Life.*

44. The first allusion is to a memorable line in a play written by James Thurber more than half a century ago. In a scene from *The Male Animal,* an all-American football hero visits a favorite former teacher of his, a professor of English literature. Upon the teacher's inquiry concerning what he might be reading now, the successful and affluent alumnus explains that he regrets to report that, owing to demanding involvements, he really has time to read only *The Reader's Digest.* "I see," said the professor, "so you like bouillon cubes!"

The second allusion is to the Inter-Church Center, 475 Riverside Drive, in New York City, often referred to as "the God-box."

covenantal story of trustworthiness and liberation for human freedom and fulfillment. It is not being implied that Luther himself was, or is, exempt from the patriarchal violation of God's name. Brother Martin would certainly have been confounded by *The Woman's Bible*.[45] But if Heine is correct at all, Brother Martin could not be imagined as a scholarly editorial consultant — well-compensated or otherwise — in an enterprise aimed at a *biblia digesta lectorem* and designed to keep "the view from below" well below any effective obstruction of the view from above. The congruence of Luther's perceptive probing of the heart and its trust with his gifted provision of language for liberty was its own shield and buckler against the expropriation of Scripture by "the proud, powerful, and rich."

More central to the heart and its words is the dissolution of the heart and its trust, when the self — in its quest and need for a focal and fulfilling conjunction of ultimacy and intimacy — turns in upon itself. The dehumanizing impact of the violation of God's name is painfully and poignantly evident in the passionate pursuit of the heart and its goddess.[46] In Carol Christ's forceful essay "Why Women Need the Goddess," the critical significance of this pursuit for faith and for self-identity as a human being is gathered up in a line from a successful Broadway play by the African playwright Ntosake Shange. At one point in the play, "a tall beautiful black woman rises from despair to cry out, 'I found God in myself and I loved her fiercely.' "[47] According to Carol Christ, this line expresses the quintessential meaning of the symbol of the Goddess. It affirms "the legitimacy of female power as a beneficent and independent power. A woman who echoes Ntosake Shange's dramatic statement is saying 'Female power is strong and creative.' She is saying that the divine principle, the saving and sustaining power, is in herself, that she will no longer look to men or male figures as saviors" (p. 277). One may be permitted to wonder whether in the context of the play itself, the pain and despair of that "dramatic

45. Cady Stanton, *The Woman's Bible* (1895 and 1898). See the instructive and important discussion of this edition by Schüssler Fiorenza, pp. 7-13.

46. For a statement of this pursuit that is more eloquent in its passion than in its trust, and hence poignantly exposed to the vulnerability of ideology to idolatry, see Carol Christ, "Why Women Need the Goddess: Phenomenological, Psychological and Political Reflections," in *Womanspirit Rising: A Feminist Reader in Religion,* ed. Carol P. Christ and Judith Plaskow (San Francisco: Harper & Row, 1979), pp. 273-86. Subsequent references to this essay will be given parenthetically in the text.

47. Ntosake Shange, *For Colored Girls Who Have Considered Suicide, When the Rainbow Is Enuf;* cited by Carol Christ, p. 273.

statement" are as remote from the cry of dereliction (Mark 15:34) as Carol Christ's interpretation suggests. Nevertheless, the awesome disjunction between the ultimacy and intimacy of the heart and its trust, which this claim to recognition and confidence is designed to overcome, is awesomely congruent with God's own wrath, which "does not abate until the fourth generation" (LCT, 369:32) whenever and wherever "truth and justice" are disjoined from one another (LCT, 373:66). When, as in our time, the patriarchal violation of God's name is at once pervasive and tenacious, the refusal any longer to "look to men or male figures as saviors" can be a sign of the use of God's name "properly," in faithfulness to the heart and its trust, to the reciprocity between faith and God set free under the right tablet of Moses. Under the Decalogue, "the power of anger," in Beverly Harrison's arresting phrase, can indeed be "in the work of love."[48]

A shared concern for and commitment to the use of God's name properly, however, must disavow the symbol of the Goddess for two basic and critical reasons. Carol Christ herself has properly noted them in her account of the meaning and importance of the symbol. The first reason is expressed in the word *legitimacy;* the second relates to the fundamental bond between the Goddess and the self. As to the first reason, the ascription of "legitimacy" to the acknowledgment of female power "as a beneficent and independent power" delivers the acknowledgment over to the identical idolatry of power that marks the patriarchal co-optation of God's name. The egregious violation of the first and second commandments by the patriarchal confusion of God with maleness is an inadmissible and idolatrous confusion of the self-identity of the creature with the self-identification of God. The operation of this idolatry is a matter of record. It exalts the independence of power over responsibility for power, and in so doing inverts both. The independence of power is inverted as bondage to power. The responsibility for power is inverted as the justification of power. Owing to this double inversion, the "power of anger in the work of love" becomes the fury that hides the idolatry to which the ideology of power is destructively vulnerable.

The primary and primordial casualty of this double inversion is the second reason for the disavowal of the symbol of the Goddess. This has to do with the bond between the Goddess and the self. The inversion nurtures the self-destruction of the self as the liberation of the self. "Evil,

---

48. Beverly Harrison, "The Power of Anger in the Work of Love," *Union Seminary Quarterly Review* 36, supplementary issue, "Inaugural Addresses" (1981): 49.

be thou my good!" The delivery of the self over to its own destruction, of "the willing acquisition of vulnerability" over to the security of recognition, achievement, and arrival, identifies the place and the hour of judgment alike for androcentric and for gynocentric violations of God's name. Its unfailing sign is the displacement of trust by power in the relation between faith and God, between the heart and its trust, between the image of God as male and female and male and female in the image of God. Yet, as the threat and peril of God's watchfulness over the first commandment are bracketed by God's promise, so the place and hour of destruction are transfigured as the place and hour of the self and its search for the proper name of God. Listen again to Robert Penn Warren:

> This
> Is the hour of the unbounded loneliness. This
> Is the hour of the self's uncertainty
> Of self. This is the hour when
> Prayer might be a possibility, if
> It were. This
> Is the hour when what is remembered is
> Forgotten. When
> What is forgotten is remembered, and
> You are not certain which is which.
> But tell me: How had you ever forgotten that spot
> Where once wild azalea bloomed? And what there passed?
>   And forgotten
> That truth may lurk in irony? How,
> Alone in a dark piazza, at 3 A.M., as the cathedral clock
> Announced to old tiles of the starless city, could you bear
> To remember the impossible lie, told long before, elsewhere?
> But a lie you had found all too impossible.
> Self is the cancellation of self, and now is the hour.
> Self is the mutilation of official meanings, and this is the place. . . .
>
> The stars would not be astonished
> To catch a glimpse of the form through interstices
> Of leaves now black as enamelled tin. Nothing can astound the stars.
> They have long lived. And you are not the first
> To come to such a place seeking the most difficult knowledge.[49]

49. Robert Penn Warren, "The Place," *The New Yorker* 59, 23 (25 July 1983):

If, then, the heart and its trust are to be joined again for the healing, freedom, and fulfillment of the self in itself and in society, in solitude and in community, the difference which going about with the name of God as though it made all the difference in the world makes must be discerned and received again. The violation of the name of God through its patriarchal co-optation must be repudiated, and the hour and the place of "seeking the most difficult knowledge" must be discovered again in the covenantal journey, its story, and its Scripture. Then — in that context — it could be possible again to remember that "truth may lurk in irony" and to "bear to remember the impossible lie, told long before, elsewhere[,] but a lie you had found all too impossible."

The Fatherhood of God: A Patriarchal Distortion and a Covenantal Recovery

The determinate image of the patriarchal co-optation and domestication of God's name was and is that of a father and his household. But this image — however appropriate to and supportive of polytheistic pluralism, hierarchical social and political folkways and habits, stabilities, institutions, and achievements it could be claimed to be — was and is profoundly at variance with and opposed to the God whom the commandments of the right tablet of Moses identify as utterly and unfailingly worthy of trust. There is a radical and uncompromising contradiction and opposition between God the father — so understood and responded to — and the God of Adam and Eve, of Abraham and Sarah, of Isaac and Rebekah, of Jacob and Rachel, of Moses and Miriam, of Gideon and Deborah, of Ruth and Boaz, of David and Esther, of Israel's prophets, priests, and sages, of Jesus and the unnamed woman of Mark's Gospel (14:3-9), of Phoebe, Prisca, and Aquila (Rom. 16:1, 3), of Epaenetus and Mary (Rom. 16:5-6). This radical and uncompromising contradiction between covenantal memories and expectations and the secure and self-justifying satisfactions of the domesticated God broke open afresh with the presence of Jesus of Nazareth in the human story and in and through the community of faith and freedom, of reciprocal responsibility

---

26. For the image of the stars, see the Canticle, Benedicite, omnia opera Dei, *The Book of Common Prayer* (New York: Thomas Nelson and Sons, 1929), pp. 11-13.

toward and among all sorts of human beings and conditions, in commitment and discipleship to him.[50]

Correlative with the patriarchal co-optation and domestication of
God's name have been the domestication and distortion of the covenantal
story and its Scripture. The fatherhood of God became the principal
warrant for the dehumanizing subordination, chiefly of women, but also

50. It is a particular merit of Letty Russell's book *Human Liberation in Feminist
Perspective* (Philadelphia: Westminster Press, 1974) that she has given central attention
to the presence and significance of Jesus in the interpretation of the Bible and of the
variety of traditions rooted in Scripture. In the light of the centrality of Jesus, moreover,
Russell seeks to explore the interrelations among Scripture, tradition, and that human
liberation to which the feminist movement is committed — at least so far as its
theologians are concerned. Certain key passages (cited by Schüssler Fiorenza, pp. 15
and 27) succinctly and strikingly express Russell's christocentric discernment.

"Christ's work," Russell writes, "was not first of all that of being a male but
that of being a new human being" (p. 138). And again, "tradition is not a block of
content to be carefully guarded by authorized hierarchies but a dynamic action of
God's love which is to be passed on to others of all sexes and races" (p. 79).

From the first, Russell has sought to show that the Bible and liberation theology
do indeed go together "on the side of the oppressed." Schüssler Fiorenza correctly
recognizes this. What is puzzling about her interpretation of Russell's work, however,
is her insistence that Russell has aligned herself "too quickly with the methods and
interests of the neo-orthodox model, and in so doing fails to explore sufficiently the
function of the Bible in the oppression of the poor or of women" (Schüssler Fiorenza,
p. 15). It is difficult to see how this assessment is supported by the passages cited by
Schüssler Fiorenza or by the thematic concern of Russell's book as a whole.

Less difficult to discover is the basis of Schüssler Fiorenza's interpretation of
Russell. Indeed, Russell and Trible — and even Rosemary Radford Ruether — are
vulnerable, according to Schüssler Fiorenza, because "they adopt a feminist neo-
orthodox model that is in danger of reducing the ambiguity of historical struggle to
theological essences and abstract timeless principles" (p. 27). It can scarcely be that
Schüssler Fiorenza is ignorant of the dialectical theological method and analysis of
Karl Barth, or of the pertinence of the dialectical relation between ideology and utopia
in a sociology of knowledge, as described by Karl Mannheim. Following Peter Berger,
Schüssler Fiorenza appears to translate Mannheim's terms into those of an "Archimedian point" and "historical relativization." She cites Berger's charge — as incredible
as it is mistaken — that "this neo-orthodox hermeneutics [is] an attempt to absorb
the full impact of the relativizing perspective but nevertheless to point to an Archimedian point in a sphere immune to relativization" (p. 15).

The fact is that for "neo-orthodox hermeneutics," the Archimedian point is at
the center of a sphere caught up in the dynamics of God's action in Jesus Christ in
the world and for the world, where nothing is "immune to relativization" — unless
perhaps it be Peter Berger's "heretical imperative," tutored by Wolfhart Pannenberg
and democratic capitalism. How far one can stray from "In Memory of Her"!

of servants and slaves, of the underprivileged and the untalented. It was not discerned that God and sin were being sexualized, that reciprocal responsibilities among social beings as human beings were being socially stratified, and that the fulfilling reciprocity between difference and sameness in a world not fated by power but purposed as creation were being polarized into falsehood. The primordial, liberating, and fulfilling dynamics of hierarchical and egalitarian social structures were being steadily undermined by hierarchical hegemonies. Inequality and heterogeneity, as structures of social interaction purposed for reciprocal responsibility, were being disregarded, diverted, and deadened by a gradual but inevitable alienation of justice from truth, of love from power, and of power from love. In the end, the faith and freedom that being and staying human in the world require were being violated. The heart and its trust were being betrayed. In their stead, the principalities and powers having checkmated the household of faith, ideology, suspicion, and hatred pervaded the body politic. But, as in former times, when "the word of the LORD was rare [and] there was no frequent vision" (1 Sam. 3:1, RSV) God "did not leave himself without witness" (Acts 14:17, RSV), so now in these days, God has withheld his wrath in favor of his promise, and, in faithfulness to his Commandments, has raised up the ecclesia of women to summon the violators of his name to move into and return to the way of obedient freedom.

Such a move involves at the very least a threefold renewal of apperception. First, the scriptural witness to the covenantal story must be heard, received, and taught anew in the fullness of its promise of and bearing upon a human future. Second, the community of faith — both Jewish and Christian — to whom the scriptural witness has been entrusted and who, in the promise and fullness of this trust, have been called to a proleptic praxis of a human future, must receive and accept anew this heritage and responsibility. Third, the primacy of the promise over the threat intrinsic to God's watchfulness over the first commandment includes the assurance that the renewal of apperception thus undertaken and pursued will discern and receive again the gift of God's self-identifying and liberating name. At issue is the recovery of memory in the power of God's future giving shape to a present fit for being human in.

The hermeneutical and historical recognitions that have been occasioned for us by the feminist movement have brought us also in sight of a semantic recognition. This recognition provides the heart and its trust with an identifiable name and an identifying claim. In it, the aspirate becomes utterable in an utter and unfailing dependence that is the secret of freedom and the source of that confidence which evokes the commitment to reciprocal responsibility for human fulfillment, and thus also our participation in the human future already breaking in upon us. Some hint of this recognition has already come before us in the course of our attempt to be about the Canon in our own way — not Luther's — yet in faithfulness to Luther's concern for what belongs to the name of God "properly." The contradiction and opposition between God the father, patriarchally understood, and God the Father, covenantally understood, have directed us anew to Jesus' own sustaining instruction in apperceptive covenantal faithfulness. In naming God "Father" in the context of prayer, it is now clearer to us than when we first believed (cf. Rom. 13:11), not only how radically Jesus joined holiness and humanness together in our not going about with the name of God as though it made no difference, but also how radically he rejected the patriarchal violation of God's name.

When Jesus conjoined fatherhood with holiness and holiness with fatherhood, he was neither sanctifying a patriarchal mentality, culture, and society nor deifying parentage. He was, on the contrary, identifying the radical transfiguration of the experience of mystery in the mystery of experience. In this transfiguration, "the silence of the infinite spaces" that terrifies (Pascal) inspires wonder; the awesome indiscriminateness of nature's bounty and caprice converts resentment into patience; the enervating unpredictability of circumstance tutors humility; the intolerability of suffering and of the brutality of human frenzy, cruelty, and power exchange the paralysis of apathy and resignation for the passion for justice and healing. In this transfiguration, the fear of death is replaced by steadfastness in hope, and the subliminal roots of idolatry are withered. Oedipus and Medea, Antigone and Narcissus are freed for the full humanity that is their birthright.

In the reality and power of this transfiguration, the aspirate name and the unmistakable claim evoke a liberating and fulfilling human commitment and trust. The name "Father" identifies the one "from whom every family in heaven and on earth takes its name" (Eph. 3:14, NEB), and is freed from its conventional and constrictive sexual confinements and restored to its constitutive mythological primordiality. According to this primordiality, the presence and power of an originating initiative evoke an inviolable trust. In the presence of this initiative and by the power of this trust, the unmistakable claim is the experience of dependence as the gateway of freedom and of gratitude as the root of responsibility. In short, this is what it means to know God as creator and the world as creation. For "out of the treasures of his glory . . . strength and power through his Spirit" are granted "in your inner being, that through faith Christ may dwell in your hearts in love. With deep roots and firm foundations . . . be strong to grasp, with all God's people, what is the breadth and length and height and depth of the love of Christ, and to know it, though it is beyond knowledge" (Eph. 3:16-18, NEB).

In the course of her discussion of "The Jesus Movement as Renewal Movement within Judaism," Elisabeth Schüssler Fiorenza makes a strong and striking connection between Jesus' identification of God as Father and "the new kingship of the discipleship of equals" (*In Memory of Her,* p. 150). She finds it notable that Jesus' sustaining instruction in covenantal faithfulness occurs in the context of "sayings against wanting to be 'great' and 'first' in the community of discipleship."[51] It is precisely here, according to Schüssler Fiorenza, in the context of Jesus' discussion of discipleship and prayer and the name of God, whom the disciples and Jesus call "father" (Luke 11:2-4; 12:30; Mark 11:25) that Jesus uses the "'father' name of God not as a legitimation for existing patriarchal power structures in society or church but as a critical subversion of all structures of domination" (pp. 150-51).

The decisive text is Matthew 23:9: "Call no one your father on earth, for you have one Father — the one in heaven." Moreover, the context in which this injunction appears includes a parallelism that serves to emphasize it, whether intentionally on Matthew's part or not. The preceding verse (v. 8) declares that "you are not to be called rabbi, for you have one teacher, and you are all brethren" (RSV). But the usual antonym to "teacher" is "disciple," not "brethren"; whereas "brethren" is usual as an antonym to "father." Thus, "the original prohibition . . . juxtaposes the terms 'not to be called rabbi,' 'one teacher,' 'all disciples' in the form of an inclusion: 'But you are not to be called rabbi, for you have one teacher and you are all disciples' " (pp. 149-50). Similarly, according to Schüssler Fiorenza, the more original form of the saying on fatherhood, contrasting earth and heaven, may have read: "Call no one father for you have one father (and you are all siblings)" (p. 150).[52] Or perhaps better — since the

---

51. The interconnection between Matt. 23:8-11; Mark 11:25; and Luke 11:2-4 and 12:30 is, according to Schüssler Fiorenza, especially significant in this connection. See Schüssler Fiorenza, pp. 149-51.

52. Schüssler Fiorenza notes that Rudolf Bultmann thinks it possible that Matt.

antonymic relation between "brethren" and "father" has been changed to "siblings" and "father" — the parallelism between verse 8 and verse 9 would allow a repetition of the word "disciples." Accordingly, in the community of equals who "have one master, the Christ" (Matt. 23:10, RSV), and no one is father save God alone, kinship is transfigured as a comradeship of receiving and giving in thankfulness and trust, and the family becomes a parable of human wholeness, of that " 'solidarity from below' required by the *basileia* of God . . . challenge to relinquish all claims of power and domination over others" (p. 148). Parents and children are all disciples. As disciples, parents are receivers and givers of that authority who means freedom, whom children receive and in their turn give again as parents to their children. As disciples, parents who were children and children who are called to be parents find their freedom and fulfillment in reciprocal responsibility toward one another. In, with, under, and through the inequalities and heterogeneities concretely and reciprocally ordained as pathways and patterns of human wholeness, they enter into and are sustained by the dynamics of freedom, reciprocity, and trust.

> "When you pray, say:
> 'Father, hallowed be your name.
> Your kingdom come.' "
>
> (Luke 11:2; and parallels)

The Father-name of God is "the name that is above every name . . . in heaven and on earth and under the earth" (Phil. 2:9-10). The Father-name of God is the name that God bestowed upon Jesus the Christ, who "did not regard equality with God as something to be exploited" (v. 6), but the occasion for the identification of the truly human through self-denying servanthood in humility and obedience unto death. Through this obedience, God's exaltation of Jesus as the servant who is Lord is God's self-identification as Father: the code word for the authority who means freedom. By this authority and this self-identification, what it means to be truly human is given and guaranteed through the reality and power of God's making himself known as God. The Father-name of God identifies who God is, who Jesus is, and who we are in the similarities and the differences, the precedences and the purposes, the reciprocities and the

---

23:8-10 is an original saying of Jesus (p. 159 n. 103; citing R. Bultmann, *History of the Synoptic Tradition* [Oxford: Blackwell, 1968], p. 144).

responsibilities intrinsic to the primordial, providential, proleptic, and consummating relationships that make our world fit for being human in, and in which the mystery of experience is transfigured in the experience of mystery. In the Father-name of God, the aspirate acknowledgment of the hidden majesty in the experience of mystery and the unmistakable responsibility hidden in the mystery of experience meet in the liberating human experience of utter dependence upon the utterly dependable. The heart and its trust have come upon the secret of their freedom for fulfillment and are set free for their fulfillment in freedom in, with, and under the reciprocities between inequality and heterogeneity in this world and the next. This is the quintessential meaning and point of prayer. This is what practice of prayer — liturgically or privately, in community or in solitude, in utterance or in silence — is quintessentially about.

> When we cry, "Abba! Father!" it is the Spirit himself bearing witness with our spirit that we are children of God, and if children, then heirs, heirs of God and fellow heirs with Christ, provided we suffer with him in order that we may also be glorified with him. . . .
>
> Likewise the Spirit helps us in our weakness; for we do not know how to pray as we ought, but the Spirit himself intercedes for us with sighs too deep for words. And he who searches the hearts . . . knows what is the mind of the Spirit, because the Spirit intercedes for the saints according to the will of God. (Rom. 8:15d-17, 26-27, RSV)

> "You are not to be called rabbi, for you have one teacher, and you are all [disciples]. And call no man your father on earth, for you have one Father, who is in heaven. Neither be called masters, for you have one master, the Christ." (Matt. 23:8-10, RSV)

We have come here upon another parallelism that yields a metaphor. As we have seen in the case of the parallelism between "male and female" and "the image of God," the vehicle (or better known element) combines with the tenor (the lesser known element) in a metaphor expressive of "new meanings not available through the individual elements" (Trible, p. 17), yet which are intrinsic to the relations between God and "male and female."[53] Just so, the parallelism between father and Father — the one on earth, the other who is in heaven — yields new meanings for a familiar metaphor for the name of God. The word "father," the better

53. See above, pp. 117-18.

known element, and the word "Father," the lesser known element, meet on the boundary between earth and heaven, between the misuse and the proper use of the same word for the name of God. In this instance, not only do vehicle and tenor call attention to each other, but the tenor highlights the vehicle. As in the former instance, where "the image of God" identifies the uniqueness of "male and female" in the uniqueness, not the gender, of their sexuality, so in the present instance, the "Father-name" of God identifies the uniqueness of "fatherhood" in the uniqueness of the heart and its trust, that is, in the uniqueness of the utterly dependable in the liberating human experience of utter dependence, not the generative power and dominating authority of parenthood.[54] To paraphrase the Apos-

54. At issue is the cosmic, historical, cultural, and human difference between an originating authority who means freedom and a dominating authority whose dominion enslaves. The question is at once natural and tantalizing whether the difference between a liberating and a dominating authority could not as appropriately be identified by the word *mother* as by the word *father*.

Logically, it may be urged, the answer is affirmative, and this reply rests not only upon the canons of rationality but even more upon the relativistic findings of cultural anthropology. Matriarchal societies and cultures are a matter of record. Moreover, these anthropological findings are broadly accompanied by the mythological and ritualistic findings of the historical and comparative study of religions. Nor do the Oedipal and archetypal psychoanalytic attempts to identify formative structures and patterns of the human experience of ultimacy and depth succeed in setting at rest the question of primordiality in matters of the heart and its trust. How fierce and frenzied, self-serving and subliminal the varieties, ambiguities, and complexities of the attempt to probe and to sort out a persuasive account of primordiality and promise in the human story can be! This desultory recognition has been recently instanced again in the quarrel that has overtaken the late distinguished cultural anthropologist Margaret Mead. An ugly debate seems to have surfaced over the integrity of her method and findings.

On a nobler and loftier level, the celebrated reply of Adolf von Harnack to Max Müller may be allowed to identify the critical point at stake. Müller once declared — and with pointed reference to the ignorance of religious traditions other than the Christian tradition that is so notable in Western religious thought — "Whosoever knows only one religion knows no religion." To which von Harnack replied: "Whosoever knows this religion, knows all religions." This epigrammatic exchange sharply poses the question of monotheism and its religious and cultural alternatives. It echoes the Talmudic legend of Abraham's sudden furious and destructive revulsion against idols, as he was tending his grandfather's shop where idols were on display, particularly for the nouveau riches of Ur of the Chaldees. It echoes, too, the settlement arrived at between Abraham and Lot (Gen. 13), the Mosaic confrontation with Pharaoh (Exod. 5:1-2), the Gideon text (Judg. 7:4-8), and the theocratic

tle Paul, it is not the "fatherhood on earth" from which all Godhood in heaven and on earth is named, but "the Father of glory" (Eph. 1:17), from whom "every family in heaven and on earth takes its name" (3:15). He is "the God of our Lord Jesus Christ," who has given us

> a spirit of wisdom and of revelation as [we] come to know him, so that, with the eyes of [our] heart enlightened, [we] may know what is the hope to which he has called [us], what are the riches of his glorious inheritance among the saints, and what is the immeasurable greatness of his power for [us] who believe, according to the working of his great power. God put this power to work in Christ when he raised him from the dead and seated him at his right hand in the heavenly places, far above all rule and authority and power and dominion, and above every

---

refusal of Gideon to rule (Judg. 8:22-23). Not least, the exchange between Müller and von Harnack sharply poses the momentous and destiny-laden human decision, put unforgettably in Joshua's words, long before the present time of troubles of the "Age of Enlightenment," and long before the gnostic and/or symbolic fascination with the goddess:

> Now therefore revere the LORD, and serve him in sincerity and in faithfulness; put away the gods that your ancestors served beyond the River and in Egypt, and serve the LORD. Now if you are unwilling to serve the LORD, choose this day whom you will serve, whether the gods your ancestors served in the region beyond the River or the gods of the Amorites in whose land you are living; but as for me and my household, we will serve the LORD. (Josh. 24:14-15)

The covenantal-messianic story emerged as an unveiling of a human future coming our way, apart from which no present has any human prospect, and the human promise of every past has been deprived of a liberating memory. There can be no inquisitorial insistence upon adherence to the covenantal-messianic story. Polytheistic and ideological options abound. But the covenantal story belongs to the human record, to be remembered, shared, and attested to as the bearer of that future which makes human sense of both past and present. Accordingly, with due acknowledgment of the deep chasm that the patriarchal violation of God's name has wrought between the covenantal story, with its Scripture and tradition, and the faith and life of the ecclesia of women, particularly in this present time, it may be appropriate, nevertheless, to hope and to pray and to work for that renewal of apperception rooted in the restoration of God's name. In the promise and power of that renewal, a transfiguration could come upon the community of discipleship of equals, in the bright light and power of which the language-and-consciousness alienation of women and of men from the heritage and promise of the covenantal story could be healed through the discernment of new and liberating metaphorical possibilities of going about with the name of God, which makes all the difference in the world.

name that is named, not only in this age but also in the age to come.
(Eph. 1:17-21)[55]

Thus the Father-name of God is the appropriate name for the God of
Abraham and Sarah and their descendants, of Moses and Elijah, and of Jesus,
the "one master, the Christ," in the community with whom and through
whom and of whom we "are all disciples." Going about with the name of
God as Father is to go about with the appropriate metaphor for God, who
is the utterly dependable in the experience of utter dependence, the authority
who means freedom, and the secret of the heart and its trust. "Like a finger
pointing to the moon," to call God "Father" is to identify the God of the
covenant and its story as he has given himself to be identified.

In calling God "Father," "a transfiguration of the commonplace"
occurs in which the mystery of experience is made "luminous in holy
grace" by the experience of mystery.[56] It is a transfiguration, as Arthur
Danto puts it, in which the mystery of experience retains its identity
through a metaphorical identification "meant to illuminate it under novel
attributes" (p. 172), discerned through new meanings. In this transfiguration, the participants in the covenantal story are drawn into collaboration
in some way to be who they are and to be changed by the experience of
being who they are. Just as "art . . . is virtually the enactment of a metaphorical transformation with oneself as subject: [as] what the work ultimately is about, a commonplace person transfigured into an amazing
[person]" (p. 173), and just as "one of art's main offices may be to cause
us to view [the world] with a certain attitude and with a special vision . . . ,
to heighten and confirm faith; . . . [to effect] . . . some transformation . . .
or some affirmation of the way the world is viewed by those who experience
it fully" (p. 167) — so also is it with going about with the Father-name
of God, the name that makes all the difference in the world. Charles
Dickens "in *Great Expectations* speaks of Mr. Jagger's 'powerful handkerchief,' but he also gives us a context for appreciating this characterization
of so essentially flimsy an accessory" (p. 158). Just so, speaking of God as
Father in the context of the covenantal story enables us to understand and

---

55. It is assumed that the consensus of New Testament scholars accepts the
Pauline authorship of the Letter to the Ephesians.

56. Arthur C. Danto, *The Transfiguration of the Commonplace* (Cambridge:
Harvard University Press, 1981). Subsequent references will be given parenthetically
in the text. Further to the pertinence of Danto's work to the concerns before us in
these pages, see n. 57 below.

appropriate this characterization of so problematical and even flimsy a term. By means of metaphorical transfiguration, God is Father and Mr. Jagger's handkerchief is powerful.[57]

Pronominal Referentiality and the Interrelations among Grammar, Language, and Art

The heart and its trust, thus properly identified, are set free not only for freedom and fulfillment but also from preoccupation with sexually adjusted pronominal referentiality. The heart and its trust discern in this linguistic pursuit a recrudescence of the genderization of the name of God from which the parallelisms so carefully noted by the feminist theologians have delivered us. They discern also a recrudescence of the lamentable textual literalism that has contributed its own share to the loss and violation of God's name. The crusaders for pronominal equivocality — like their fundamentalistic predecessors and contemporaries who relentlessly insist upon univocality — may also persist indefinitely in their shared literalistic imperviousness to metaphorical transfiguration.

57. It is a particular pleasure to acknowledge my indebtedness to Professor Danto, whose splendid volume noted above has recalled Dickens's great work and alerted me to Mr. Jagger's handkerchief. Danto is concerned with the point and purpose of artistic creation and creativity. His analysis is as imaginative as it is learned, as brilliant as it is subtle. The range, variety, and perceptiveness of his artistic commentary and interpretation promise a careful and thoughtful reader a feast of enrichment of sensibility and understanding, from Socrates to Andy Warhol, that leaves an immense and lingering delight in its wake.

Professor Danto is, of course, not accountable for my interpretation of the segment of his analysis drawn upon here. Yet, inasmuch as I have long found a central and significant kinship between Christian ethics and art (see my books *Ethics in a Christian Context* [New York: Harper & Row, 1963], esp. chaps. 3 and 4, and *The Transfiguration of Politics* [New York: Harper & Row, 1975], esp. the preface and chaps. 8 and 9), the suggestion in this volume is that the Decalogue might function provisionally as a surrogate for Troeltsch's vision of an epic for "the overcoming of history by history" (Troeltsch, p. 772). Thus Danto's analysis has come to me as a welcome gift of encouragement and guidance in the present attempt to think again about the pertinence of "the right tablet of Moses" to "the prospect of a human future" (Heilbronner). Although I have paraphrased the passage drawn upon, I have nonetheless indicated in parentheses the pages on which certain of Danto's formulations may be found, and to which the reader may wish to refer in determining the correctness and appropriateness of the interpretation offered here.

Metaphorical transfiguration, however, not only recovers God's name from its patriarchal violation. It also opens the way for a further contribution of rhetorical criticism to the liberation of faith, society, and culture from misogyny. This contribution is the gift of the power of interpretation of the meaning and importance of going about with the name of God "properly." Under way is the compelling discovery (in Robert Penn Warren's words) "that truth may lurk in irony," which is bearing "to remember the impossible lie, told long before, elsewhere[;] but a lie . . . found all too impossible," being on the threshold of "seeking the most difficult knowledge." Some understanding of what this discovery really comes to in experience, in the apperception of the human, and in "the knowledge of God and of ourselves" may be gleaned from the structural interrelations among grammar, language, and art.

Phyllis Trible has pointed out, with notable clarity and candor, that there is an almost unbridgeable chasm of understanding between the Hebrew language, which employs masculine pronouns for God, and contemporary hearing and response. "Though grammatical gender," she writes, "decides neither sexuality nor theology . . . masculine pronouns reinforce a male image of God, an image that obscures, even obliterates, female metaphors for deity. The effect is detrimental for faith and its participants." Concerning this effect upon contemporary hearing, there can be little doubt. Nor can there be much doubt about "the dilemma posed by grammatical gender for deity in the scriptures themselves, since translation must answer to both grammatical accuracy and interpretive validity." Provisionally, Trible avoids pronouns for deity in her own writing, and she thinks that "an occasional resulting awkwardness of style is a small price to pay for a valuable theological statement." Yet her own analysis has taken her, as well as contemporary hearers who have ears to hear, a certain way toward that "illumination on this issue" so "pressing . . . in contemporary hermeneutics" (Trible, p. 23 n. 5).

In the course of her own commentary upon Genesis 2:4b-7, Trible notes that the very long and even "tedious sentence struggles both to present and to limit cosmic perspective . . . as a prelude to the advent and fulfillment of human life on earth" (p. 75). She then continues with what may be regarded as her crucial hermeneutical remark, one that really carries her beyond her pronominally induced neutralization of the name of God as "the deity." "The tension between cosmic perspective and earthly focus," Trible writes, "threatens to explode grammar and syntax" (p. 76). Exactly so! Grammar and syntax are threatened with explosion, yet they manage to keep their tenuous hold. Otherwise language would be bereft of its human point and purpose and would be reduced to the dehumanizing fate of an unholy fluctuation between cacophony and the tedious prosody that ends up in statistics.

In the face of this melancholy prospect, however, the sturdy structural relation between grammar and language discovers a "friend in need" in the relation between language and art. Perhaps there is a congruent relation between the problem of predication, which is so baffling to artistic discourse, and the problem of pronominal referentiality, which is no less baffling to hermeneutical and theological discourse.

As to the problem of predication in artistic discourse, we may turn again to Arthur Danto's instructive analysis for help along our way. Reflecting upon certain drawings of flowers by André Racz, upon Roy Lichtenstein's portrait of Madame Cézanne (1963), and upon the more widely known sculptures of Napoleon in the garb of a Roman emperor, Danto underlines certain particulars of the relation between vision and interpretation in understanding a work of art — that is, between what one sees and what one says about what one sees. Of Racz's drawings of flowers, Danto notes that the representation of flowers and flowers as flowers must correspond with discernible self-evidence. "Nothing will be true of the representation of flowers that will not be true of flowers as flowers" (p. 156). Of Roy Lichtenstein's *Portrait of Madame Cezanne,* Danto recalls a controversy of some intensity over the question of whether the diagram of Cézanne's wife as worked out by Erle Loran had been plagiarized by Lichtenstein's portrait. Loran's diagram, according to Danto, "is about a specific painting and concerns the volumes and vectors of it. Lichtenstein's painting is about the way Cezanne painted his wife: it is *about* the wife, as seen by Cezanne" (p. 142). The issue of plagiarism could arise because Cézanne applies to his wife "a kind of Pythagorean vision of the ultimate forms of reality," with the result that she appears "as though she were a Euclidean problem!" Accordingly, the portrait "entailed a certain dehumanizing transfiguration of the subject; as if the person were so many planes, treated with no more and no less intensity and analytical subversion than a wax apple." For Danto, Loran's diagram is "not a work of art at all, but just, after all, the diagram of a painting." Consequently, "the issue of plagiarism is silly" (p. 143). Can the same be said for Scriptural or pronominal literalism?

Of Napoleon as a Roman emperor, it must be understood that "the sculptor is not just representing Napoleon in an antiquated get-up. . . . Rather the sculptor is anxious to get the viewer to take toward the subject —

Napoleon — the attitudes appropriate to the more exalted Roman emperors — Caesar or Augustus. . . . That figure, so garbed, is a metaphor of dignity, authority, grandeur, power, and political utterness" (p. 167). To be sure, participation in the artist's intention and creation presupposes a certain knowledge of how Napoleon really did dress and of the fact that he was a French and not a Roman emperor, and lived in the nineteenth century, not the first. "In brief, . . . the locus of metaphoric expression is in the representation — in Napoleon-as-Roman-emperor — rather than in the reality represented, namely, Napoleon wearing those clothes. . . . Napoleon was a very powerful figure. The purpose of the rhetorical portrait was to have that piece of common knowledge put in the light of Roman power" (p. 171).

With these particular cases in point before us, we may now venture upon some attempt at a summation of Danto's account of what is involved in artistic predication. Owing to its possible pertinence to the grammatical problem of pronominal referentiality, it is necessary to attend to several passages in Danto's own words. "The language of art," he writes,

> stands to ordinary discourse in a relationship not unlike that in which artworks stand to real things. One can almost think of it as an imitation of real speech. There are terms that apply to artworks that do not apply to real things, or do so only by metaphoric extension. . . . We cannot characterize works of art without in the same breath evaluating them. . . .
> . . . Thus nothing will be true of the representation of flowers that will not be true of flowers as flowers. . . .
> . . . We cannot proceed from "are powerful drawings of flowers" to "are drawings of powerful flowers." We cannot because there are none, or at least these flowers are not powerful. So in cases where it seems licit, some essential grammatical or lexical structure is concealed — as "are powerful drawings of athletes" to "are drawings of powerful athletes," or . . . "is a beautiful painting of x" to "is a painting of a beautiful x." . . .
> . . . It is part of the structure of a metaphoric transfiguration that the subject retains its identity throughout and is recognized as such. Thus transfiguration rather than transformation: Napoleon does not turn into a Roman emperor, merely bears the attributes of one. (pp. 156-57, 168)

It may just be one of the main offices of art less to represent the world than to represent it in such a way as to cause us to view it with a certain attitude and with a special vision. This had been the explicit aim in the period of the High Baroque in Italy, where artists were mandated to cause feelings in viewers in order to heighten and confirm faith; and it remains the clear aim of Socialist Realist and political art generally in the world today. But it is difficult to imagine an art that does not aim at some effect and insofar at some transformation in or some affirmation of the way the world is viewed by those who experience it fully. (p. 167)

Metaphor constitutes the *living edge* of language. . . . The locus of metaphoric expression is in the representation . . . rather than in the reality represented. . . .

. . . In order for the viewer to collaborate in the transfiguration, he must of course know the portrait . . . and accept certain connotations of the concept . . . and then he must infuse that portrait with those connotations. So the artwork is constituted as a transfigurative representation rather than a representation *tout court*. . . . To understand the artwork is to grasp the metaphor that is, I think, always there. (pp. 171-72)

Turning, then, to the relation between grammar and language, and giving special attention to the question of pronominal referentiality, it seems both licit and of no trivial significance to note that in pronominal referentiality, as in artistic predication, a structural concealment occurs. In faithfulness to the second commandment, this concealment is properly acknowledged by the discernment and acceptance of the grammatical fact that the masculine pronoun referring to the proper name of God as Father cannot be interpreted or understood as a gender identification, since the noun to which the pronoun is syntactically bound is devoid of sexuality and signifies instead an utterly unique relation between God and the human creatures with whom God is covenantally related. As Karl Barth has put it, "Creation is the external ground of the covenant; covenant is the internal ground of creation."[58] This is, indeed, the context of that metaphorical parallelism we have already noted between Genesis 1:27 and Matthew 23:9. If androgyny is excluded, misogyny yet more so! "It is part of the structure of a metaphoric transfiguration that the subject retains its identity throughout and is recognized as such." The subordination of the noun to the pronoun that is syntactically bound to it, by an insistence

---

58. Karl Barth, *Die Kirchliche Dogmatik*, III/1 (Zurich, 1945), pp. 103, 258; my translation.

upon the genderization of the noun owing to the gender associations of the pronoun, is the disavowal of the transfiguration of the experience of mystery in the mystery of experience.

This transfiguration links the pronoun with its noun in such a way as to underscore both its subordination to the noun to which it is structurally attached and its indicative power to bring syntax to the aid of the noun, so that precisely in this relation the noun may say what it means and mean what it says. Like a finger pointing to the moon, "our Father" or "their Father" or "your Father" or "his Father" or "her Father," as well as "His will," "His grace," "His ways for His world," all refer to that "one heavenly father" by whom "the new kinship of equals" is established and in relation with whom "patriarchal power and esteem" are disestablished (Schüssler Fiorenza, p. 150). The disregard of "the living edge of language" by the literalistic intrusion of genderization upon the "grammatical or lexical structure . . . concealed" signals an exchange of participation in the covenantal story for participation in the cultural story. In this exchange, the human birthright and its prospect are being bartered, and both covenant and culture become vulnerable to the dehumanizing disregard of the promise of freedom and fulfillment.

What, then, shall become of the fathers on earth? What of the mothers? What shall become of the girls and the boys — and of the women and the men they are created and purposed to be? The answer is this: in the community of disciples, wherein they may be nurtured in the apperception and praxis of the human through the transfiguration of the mystery of experience in the experience of mystery, the moment of truth and point of no return have come upon them. The future coming their way is open to them in the pathways and patterns of human freedom and fulfillment through reciprocal responsibility. In the community of disciples, male and female, who bear in themselves and in the reciprocity of their identity and difference the secret of their humanity, find their humanity and fulfillment in, with, and through one another. As the image of God, their sexuality is not threatened by their gender nor their gender by their sexuality, since God, who is beyond both creaturehood and sexuality, has called them into being after his likeness and has ordained their sexuality as the sign of the reciprocity in identity and difference between the Creator and those creatures purposed above all others to share with him in the celebration of his Shabat and shalom. Thus, going about with the name of God, which makes all the difference in the world, prepares the heart and its trust for making a day of celebration holy.

Shabat, Shalom, and Responsibility for Creation

The Third Commandment:

"You Shall Make a Day for Celebration Holy"

If the second commandment has been trivialized beyond measure, the so-called sabbath commandment has been legalized beyond measure. As we have just suggested, the third commandment is the infusion of the first and the second into the common life. As Luther stated it in the Large Catechism, it reads: *"Du sollst den Feiertag heiligen!"* ("You shall make a day of celebration holy.")

I venture this translation partly because Luther himself expressly departs from the biblical form of the commandment, and partly because, in so doing, Luther freed us from all prescriptive Sabbatarianism. Somewhere in Heine's praise of Luther for the benefit of the French, he remarks that Luther used the familiar German word *Feiertag,* in lieu of the transliteration of the Hebrew word *Shabat,* in order to make plain that the Bible does not belong to Jews only. In German, the word *Feiertag* can mean "to celebrate a festival, or simply to take time off from work" (LCT, 375 n. 1). Luther, as was his wont, appropriated common folk expressions, such as *Feierabend machen,* or *heiligen Abend geben* ("to make an evening for celebration," or "to give a holy evening") which literally means "observing (or granting) a holy day, originally the eve of a festival" (LCT, 375 n. 1). In English, a similar interchangeability between "holy day" and "holiday" has come down to us, but the Sabbath tradition has rather preempted this flexibility for liturgical purposes.

When one considers the joylessness with which blue laws and checklists of things not to be done "on the Sabbath day," as the going phrase went, have infected "the making of a day of celebration holy," it is difficult to repress at least a *Te Deum* sotto voce for the creeping intrusion upon the once widely observed weekly calendar respite that religious pluralism and an insatiable passion for commercial advantage have irreversibly brought about. The pious regard for the Lord's day had slowly but surely been despoiled of celebration, the making of a holy day, in flagrant violation of the precedent set by the Creator, who took time off to enjoy all that he had made, and of creation's own way of replenishing its energies. The ancient Bedouins, who wandered to and fro across their desert habitations, paid impressive heed to nature's own shabat. They steadfastly refused to return to whatever oasis had sustained them with energies indispensable to life until an interval of at least five years had made it possible for the oasis to catch its breath, to make its own time of celebration holy. Crop rotation is, of course, a more familiar case in point, although its observance has been rather more a routine order than a sign of the indispensability of making a day of celebration holy.

> Therefore according to its literal, outward sense, this commandment does not concern us Christians. It is an entirely external matter, . . . from . . . which we are now set free through Christ.
> . . . We keep holy days not for the sake of intelligent and well informed Christians, for these have no need of them. We keep them, first, for the sake of bodily need. Nature teaches and demands that the common people — man-servants and maid-servants who have attended to their work and trades the whole week long — should retire for a day to rest and be refreshed. Secondly and most especially we keep holy days so that people may have time and opportunity, which otherwise would not be available, to participate in public worship, that is, that they may assemble to hear and discuss God's Word and then praise God with song and prayer.
> . . . However, the observance of rest should not be so narrow as to forbid incidental and unavoidable work.
> . . . Since all people do not have this much time and leisure, we must set apart several hours a week for the young, and at least a day for the whole community, when we can concentrate upon . . . the Ten Commandments, the Creed, and the Lord's Prayer. . . . Non-Christians can spend a day in rest and idleness too, and so can the whole swarm of clerics in our day who stand daily in the churches, singing and ringing bells, without sanctifying the holy day because they neither preach nor practice God's Word but teach and live contrary to it.
> Therefore this commandment is violated not only by those who grossly misuse and desecrate the holy day like those who in their greed or frivolity neglect to hear God's Word, or lie around in taverns dead drunk like swine, but also by that multitude of others who listen to God's Word as they would to any other entertainment, who only from force of habit go to hear preaching and depart again with as little knowledge of the Word at the end of the year as at the beginning. (LCT, 376:82-84, 86; 377:89-90; 378:96)

Clearly, Luther's focus is upon the apperceptive self-evidence of the first three commandments and their nurture of the common life in the art of taking fulfilling responsibility for creation. He is aware that "from ancient times Sunday has been appointed for this purpose" and that the better part of wisdom is probably not to change it. "In this way a common order will prevail and no one will create disorder by unnecessary innovation" (LCT, 376:85). It could be, however, that in the common life today, faithfulness to the third commandment calls for imaginative alternatives to making a day of celebration holy.

Such alternatives would seek to rescue the basic structure of social reality from the dehumanizing depersonalization that infects the parameters of social interaction when roles, functions, and population differentiation and distribution determine the mobility and reciprocity required for the extension of heterogeneity and the reduction of inequality. Such celebrative alternatives would endeavor to gather people together, as and where they are, upon occasions of "time for catching one's breath," a time in which an apperceptive discovery could become the experience of each in the company of all. The discovery is that, in returning and in rest, in quietness and in confidence reside the experience of the authority who means freedom, in and through commitment to whom the parameters of social interaction might become avenues of freedom and reciprocal responsibility. Meanwhile, since the ecological and energy crises of our day are more directly congruent with a Sabbatarian default than we have been wont to suppose, let us keep the appointed time for making a day of celebration holy, and press ahead toward such other celebrative makings as may be given us along the way. "These things you ought to have done, and [without leaving] the other undone" (Matt. 23:23; Luke 11:42, AV).

As regards the question of ecology and energy, the "significant in the factual" is that they exhibit the correlative limits that the nonhuman order of the world sets to its use for purposes of human freedom and fulfillment. In the economy of the Creator of his creation, nature is guaranteed a freedom peculiar to itself, which is inviolate against the human probing of the mysteries and resources of nature. The violation of this freedom converts the assigned human dominion over nature into exploitation and responsibility for creation into expropriation. It signifies a passionate limitlessness that anesthetizes gratitude and culminates in the Titanism that serves some other god. In short, nature's own way of making a day of celebration holy is transgressed. The result is the consequence of all idolatry: the reduction of heterogeneity to monotony and the intensification of inequality, until the order of freedom is forced to the nearer edge of anarchy, and chaos once again, as at the beginning, threatens creation.

The humanizing exploration and organization of energy is thus correlative with a responsible recognition of the limits set by the freedom of nature to be what it was made to be: the environment of humanization. It is no accident that the hierarchical orientation of traditional societies has nurtured a livelier awareness of these limits than has the egalitarian society of the modern Western world, in which things are preeminent over people and productive wealth is preeminent over land. At the same time, the burden of inequality is scarcely less grievous in modern society than in traditional societies, since the gap between developed and developing countries tends increasingly to be a fiscal and technological one. The globalization of the question of ecology and energy seems to have impaled the responsibility for creation upon a fateful dilemma between an "ethic of risk" and an "ethic of fear." An "ethic of fear" stresses the preeminence of ecology over energy and exhibits a vulnerability to an ideological reduction of the questions of ecology and energy to the question of industrial ownership and control. An "ethic of risk," on the other hand, stresses the preeminence of energy over ecology and is vulnerable to a reduction of the complexities of these questions to a self-evident and self-justifying bond between private ownership and control and the public good.

A third possibility is at hand, however, in the apperceptive correlation of the Decalogue with the common life. An apperceptive regard for the responsibilities reciprocal to an order of freedom that joins God and humanity and nature in a humanizing concern of *authority* and *gratitude* and *trusteeship* is the fruit of a way of looking at life and of living it that is rooted in the first three commandments. Living by the Commandments in the sense intended by the authority who gave them and who means freedom must lead to the abandonment of an "ethic of fear" and the adoption of an "ethic of risk," within the parameters of reciprocal responsibility, that is, with due regard for a humanizing relation between inequality and heterogeneity.

It could be that an alert and sensitive faithfulness to "the right tablet of Moses" would require praying without ceasing, and with both eyes open: keeping one sharp eye on Texaco, Mobil, Standard of California, Middle South Utilities, and their lobbying kith and kin, and the other eye sharply on the shining of the sun.

CHAPTER FIVE

The Family, Abortion,
and Homosexuality

(The Fourth, Fifth, and Sixth Commandments)

The "Left Tablet of Moses"

We now turn toward Moses' left hand. To Luther's imagination, the "left tablet of Moses" *(linke Tafel Mosi)* is directly parallel to the tablet he held in his right hand as he descended from the mountain of God. As the right tablet directs us in the parameters of reciprocal responsibility toward God, so the left tablet directs us in the parameters of reciprocal responsibility toward our neighbor. As the right tablet tells us what is involved in a realistic, liberating, and fulfilling commitment between God and humankind, so the left tablet tells us what is involved in a realistic, liberating, and fulfilling commitment between persons and neighbors. In Luther's words, we are directed toward "what a person owes to another person and his neighbor to refrain from and to do" *(was er den Menschen und seinem Nähsten schuldig ist zu lassen und zu thun)*.[1]

According to Luther, we have only to look squarely at the facts of these human relations to discern the "significant in the factual," which is "how cost-less and alike *[billig und gleich]* all these commandments are, since they command nothing relating to God and the neighbor which any one would not wish for himself were he in God's and his neighbor's place *[an Gottis und seines Nähsten statt wäre]*.[2]

1. Martin Luther, *Kurze Form der Zehen Gebote, des Glaubens und des Vater Unsers* (1520). In *Dr. Martin Luther's sämmtliche Werke*, ed. Johann Konrad Irmischer, Erlangen, Carl Heyder, 1833, vol. 22 *(Dr. Martin Luther's katechetische deutsche Schriften)*, pp. 6-7.
2. Luther, *Kurze Form*, pp. 6-7.

The Paradigm of Human Wholeness
and the Question of the Family

The Fourth Commandment:
"You Shall Honor Your Father and Mother"

Reciprocal Responsibility between Parents and Children

While Luther's enumeration of the Commandments in the shorter preface to the Large Catechism states succinctly: "You shall honor father and mother," when he addresses himself to what this commandment involves, he adds the possessive personal pronoun: "You shall honor *your* father and mother," The force of the addition is plain. We have to do here with the paradigmatic relation upon which human wholeness radically and realistically depends. Wrapped in the four-letter word *your* is the secret of belonging, the freedom and fulfillment that come to whomsoever the secret is given.

> To fatherhood and motherhood God has given the special distinction above all estates that are beneath it, that he commands us not simply to love our parents but also to honor them. With respect to brothers, sisters, and neighbors in general he commands nothing higher than that we love them. Thus he distinguishes father and mother above all other persons on earth, and places them next to himself.

Thus, of the seven commandments of the left tablet of Moses, "the first and greatest is: *You shall honor your father and mother.*"[3]

In Luther's view, it is a greater thing to honor than to love. Not that love is a second-order relation, anymore than motherhood is a second-order relation to fatherhood. On the contrary! Just as the sequence from fatherhood to motherhood is an ordination to parenthood, anchored in the Creator's purpose that the wholeness of the creature shall be experienced and nurtured in reciprocal responsibility, so the sequence from honor to love is an ordination to reciprocal responsibility toward the gift of parenthood, on the part of those to whom the gift is given. "For," says Luther,

3. Martin Luther's Large Catechism, in *The Book of Concord*, trans. and ed. Theodore G. Tappert (Philadelphia: Fortress Press, 1959), p. 379, pars. 104-5. Subsequent references will use the abbreviation LCT and will give page and paragraph numbers. I have ventured my own translation in a few places, indicated with brackets.

it is a much greater thing to honor than to love. Honor includes not only love, but also [a self-discipline *(Zucht)*, humility and shyness *(Scheue)*, as toward a majesty therein hidden]. It requires us not only to address them [(i.e., our parents) in friendship *(freundlich)* and with reverence, but above all, so to relate to them both from the heart and with the body, as to show that one thinks much of them and regards them as next to God the highest]. (LCT, 379:106)

On the other hand, Luther has no illusions about parents. He is as aware as we are that there is much at the level of experience to call such an ordination to parenthood severely into question.[4] Nevertheless, parents, according to Luther, "are not to be deprived of their honor because of their ways or their failings. . . . We are not to think of their persons, whatever they are, but of the will of God, who has created and ordained them to be our parents." In other words, we are "not [to] address them discourteously, critically, and censoriously, but [to] submit to them and hold [our] tongue, even if they go too far." We are to honor them also in our actions, "serving them, helping them, and caring for them when they are old, sick, feeble, or poor"; and we are to do all this "not only cheerfully, but with humility and reverence, as in God's sight." Indeed, "he who has the right attitude toward his parents will not allow them to suffer want or hunger, but will place them above himself and at his side and will share with them all he has to the best of his ability" (LCT, 379-80:108, 110-11).

On the other hand, Luther is fully aware that the fourth commandment is not a one-way street. "Nothing," he declares,

> ought to be considered more important than the will and word of our parents, provided that these, too, are subordinated to obedience toward God and are not set into opposition to the preceding commandments.
> . . . [Indeed,] if we were to open our eyes and ears and take this [commandment] to heart so that we [would] not again be led astray from

4. Even with Geritol, we are scarcely in better shape. Indeed, the population statistics nowadays forecast an almost frightening prospect of a gerontocracy that threatens to reduce Luther's realism about the aged and the aging to naiveté. On the one hand, the phrase "the Golden Years" is a Madison Avenue fantasy designed for real estate and insurance developers and to add lustre to the tarnish for people of deteriorating vision. On the other hand, Maggie Kuhn is certainly on the side of divine righteousness in her passionate crusade against the ghettoization of the elderly as a way of facilitating their not so benign neglect.

the pure Word of God to the lying vanities of the devil . . . parents would have more happiness, love, kindness, and harmony in their houses, and children would win their parents' hearts completely. [But] now, as every one complains[,] both young and old are altogether wayward and unruly; they have no sense of modesty or honor; they do nothing until they are driven with blows; and they defame and depreciate one another behind their backs in any way they can. . . . Neither can parents, as a rule, do very much; one fool trains another, and as they have lived, so live their children after them. (LCT, 381-82:116, 121-24)[5]

The Family and Civil Society

The crux of Luther's interpretation of the fourth commandment is its insistence that the relations between parents and children are paradigmatic of human wholeness. This is the case because the relations between parents and children are pivotal to the nurture of a humanizing apperception that converts the otherwise dehumanizing polarization between inequality and equality, and between authority and freedom, into a creative and fulfilling congruence. The secret of this conversion is the reciprocal responsibility in, with, and under which inequality and equality, authority and freedom are joined. In the wisdom and power of this secret, rights are transfigured as responsibilities, and politicization, with its bittersweet fruits in fragmentation, competition, and mistrust, is transfigured into a *politeia*.

An essay by Jacques Maritain, written many years ago, sheds light upon the perennial and vexatious problem of inequality and equality in human society. The unique contribution of Christianity to this problem, Maritain suggested, was its refusal to disregard inequality, owing to an egalitarian vision and hope, or to deny equality in deference to the overwhelming impact of inequality upon the common life. Conjoined with this refusal was the way in which Christian faith and life related inequality and equality to each other.[6] So, Luther can say, with respect to the ordination of father and mother to parenthood,

---

5. The phrase "one fool trains another" echoes a proverb of the time: "ein Tor bringt einen zweiten Tor mit sich" ("one fool brings another along"). So Georg Buchwald, *Dr. Martin Luther's Grosse Katechismus* (Leipzig: Bernhard Liebisch, 1912), p. 30, Anmerkung 5.

6. Jacques Maritain, *True Humanism*, trans. M. R. Adamson (London: Centenary Press, 1938).

in other respects, indeed, we are all equal in the sight of God, but among ourselves there must be this sort of inequality and proper distinctions. [Since this inequality is also commanded of God, it follows that you are to be obedient to me, as your father, and to acknowledge my authority *(das ich die Überland habe).]* (LCT, 380:108)

According to Christian faith and responsibility, at any rate, the primary mark of the relation between inequality and equality is not subordination, in the sense of a value determination, which finds unequals related as inferior to superior. Inferiority means secondariness; and secondariness is strictly a matter of sequence, not significance. In accord with the precise meaning of the Latin terms *superior* and *inferior,* the accent falls upon first and second in time and place. The accent does not signify worth. On the contrary, inequality and equality are related according to a ranking order of *responsibility,* not according to a ranking order of *power.*

In ancient India, according to Louis Dumont, a clear hierarchical distinction was made and maintained between status and power. At the top of the social structure was the priest, who exercised preeminent authority but not preeminent power. Second in rank was the king, who bore principal responsibility for power, but under the primary authority of the priest.[7] A parallel ordination of status in relation to authority and power is exercised, in the West, in the doctrine of the divine right of kings, and more broadly, since Gregory I, in the doctrine of the two swords. The doctrine is the cornerstone of the tortuous story of the relations between the spiritual and the temporal powers, institutionalized as church and state, and personalized as pope and emperor.

In the West, however, it would appear that authority by divine right was, rather more easily than not, transposed into the divine right of authority. Emperors behaved like popes, and popes behaved like emperors — a precedent that reached across half the globe, all the way to the Casa Pacifica, and into the imperial presidency through which the Casa Pacifica was built. Even Robespierre insisted that the exercise of power required "an ever-present transcendent source of authority that could not be identified with the general will of either the nation or the Revolution itself," but which "might function as the fountainhead of justice from which the laws of the new body politic could derive their legitimacy."[8]

7. See Louis Dumont, *Homo Hierarchicus: The Caste System in India* (Chicago: University of Chicago Press, 1974), esp. chap. 3.

8. Hannah Arendt, *On Revolution* (New York: Viking Press, 1965), p. 1985. See also my book *The Transfiguration of Politics* (New York: Harper & Row, 1975), chap. 2.

Wisdom, however, is seldom justified of her children. Hierarchical social structures became the Azazel of the egalitarian vision, and its passionate enthusiasm. Expunged into the wilderness from the community of promise, Azazel has now returned without atonement. Can there really be Rosh Hashana without Yom Kippur? A New Year without a Day of Atonement? Inequality is a structure of social reality, and rights cannot upstage responsibilities if equality is to be something other than the nemesis of inequality, if it is to be the extension of heterogeneity instead. This, I take it, is what the Letter to Philemon is all about, as well as the "year of Jubilee" and the Deuteronomic "year of release."

It must be admitted that the egalitarian repudiation of subordination was not without warrant. Luther himself was both in word and in deed readier with the rod and with invective — and even with the sword — than he was in "pausing for station identification." His own ground-breaking perception of the apperceptive bond between the Commandments and the common life faltered in the breach. The apperceptive affirmation of the liberating mobility of equality within the parameters of inequality and heterogeneity still waits upon the steadfast implementation of Luther's lead. Failing such implementation, the freedom intrinsic to the ordination was attacked. Consequently, the pioneering revision of the relations between inequality and equality, rooted in Christian faith and life, has not been fulfillingly linked with the similarly pioneering revision of the relations between authority and freedom. The unique Christian perception of the God of the Decalogue, as the only God worth trusting because he commands, has been too intermittently conjoined with the structural realism of the Decalogue itself. Jesus' radical reduction of the Decalogue to the love commandment, however, and his radicalization of the love commandment as the breakthrough of the freedom of the self for the neighbor and of the neighbor for the self, promise to those who are faithful to it the discovery, in the reciprocity of each toward the other, of the fulfillment of responsible freedom. The discovery is that authority is the presupposition, not the nemesis, of freedom; and freedom is the test case, "an ever present transcendent source of authority," whose power and purpose are human fulfillment in freedom. Thus Luther can say:

> Out of the authority of parents all other authority is derived and developed. . . .
> The civil government . . . is to be classed with the estate of fatherhood,

the most comprehensive of all relations. In this case a man is father not of a single family, but of as many people as he has inhabitants, citizens, or subjects. Through civil rulers, as through our own parents, God gives us food, house and home, protection and security. Therefore, since they bear this name and title with all honor as their chief glory, it is our duty to honor and magnify them as the most precious treasure and jewel on earth. . . .

. . . Why, do you think, is the world now so full of unfaithfulness, shame, misery, and murder? It is because everyone wishes to be his own master, be free from all authority, care nothing for anyone, and do whatever he pleases. So God punishes one knave by means of another. . . .

Of course, we keenly feel our misfortune, and we grumble and complain of unfaithfulness, violence, and injustice; but we are unwilling to see that we ourselves are knaves who have roundly deserved punishment and that we are not one bit improved by it. . . . All this I have been obliged to set forth with such a profusion of words in the hope that someone may take it to heart, so that we may be delivered from the blindness and misery in which we are so deeply sunk and may rightly understand the Word and will of God and sincerely accept it. . . .

Thus we have three kinds of fathers presented in this commandment: fathers by blood, fathers of a household, and fathers of the nation. Besides these, there are also spiritual fathers — not like those in the papacy who applied this title to themselves but performed no fatherly office. For the name spiritual father belongs only to those who govern and guide us by the Word of God. . . .

. . . It would be well to preach to parents on the nature of their office, how they should treat those committed to their authority. . . . God does not want to have knaves or tyrants in this office and responsibility; nor does he assign them this honor (that is, power and authority to govern) merely to receive homage. Parents should consider that they owe obedience to God, and that, above all, they should earnestly and faithfully discharge the duties of their office, not only to provide for the material support of their children, servants, subjects, etc., but especially to bring them up to the praise and honor of God. Therefore, do not imagine that the parental office is a matter of your pleasure and whim. It is a strict commandment and injunction of God, who holds you accountable for it. (LCT, 384-88: 141, 150, 154-55, 157-58, 167-69)

The Family between Rights and Responsibilities

This eyewitness report by Luther of his own times scarcely requires an update. The patriarchal household toward which Luther directed his concerns has, of course, given way to the nuclear family, and this in turn seems to have entered upon its own "time of troubles" and to be beset by various experiments with so-called "extended families" and, more recently, by the phenomenon of the "single-parent family." Feudal patterns of social interrelatedness have been exchanged for industrial patterns as rural contexts have given way to urban ones.

Perhaps the greatest distance between Luther and ourselves, however, is marked by two principal developments. The first is the pervasive loss of stability in the relations between parents, and between parents and children. The inevitable corollary is the loss of concern about and confidence in the indispensability of the family to the nurture of humane apperception. The second development is the virtually total breakdown of the link between the family and civil society. Indeed, if any residue of Luther's perception of the family as the laboratory of reciprocal responsibility for a reciprocally responsible society remains, it is discernible in the inversion of Luther's sense of direction. Society now is widely expected to come to the aid of the family in crisis.[9]

The nuclear family is the achievement of egalitarian ideals, aspirations, and practices. As Peter Gay describes the development in a rather extended passage:

> The old clean-cut social hierarchies retained much of their prestige, but they were on the defensive in the face of powerful social aspirations and a growing desire for mobility. Especially in the middle ranges of Western European society, the father's power over his children and the husband's power over his wife markedly declined. The patriarchal family, still the pattern in the seventeenth century, was giving way to the nuclear family, with its well-defined boundaries against the community and its growing

9. See two older but particularly instructive essays on this aspect of the family crisis in *Daedalus* 106, 2 (Spring 1977). One essay is by Colin C. Blaydon and Carol B. Stack and is entitled "Income Support Policies and the Family," pp. 147-61. The other is by Suzanne H. Woolsey and is entitled "Pied Piper Politics and the Child-Care Debate," pp. 127-45. This entire issue of *Daedalus* is devoted to the family. *Daedalus* is published as the *Journal of the American Academy of Arts and Sciences,* 7 Linden Street, Cambridge, MA 02138.

intimacy and equality. Within certain limits, still rather rigid but distinctly commanding, young girls were being permitted to choose their partners. . . . As a writer put it in 1739, "the choice of a husband or wife more nearly concerns the happiness of the parties themselves than it does the parents; it is the young couple who are to abide by the choice; by consequence they ought to choose for themselves." The world of the family was changing, in the direction of freedom. . . .

In consequence, marriage, which through the seventeenth century had been regarded as a sacred institution and as a legal device for the management of property and the regulation of inheritance, came to be spoken of in the age of the Enlightenment as a partnership, a contract, honorable and grave but secular in nature. Monogamy, long a Christian ideal, became for many a comfortable reality, and even those philosophers whose own marital experience was unhappy felt that they owed it to the philosophy to praise marriage as an institution. . . .

In this atmosphere, which was clearer and less oppressive than the atmosphere of preceding centuries, women and children secured new respect and rights. In the seventeenth century — as Milton's portrayal of Adam and Eve made plain to all — no one had doubted that women were inferior to men. But then, at the end of the 1690s, Daniel DeFoe, who was always a pioneer, sharply took his fellow-men to task for their scurvy treatment of women: had women the education of men, he argued in his *Essay upon Projects,* their supposed inferiority would soon vanish. And it was Defoe, not Milton, whom the eighteenth century was to follow.[10]

The expansion of rights for women and children against the patriarchal conversion of responsibilities into rights was a move in the direction of freedom. The move not only forbids any return to the *status quo ante* but also excludes any wish to do so. Nevertheless, the crisis of the family in these days is so advanced and sobering as to give rise to the question whether the move from responsibilities to rights, which began as a move in the direction of freedom, was designed in the long run to further a corresponding move from rights to responsibilities, or whether the initial move in the direction of freedom was mainly — if not solely — a move against the patriarchal subversion of the humanizing relation between responsibility and rights. A steadily mounting divorce rate has been, if

10. Peter Gay, *The Enlightenment: An Interpretation,* vol. 2: *The Science of Freedom* (New York: W. W. Norton, 1977), pp. 31-33.

not matched, at least notably accompanied by an increasing rate of wife-beatings, child-beatings, and lately husband-beatings.

One informed and thoughtful discussion of the crisis of the family argues that "crisis" is not an accurate description of what is happening.[11] Such a "crisis" view fails to take account of the course of family events since the Middle Ages. In traditional Western societies, the community was more important in determining the individual's place and possibilities than was the family. From the standpoint of the individual, more important than either the community or the family was a relation best described as "the consent of domain." Domain was the place determined by the individual within the limits set for the individual as he or she discovered the limits of his or her authority — that is, it was the discovery of "what he could do, and how far he could go before encountering resistance from others — his parents, his wife, his neighbors, and the community as a whole" (p. 227). Domain was neither private nor public, but both. It was private because it had to do with individual behavior, "with a man's personality, with his manner of being alone or in society, with his self-awareness and his inner being; public because it fixed a man's place within the community and established his rights and obligations. . . . The role of the family was to strengthen the authority of the head of the household, without threatening the stability of his relationship with the community" (p. 228).

For reasons which Philippe Ariès, our informant, indicates, but which cannot detain us here, a far-reaching change overtook the family during the eighteenth and nineteenth centuries, a change with which the twentieth century must still come to terms. The family went nuclear, and, with the development of urbanization and industrialization, a cleavage emerged between "the growing privacy of the family" and "a new and lively form of social intercourse [that] developed in even the largest societies" (p. 232). Ariès singles out the cafe as the symbol of this development. He concludes that

> In the so-called post-industrial age of the mid-twentieth century, the public sector of the nineteenth century collapsed and people thought they could fill the void by extending the private, family sector. They

---

11. Philippe Ariès, "The Family and the City," *Daedalus* 106, 2 (Spring 1977): 227-35. Subsequent references will be given parenthetically in the text. Ariès is a French sociological historian whose books include *Centuries of Childhood* (1960), *Western Attitudes Toward Death* (1974), and *On the History of Death in the West from the Middle Ages Until Today* (1975).

thus demanded that the family see to all their needs. . . . This tendency to monopolize its members is the family's way of coping with the decline of the public sector. . . . The twentieth century post-industrial world has been unable so far either to sustain the forms of social intercourse of the nineteenth century or to offer something in their place. The family has had to take over in an impossible situation; the real roots of the present domestic crisis lie not in our families, but in our cities. (pp. 234-35)

The price of this overstrain has been the politicization of the family, as opposed to the humanizing purpose for which the family was intended.

At the other end of the spectrum of the diagnosis of the family is an incisive, provocative account by Alice S. Rossi in an essay entitled "A Biosocial Perspective on Parenting."[12] Rossi notes a remarkable shift in the opinion of the family during the 1970s. The shift spans the value spectrum "from a general endorsement of the family as a worthwhile and stable institution to a general censure of it as an oppressive and bankrupt one whose demise is both imminent and welcome" (p. 1). Rossi continues:

Not so long ago, many sociologists were claiming that the nuclear family was neither as fragile nor as isolated as it had been claimed, but was in fact embedded in a viable, if modified, extended kin network. Today, one is more apt to read that the nuclear family will oppress its members unless couples swap spouses and swing, and young adults are urged to rear their children communally, or to reject marriage and parenthood altogether.

Age and sex are fundamental building blocks of any family system. . . . When functional theory dominated family sociology, the key was age: the treatment of generational continuity and parent-child relationships received central attention. . . . More recently, the emphasis in family analysis has been on sex, with a heavy reliance on egalitarian ideology that denies any innate sex differences and assumes that a 'unisex' socialization will produce men and women that are free of the traditional culturally induced sex differences. This egalitarian ethos wages several programmatic changes in family organization: a reduction of material investment to permit greater psychic investment in work outside the family, an increased investment by men in their fathering roles, and the

12. Alice S. Rossi, "A Biosocial Perspective on Parenting," *Daedalus* 106, 2 (Spring 1977): 1-31. Subsequent references will be given parenthetically in the text.

supplementation of parental care by institutional care. Frequently associated with this emphasis on equal commitments to work and family for both men and women is a corollary emphasis on the autonomy and the "rights" of the child. (p. 1)

Thus we are well on the move in the direction of freedom — "beyond the nuclear family" or "beyond monogamy" (p. 1).[13] According to Rossi,

in sociology . . . it is easy to forget that the basic facts of family life consist in the coming together of people with physical bodies to mate, to reproduce, and to rear the young. In its tendency to define sociological variables in terms of script, roles, status, and systems, a further barrier is created to any easy linkage of body process and personality to social relations and social systems. (pp. 12-13)

If the family amnesia of this sort were only a defect of sociologists, the prospects of recovery of human apperception would be more promising than they are. The sociologists, however, have been joined by a host of others in and outside the church who have embraced "a depressing bias toward middle-class individualistic elevations of the will."[14]

Indeed, the psychodynamics of consciousness have already reached cultic proportions, both personal and political, which have carried the consciousness of self and other confidently across the bound of protecting it against the self-consciousness of self and other. Thus, the Fall keeps being reenacted as fulfillment, as though Genesis 3 had been erased from the human mythological and historical record. Augustine has been am-

---

13. A proposal of "flexible monogamy" put forward by a psychiatric counselor is at once touching and pathetic in its serious attempt to find a way "beyond monogamy" that takes account both of the sustaining significance of monogamy and of the contemporary persuasion that sexual satisfaction contributes more reliably to human wholeness than does sexual fidelity. See Raymond Lawrence, "Toward a More Flexible Monogamy," in *Christianity and Crisis* 34, 4 (18 March 1974): 42-47. See also Raymond Lawrence, *The Poisoning of Eros: Sexual Values in Conflict* (New York: Augustine Moore Press, 1989). Lawrence seeks to explore the viability of the distinction between "a primary loyalty" and "an exclusive allegiance which will permit a satellite relationship, so long as the primacy of the original relationship is maintained." Perhaps. But certainly not without more careful attention both to Martin Luther and to Alice Rossi. We are not all cosmonauts yet!

14. Quoted by Rossi, p. 15, from B. Berger, B. Hackett, and R. M. Millar, "The Communal Family," in *The Family Coordinator* 21, 4 (1972): 422.

bushed by Kinsey, Rogers, Masters and Johnson, and EST. Even David was up against fairer odds.

Following Rossi's discussion a brief moment longer, we learn that "a new genre of family sociology" seems to be carrying the day. "The implicit premise in much of [its] literature is the right of the individual to an expanded freedom in the pursuit of private sexual pleasure: I want what I want when I want it" (p. 14). Moreover, a probing study of communal families analyzes the extent to which communal ideology includes "children through the notion of equality defined as identity, so that children are viewed as 'autonomous human beings, equal to adults.'"[15] The study reports "one mother who aptly caught the dilemma of this ideology in action. 'What I wanted was a baby; but a kid, that's something else'" (p. 15). So, there is a "sex script" and a "parenting script in the new family sociology." Both scripts seem to be modeled

> on what has been a male pattern of relating to children in which men turn their fathering on and off to suit themselves or their appointments for business or sexual pleasure. The authors and dramatists of both the mating and parenting scripts in the new perspectives on the family are just as heavily male as the older schools of thought about the modern family, if not in the generic sense, then in the sense that parenting is viewed from a distance, as an appendage to, or consequence of mating, rather than the focus of family systems and individual lives. It is not at all clear what the gains will be for either women or children in this version of human liberation. . . . It is questionable whether the single mothers who head the households that include eight million children under eighteen retain responsibility for their children because they are "stuck with the kids" simply as a result of cultural pressure, as some current family critics claim. It is more likely that the emotional ties to the children are more important to the mothers than to the fathers. It is probably still the case that the vast majority of women can have ex-spouses but not ex-children. (pp. 16, 18)

There will be those, of course, who will regard the present recourse to Rossi's analysis and judgment as a fragile reed upon which to rest the suggestion that she has provided a corroboration of Luther's account of the family, according to the fourth commandment, as a paradigm of

---

15. Rossi, p. 15, quoting Berger, Hackett, and Millar, p. 427.

wholeness. They will choose instead to see in this undertaking a retreat to the *status quo ante*, to traditional family and work roles for men and women. Denial merely confirms the ideological suspicion. By her own admission, Rossi finds herself in similar case, with neither help nor hindrance from Luther. This is, as she says,

> a risk one takes to reach those who will see a more radical vision in the analysis: a society more attuned to the natural environment, in touch with, and respectful of, the rhythm of our own body processes, that asks how we can have a balanced life with commitment both to achievement in work and involvement with other human beings. In my judgment, by far the wiser course to such a future is to plan and build from the most fundamental root of society in human parenting, and not from the shaky superstructure created by men in that fraction of time in which industrial societies have existed. (p. 25)

That was Luther's point, too. Parenting is an ordination to responsibility, not a function of procreative (in distinction from recreative) sex, as the current ideology of freedom has it. This ordination provides for the wholeness of human life in and through the family, where rights are nurtured in trust and transformed into the responsibilities through which the freedom to be fulfilled is experienced, sustained, and enlarged.

It could be that here again Luther is not behind us but is, in fact, our contemporary, as we seek to find our way toward a theological and biosocial perception of the family as a paradigm of human wholeness. The paradigm informs and enables us to discern and to practice the family as a community of parents and children ordained for human wholeness. It is the indispensable matrix of the nurture of an apperceptive perception of and participation in what is required for being and staying human in the world. What is required is the practice of freedom — given, experienced, and anchored in a purposed ordination to reciprocal responsibility along the structured parameters of social interaction in the world. The practice of this freedom is the formative factor in the social mobility that facilitates the enlargement of heterogeneity and the reduction of inequality as the concrete structures that determine the limits and the direction of humanness in society. Human wholeness, as the fruit of the practice of freedom, is also the foretaste of human fulfillment in the world of time, and space, and things, and relations — and beyond the world of time, and space, and things, and relations. Since the Commandments are the substantive indicators of what an apperception of the human is about, they function as barometers of the common life as human life.

The Question of Abortion

The Fifth Commandment:
"YOU SHALL NOT KILL"

To Whom Does the Commandment Apply?

> In this commandment we leave our own house and go out among our neighbors to learn how we should conduct ourselves individually toward our fellow men. Therefore neither God nor government *[die Oberkeit]* are included in this commandment, yet their right to take human life is not abrogated. . . . What is forbidden here applies to private individuals, not to governments. (LCT, 389:180-81)

The distinction between what God and governments can do and what is permitted to individuals is a familiar one in biblical and Christian ethical and political theory. Luther certainly did not invent the distinction, although he has often, and rather too persistently, been held culpable for inordinate encouragement to the powers that be. Unlike Calvin, who, as we know, followed the Platonic tradition, which assigned to the Laws and to rulers the responsibility for the common good as well as for the restraint of evil, Luther seems to have been unable to divert his attention from the craftiness of the devil and from the intensity and the subtlety of evil in the world. "The world," he declares,

> is evil and this life is full of misery. [God] has therefore placed this and the other commandments as a boundary between good and evil. . . .
> Briefly, he wishes to have all people defended, delivered, and protected from the wickedness and violence of others, and he has set up this commandment as a wall, fortress, and refuge about our neighbor so that no one may do him bodily harm or injury. (LCT, 389-90:183, 185)

Elsewhere, I have tried to explore the sense in which the divine ordination of "higher powers" (Rom. 13:1) sets its own boundaries and direction to the authority that they are instituted to exercise.[16] In no sense are the authorities interchangeable with God; nor can they claim self-justifying legitimation. On the other hand, if the family is, for Luther, the paradigm of human wholeness — and, as such, the laboratory of human apperception — the question of the rights of rulers and the rights of individuals is transposed into the question of the reciprocal responsibilities of each toward the other. Only a tendentious interpretation of Luther would insist that Luther must have meant something else because he sometimes forgot what he knew.

How Should the Commandment Be Applied?

I take it that in referring to "the other commandments" in connection with the fifth commandment Luther means that everything on "the left tablet of Moses" has been set up "as a wall, fortress, and refuge about our neighbor" so that he may be saved from us and we may be saved from him, "so that no one may do him bodily harm or injury." But there is a positive side to Moses' left hand, no less intrinsic to its parameters than is the negative side. As Luther goes on to explain:

> This commandment is violated not only when a person actually does evil, but also when he fails to do good to his neighbor, or, though he has the opportunity, fails to prevent, protect, and save him from suffering bodily harm or injury. If you send a person away naked when you could clothe him, you have let him freeze to death. If you see anyone suffer hunger and do not feed him, you have let him starve. Likewise, if you see anyone condemned to death or in similar peril and do not save him although you know ways and means to do so, you have killed him. It will do you no good to plead that you did not contribute to his death by word or deed, for you have withheld your love from him and robbed him of the service by which his life might have been saved. . . .
>
> It is just as if I saw someone wearily struggling in deep water, or fallen into a fire, and could extend him my hand to pull him out and save him, and yet I did not do it. How would I appear before all the world in any other light than as a murderer and a scoundrel?
>
> Therefore it is God's real intention that we should allow no man to

16. See my book *The Transfiguration of Politics*, pp. 34ff.

suffer harm, but show to everyone all kindness and love. And this kindness is directed . . . especially toward our enemies. (LCT, 390-91:89-90, 92-94)

War and the Fifth Commandment

More than a generation ago, William Temple, then Archbishop of Canterbury, was addressing a national student conference in this country. We were between the two world wars, and the pacifist issue was much on the consciences of students. In the course of a long and informal discussion session, the inevitable question came. Could one reconcile participation in war with the commandment "You shall not kill," and if so, how? Dr. Temple's reply was as tantalizing as it was instantaneous. "The sixth commandment," he said (for he went by Calvinist and Anglican reckoning) "does not mean: you shall preserve life." He then went on to explain that what was involved was vastly more than merely refraining from killing, or merely keeping life going — as though life and death were fundamentally and basically divided one from the other by a biological criterion. The critical issue at the core of the fifth commandment is the issue of *responsibility* for life, as against the *right* to life! "If you send a person away naked when you could clothe him, you have let him freeze to death. If you see anyone suffer hunger and do not feed him, you have let him starve. Likewise, if you see anyone . . . in peril [of death] and do not save him although you know ways and means to do so, you have killed him." Moses and Jesus never were, and were never intended to be, bound by the Hippocratic oath. Neither was Luther! And in Luther's view, neither were Christians to be!

Well, it seems that from Archbishop Temple's time until now the focal concern of the fifth commandment has been thought to be the question of war. The concern now often centers upon the nuclear arms race as a violation of creation and therefore unqualifiedly sin. This shift from the left hand of Moses to the right hand of Moses must be regarded not only as more than welcome but as more than long overdue. It accords not only with the grim realities of nuclear madness but also with Jesus' insistence that war belongs with the signs of the end of one world and the ingression of the next. The signs are not merely coincidentally drawn from the awesome and terrifying "No!" that creation says to all transgression of its limits.

Abortion and the Fifth Commandment

There is no intrinsic reason, of course, against a shift in the discernment of the cutting edge of the Commandments in and for the common life. Luther had a better reason for excluding war from the concerns of the fifth commandment, even when the shift was to the first three commandments for which he opened the way, or the one which he by implication gave. The reason is that in matters of life and death, and living and dying, neighbors are critically involved with one another in such a way as to expose the inviolable bond between "the edges of life" (as Paul Ramsey has taught us to refer to them) and the humanness of life. The stakes are indeed a life and death matter. So God "always wants to remind us to think back to the First Commandment, that he is our God; that is, he wishes to help and protect us, so that he may subdue our desire for revenge" (LCT, 391:95). Thus we are virtually catapulted by the fifth commandment into critical questions of bioethics — and by critical questions in bioethics into the fifth commandment. Once again we have come upon a point of intersection between the structural realism of the Decalogue and the common life today. Among these questions, and clearly among the more complex and agonizing for any attempt to take responsibility for life, are those relating to birth — namely, contraception, abortion, and what I learned from Paul Ramsey to identify as "neo-natal infanticide" — and those relating to death — namely, suicide, euthanasia, and "the whole ambulance load of pain," in J. D. Salinger's phrase.

On the way from birth to death, there is increasing concern among sensitive and competent scientists, moralists, and theologians arising from genetic research, and there is also the thorny thicket of technological prolongation of death and dying, with its cultic concomitant of psycho-pastoral ministrations on how to die with dignity and tranquility, if not with faith and hope. What *would* seminary departments of practical theology, not to mention psychiatry and religion, have done without Elizabeth Kübler Ross! Having sown the wind, we are now beginning to reap the whirlwind in a gathering right to life movement in which the cultic crosses over into the occult, and on which, at least, the Pentateuch and Jesus blow the whistle. Necromancy — with or without ectoplasm — is simply a dead option!

We must now, however, confine ourselves to the question of abortion. On 1 July 1976, the United States Supreme Court gave us its decision opening the way for the legalization of abortion in this country. Paul

Ramsey noted that the decision was misleadingly hailed as a victory for unlimited abortion.[17] Actually, however, the subtleties of the decision and the concurrences and dissents of the several justices make the decision a more carefully circumscribed one. Nevertheless, abortions are no longer unexceptionally proscribed. Strictly speaking, of course, they never have been unexceptionally proscribed, either in common law or in criminal law. The "rights" of the mother and the "rights" of the fetus have always constituted exceptions under certain circumstances.

I find myself in complete agreement with Ramsey that "an opportune moment" has come for "moral dialogue" about this question, about "perils and problems ahead, if we are to avoid further descent into technological barbarism." With Ramsey, I want to take with full seriousness "the preciousness of unborn life" (p. 46). Moreover, the medical, legal, and institutional evidence brought together in the pages of *Ethics at the Edges of Life* is ominous indeed, with its ambiguity, its diversity, and even worse, its capriciousness. Particularly horrendous is the dehumanizing waste that goes on day after day in hospitals and clinics as human fetuses are treated with such professional callousness as to make the phrase "disposed of" a grim euphemism for "thrown away." If nothing else, it is a matter of record that abortion practices and procedures are a terrifying indication of the depth and range of dehumanization that ensues from the quantification of life.

According to the report of a distinguished committee, submitted to a major conference on abortion in the United States as early as 29 May 1957: "The frequency of induced abortions in the United States could be as low as 200,000 [or] as high as 1,200,000 per year, depending on the assumptions made. . . . There is no objective basis for the selection of a particular figure between these two estimates as an approximation of the actual frequency." These raw and rough data are more than enough to drive one to take cover behind the time-honored position of Christian theological and ethical teaching that the fifth commandment simply proscribes abortion. The inviolability or "sanctity" (Ramsey's preferred word)

---

17. Paul Ramsey, *Ethics at the Edges of Life* (New Haven: Yale University Press, 1978). Subsequent references will be given parenthetically in the text. A portion of these reflections on the abortion debate have been published earlier in my essay entitled "Responsibility for Life: Bioethics in Theological Perspective," in *Theology and Bioethics: Exploring the Foundations and Frontiers,* ed. Earl E. Shelp (Dordrecht: D. Reidel Publishing Co., 1985), pp. 283-302.

or "dignity" (his allowed term) of human life defines a boundary that one dares not cross.

Yet — as we all know — the tradition itself never disallowed exception. Ramsey reminds us that Jewish and Roman Catholic "moral theology" are "operationally very similar" (p. 47). Jewish teaching undertakes to identify "individual human life only after the head or the greater portion of the fetus has passed through the birth canal" (p. 46). At the same time, Jewish teaching says that "one should violate the most holy days . . . to save a fetus, which is only potentially a human being. One violates for him this Sabbath so that he will remain alive to observe many Sabbaths" (pp. 46-47). In Roman Catholicism, "abortion is justified only to save the mother's life" (p. 47).

So there are exceptions to the unexceptionable. And this is where my troubles with Paul Ramsey begin to be troublesome. I am comforted that Ramsey finds himself vis-à-vis Charles Curran in my corner — and vis-à-vis Paul himself. "I have studied and studied Charles Curran's chapter 'Cooperation in a Pluralistic Society,'" Ramsey writes, "and still cannot comprehend the reasoning in it" (p. 84). Well, much as I have admired Charles Curran's effort to demanualize moral theology and at the same time to have it without causality, I have been content to conclude that such confusions of face are the proper due of moral theologians in a pluralistic society or any other kind. Nor can I report that I have studied and studied *Ethics at the Edges of Life*. I have only studied it. But when Ramsey writes, "A general obligation to provide abortion services cannot be made consistent with freedom of conscientious refusal" (p. 53), I can comprehend the logic but cannot commend the reasoning. The "significant in the factual" seems to me to have escaped Ramsey's notice for the moment. Either that, or the significant in the factual has been caught in a logical trap. Rights are indeed amenable to logic, but responsibilities always break out of logic into relational reality. Or again, Ramsey writes,

> Most people in all ages act *sub specie boni*. In any case, the issue to which past discussions of cooperation and conscientious refusal to cooperate were addressed had to do with what *the cooperator* understood *himself* to be doing and was actually doing in the moral order — not first of all with what the primary agent thought *he* was doing. That issue still remains with us, despite all attempts to dissolve it. (pp. 85-86)

Agreed! But somehow I sense that for Ramsey the "refuser" is more faithful to the conscience as the guardian of the moral order than is the cooperator.

Along that road lies the dehumanizing vulnerability to self-righteousness that is in every ethical view that insists that there is always only one right thing to do; or if not that, there is the only less dark counsel that there are degrees of approximation and faithfulness to the moral order. The current Right to Life movement is one of the most frenzied and fanatical indications of moral self-righteousness that I know. Luther's perception that the fifth commandment is violated not only when a person actually does evil but also when one fails to do good to one's neighbor is unhappily altogether overlooked.

What does the cooperator understand himself or herself to be doing, and what is he or she actually doing, in the moral order where abortion is concerned? He or she is taking responsibility for life. What, on the other hand, is the conscientious refuser to cooperate doing? At least so far as most current discussions go, he or she is defending the right to life!

It has been noted that the abortion debate may be divided into three major segments.[18] At one extreme there is the "no abortion" position. At the other extreme is the "abortion on demand" position. And in between, there is a view that may be called the position of "justifiable abortion." The common point around which all three notions gravitate is the notion of rights. "Abortion on demand" seeks to further and defend the "rights of the woman." "No abortion" seeks to further and defend the "rights of the unborn." The position of "justifiable abortion" seeks somehow to adjudicate the rights of both. In any case, a grievous politicization of a critical human situation has taken place and is now taking place. At the very least, the whole discussion goes on at a subcatechetical level, unmindful of Luther's perception that "it will do you no good to plead that you did not contribute to [your neighbor's] death by word or deed, for you have withheld your love from him and robbed him of the service by which his life might have been saved" (LCT, 391:90).

The human fact is — whatever the social, legal, political, and moral circumstances may be — that the unborn has no rights, but only a divine ordination to the responsibility *for* life on the part of the born. The human fact is that the woman has no rights on demand, but only a divine ordination to the responsibility for life under which she, together with all the born — male and female, man and woman and child — are called to be. And they are called to be born as surely as "a world of made is not a world of born," in E. E. Cummings's finely honed phrase.

18. R. Potter, "The Abortion Debate," in *The Religious Situation,* ed. D. Cutler (Boston: Beacon Press, 1968), pp. 112-61.

The Right to Life movement is, in my judgment, in thorough violation of the fifth commandment since it subsumes responsibility for life so tightly under the right to life as to foredoom the fetus brought to birth to a less than fully human life. This is most evident, of course, from the fact that the denial of abortion most grievously afflicts the poor. And it is only a little less evident, amid the sound and fury, from the fact that the privileged life into which the forcibly unaborted fetus comes is the life that values property over people and moves increasingly in treadmill fashion from the value-producing, to the solitary, to the isolated individual. The "abortion on demand" position is more open to the dehumanizing reality of a pregnancy in which the woman is left to bear the major torment, pain, and bitterness in a society whose principles and patterns for living increasingly deprive the woman with child of a sustaining community of shared concern and drive her into isolation. The nadir of this societal repudiation of the fifth commandment and its parametric indication of the responsibility for life in terms of the reduction of inequality and the enlargement of heterogeneity is described in a recent press report concerning a shelter for pregnant teenage girls in Los Angeles. The report says that almost without exception these girls did not want abortion but wanted to bring the fetus to birth. Their reason was that then they were sure they would have somebody who would love them. How isolated can you get? How dead can you be while living? How dehumanizing can the proscription of abortion become?

Although Bonhoeffer's discussion of "the right to bodily life" in the *Ethics* seems itself to remain in the context of rights, it must be remembered that he was manning the frontier of freedom against totalitarian tyranny, of humanization against dehumanization in a society that was in effective repudiation of the Commandments of God. Bonhoeffer is clear that "the question whether the life of the mother or the life of the child is of greater value can hardly be a matter for human decision." He is no less clear that "the simple fact is that God certainly intended to create a human being and that this nascent human being has [in abortion] been deliberately deprived of his life. And that is nothing but murder." At the same time, however, Bonhoeffer notes that "a great many different motives may lead to an action of this kind; indeed in cases where it is an act of despair, performed in circumstances of extreme human or economic destitution and misery, the guilt may often lie rather with the community than with the individual." Precisely in this connection, Bonhoeffer says, "many may conceal many a wanton deed, while the poor man's reluctant lapse may far more easily be disclosed."[19]

Exactly so! The "rights" approach to the question of abortion is out of phase both with the Decalogue and with social reality. It presupposes and perpetuates a view of conscience according to which the conscience has been cut off from its covenantal context, and the individual is left to the devices and desires of his or her own heart, which both subvert and are nurtured by deeds made rules in Christian ethics. Responsibility for life, on the other hand, rescues the individual both from solitariness and from the tyranny of conscience by drawing him or her into the social as well as the private making of room for the freedom to be human. In this context, nurture in the Commandments would lay bare that *all* are murderers in sheer dependence upon the gift of forgiveness and the grace of life, and that *all* are called to take responsibility for life in the power of the strength that is made perfect in weakness.

So when I am asked directly whether I am for abortion or against it, my reply is that I am against it and for it — and in that order, trusting, as the Heidelberg Catechism so beautifully puts it, that "my only comfort in life and in death" is God, who means freedom and who is against sin, and yet in the midst of that sin summons precisely the sinners to take responsibility for life. In short, abortion is not justifiable, but it is forgiveable! The proscription of abortion by law, constitutional amendment, or other means exhibits a sterilization of faith. Such a legal proscription threatens an obedience of faith in which one moves in the direction of freedom and justice regardless of the incongruities between law and morality (making human life human) encountered on the way. Faith, not law, makes room for freedom and justice — or to state the same idea differently, I cannot pursue my own righteousness in disregard of my neighbor. As surely as the letter kills, the spirit gives life (2 Cor. 3:6).

19. Dietrich Bonhoeffer, *Ethics* (New York: Macmillan, 1965), p. 176.

Sexuality and Human Fulfillment:
The Question of Homosexuality

The Sixth Commandment:
"You Shall Not Commit Adultery"

What follows from the sixth commandment on, Luther explains, is "easily understood from the preceding one. They all teach us to guard against harming our neighbor in any way. They are admirably arranged. First they deal with our neighbor's person. Then they proceed to the person nearest and dearest to him, namely his wife, who is one flesh and blood with him" (LCT, 392:200).

For Luther, the sixth commandment "is concerned specifically with the estate of marriage." "Significantly," he says, God "established it [i.e. marriage] as the first of all institutions, and he created man and woman differently . . . not for lewdness but to be true to each other, be fruitful, beget children, and support and bring them up to the glory of God" (LCT, 393:206-7).

In concert with the biblical and theological tradition, sexuality is the paradigm of human fulfillment. Indeed, we could say that, just as the family is the paradigm of human wholeness, sexuality is the paradigm of human fulfillment. Where there is no human fulfillment in and through sexuality, there can be no human wholeness, for as we have already suggested, the family is the laboratory for the nurture of the apperception of what it takes to be and to stay human in the world.

Karl Barth is the only theologian, so far as I know, who has identified sexuality as the concrete mode of the image of God. This may be the best reason for not following Barth into that thicket of perils and problems, but two merits at least appertain to Barth's suggestion. The first is that, in linking sexuality with the image of God, Barth has rescued biblical and Christian faith and life from Augustine's unfortunate libidinal stranglehold. In the second place, Barth's linkage underscores the fact that the divine image in the human creature as male and female is not an attribute of their creaturehood but a relation between male and female that expresses *who* they are, as and where they are, exactly as the image of the Creator in creation expresses the true relation between Creator and creatures, who and as and where they are — that is, in relation to each other.

Now, according to Barth, the order "male and female" is a subordinate order only as a matter of sequence, in no sense as a matter of worth.

Indeed, as far as worth goes, according to Genesis 2 the woman is worth more to the man than the man is to the woman. One gets the impression that it occurred to God one day that Adam was in danger of taking himself too seriously and was showing signs of both humorlessness and boredom. What he needed was an Other whose apperceptive grasp of what being human involves could get through to the man, thereby keeping him mindful that he was after all a creature, not God, and as a creature a big wheel only because God had given him a humanizing companion — a "helpmeet" or "help-mate," as the Bible records it. In short, Adam's "meet for help" was given Eve as a gift, a "mate-for-help." And in the reciprocal responsibility of that "mate-ing," the reciprocal and responsible relation of Creator to creature is a matter of daily experience. One remembers the vivid lines of Sister Corita: "Three things there are that keep life from being so daily: to make believe, to make hope, to make love." Well, Barth and Sister Corita have both latched on to what it is that really makes Adam and Eve tick.

It's a long story, of course, but let me just say in passing that the more I ponder the image of God in this sense the more baffling it becomes for me to understand how the church could have so disastrously mixed up worth and sequence in the matter of subordination. The patriarchalization has obviously been first in the line of default. Its defection and correction have been long overdue. We can only be grateful to the women's movement in our time for making assurance doubly sure that the defection stays corrected for good. At the same time, it must be noted that the human point and purpose of the correction is undergoing an increasing politicization as sexuality becomes more and more a struggle over rights and less and less an ordination to reciprocal responsibility in freedom and fulfillment.

Since Luther notes that this commandment is concerned specifically with the estate of marriage, I venture to suggest that his exposition of the commandment does not exclude a move from heterosexual to homosexual married life, as well as "others whom [God] has released by a high supernatural gift so that they can maintain chastity outside of marriage" (LCT, 393:211). Luther was, of course, referring to monastic life, but not only to monastic life, for he thought of marriage as a humanizing check upon sensuality for its own sake and purposes — but not only as a check upon sensuality.

"Let it be said in conclusion," he writes, "that this commandment requires everyone not only to live chastely in thought, word, and deed in his particular situation, . . . but also to love and cherish . . . each other wholeheartedly and with perfect fidelity" (LCT, 394:219). Luther, I submit, was more open than his Lutheran progeny to the fact that a divine ordination is not a *limiting* instance, but a *foundational* one. As a limiting instance, the divine ordination to sexual otherness and reciprocity is put forward as the normative mode of sexuality, in relation to which variants are excluded as deviants from the heterosexual norm. As a *foundational* instance, the divine ordination to sexual otherness and reciprocity becomes the liberating instance in relation to which divergent possibilities may be pursued and assessed. As a *limiting* instance, heterosexuality necessarily excludes homosexuality from the divine purpose of and for human fulfillment. As a *foundational* instance of otherness in differentiation and commitment, inequality and heterogeneity, reciprocity and fidelity, heterosexuality becomes the liberating occasion and sign of human fulfillment in relation to which homosexuality may also be affirmed. Just as in Scripture and tradition, a central and indispensable correlation between monotheism and monogamy has been discerned and affirmed, yet without requiring the instantaneous and intransigent rejection of concubinage, polyandry or polygamy, or even interracial and/or interfaith marriage as a test case of the obedience of faith, so the foundational and liberating instance of heterosexuality as a parable of human fulfillment does not require an intransigent rejection of homosexuality as a test case of the obedience of faith.

This consideration is more pertinent when one remembers that the word *homosexuality* springs from a Greek root, not a Latin one. *Homo* in Greek means "the same" (as against "different"); in Latin, it means "male" in distinction from "female." Thus the critical issue posed by homosexuality, in distinction from and in relation to heterosexuality, is (and this is where our ongoing work as Christians, it seems, is to have a special item to raise to the top of the agenda) whether sameness or otherness bears within itself the human secret of fulfilling differentiation and whether it can be so discovered to do.

At least under the parameters of marriage and chastity exalted by Luther's explication of the sixth commandment, this possibility of sameness in relation to otherness must be regarded as open and accepted as conformable to the obedience of fiat. The foundational instance of heterosexuality as the liberating instance of human fulfillment must be viewed as open to and not exclusive of homosexual discoveries of human fulfillment, and this for at least four momentous reasons.

(1) The first is the sinful violation of the image of God, which as the critical instance of sexuality takes heterosexual as well as homosexual forms. Homosexuals do not have a monopoly on sexual sinfulness. Romans 1:18-32 is an eloquent case in point.

(2) The second reason is that the cultural revision and renewal occasioned by the Abrahamic-Messianic intrusion upon the human story is a movement from the particular and exclusive toward the human and inclusive, refusing to stop short of the whole of humankind.

(3) The third reason is that the cultural rejection of homosexuality under the impact of Hebrew-Christian perceptions of faith and obedience has overreached itself to such an extent that homosexuality now emerges as perhaps the most painful instance of the politicization of sexuality in a struggle for rights as the precondition of any promising prospect for a responsible rediscovery of the parabolic relation between human sexuality and human fulfillment.[20]

(4) The fourth reason is rooted in the arresting conjunction of the mystery of human sexuality with the mystery of the presence of God in the midst of and in and with the community of those called out by Jesus Christ to and for discipleship in the world. Perhaps the best-kept secret of the Blessed Trinity is the divine ordination according to which sexuality, as the sign of the image of God in human creaturehood, is remembered, celebrated, and nurtured in and through the regeneration of that image in baptism and the eucharist. "We all, with unveiled face, beholding the glory of the Lord, are being changed into his likeness from one degree of glory to another" (2 Cor. 3:18, RSV) to be "conformed to the image of his Son, in order that he might be the firstborn within a large family" (Rom. 8:29).

If Augustine had only completed the move he began, instead of halting at midpoint! Think how he might have liberated sexuality *from* sin, instead of converting the linkage between sexuality and sin into a fixation! And think of the overload of neurotic guilt over and fear of concupiscence from which Western piety and morals might have been spared! If only Augustine had conjoined in infant baptism, in the release from the guilt of original sin, along with the release of sexuality from the

20. See John Boswell's thoroughgoing examination of the homosexual question in history, *Christianity, Social Tolerance and Homosexuality: Gay People in Western Europe from the Beginning of the Christian Era to the Fourteenth Century* (Chicago: University of Chicago Press, 1980).

dominion of sin and for its purposed freedom for human fulfillment and wholeness! If he had done that, the Baptists and even Karl Barth might have been spared their appointed task of rescuing faith and commitment, sin and regeneration, from the sacramental magic and superstition in which the Catholic Church, both Roman and Reformed, had imprisoned the unsuspecting infants in baptism. All of us — Baptists, Barthians, Romans, and Reformed (not to mention the Greek Orthodox) — might have noticed instead what the *New Yorker* might have reported as "the neatest trick of the week the world was made" — and that is the divine ordination according to which infants are readied to be received into the household of faith before their sexual formation has moved from "the invisible to the visible things that were made." The third person of the Blessed Trinity also has a sense of humor.

Attention to this point opens the way for a momentous and liberating reversal. According to this reversal, sexuality is not a criterion for sacramental participation; on the contrary, sacramental participation is the guardian of the primordial relation between sexuality and human fulfillment! A corrected Augustinian consequence of this reversal would be the discernment, by and within the community of faith, that homosexuality and holy orders are *not* in contradiction or in conflict one with another and that ordination can no more be denied to one whose mode of sexual chastity is homosexual than the grace of regeneration at baptism can be withdrawn or denied on the grounds of homosexuality. Sexuality is not a criterion of ordination, of calling into the ministry; there is no sexual criterion for ordination. The criterion for calling to ministry is a vocational sense of commitment as a baptized member of the household of faith to the ministry of Word and Sacrament.

Admittedly, Luther would not have gone *this* far — then! As our contemporary, however, his high view of marriage and chastity, together with his expressed acknowledgment that "there are some who are unsuited for married life, others whom [God] has released by a high supernatural gift so that they can maintain chastity outside marriage," would seem rather to open the way toward than to preclude the search for "the best possible knowledge about events without becoming dependent on this knowledge." Instead, such a search might be a prelude to receiving the gift of "discerning the significant in the factual," bestowed upon the obedience of faith. "In short," as Luther said, "everyone is required both to live chastely and to help his neighbor to do the same."

The community of faith has been disobedient to God's ordination to sexuality in driving our homosexual brothers and sisters into seclusion. It could be that there are perspectives and parameters in the sixth commandment that point to, and point up, a heterosexual apperception in our times, which in grateful obedience to the divine ordination of sexuality for human fulfillment will transform politicization in sexual matters to humanization. In this case our brothers and sisters may come out of their isolation to a sustaining community of faith and freedom and fulfillment. At any rate, I venture the judgment that this is an intrinsic human item on our post-Westphalian agenda set for us by Brother Martin, our contemporary.

CHAPTER SIX

Property, False Witness, Vocation, and Belonging

(The Seventh, Eighth, Ninth, and Tenth Commandments)

Christianity and Property

The Seventh Commandment:
"YOU SHALL NOT STEAL"[1]

A person steals not only when he robs a man's strong box or his pocket, but also when he takes advantage of his neighbor at the market, in a grocery shop, butcher stall, wine and beer cellar, workshop, and, in short, wherever business is transacted and money is exchanged for goods or labor. . . . Daily the poor are being defrauded. New burdens and high prices are imposed. Everyone misuses the market in his own willful, conceited, arrogant way [it's called, I think, cost effectiveness] as if it were his right and privilege to sell his goods as dearly as he pleases without a word of criticism.[2]

Luther's reflections on the seventh commandment bring us to the question of property. In examining Luther's as well as Calvin's view, one

---

1. These reflections on the seventh commandment were originally published under the title "The Standpoint of the Reformation," which appeared as chapter five of *Christianity and Property*, ed. Joseph Fletcher (Philadelphia: Westminster Press, 1947), pp. 100-123.

2. Luther, *The Large Catechism of Martin Luther*, trans. Robert H. Fischer (Philadelphia: Fortress Press, 1959), pp. 39, 41. All of the quotations in this chapter from Luther's reflections on the Decalogue will be taken from this translation. Subsequent references will be noted parenthetically in the text.

discovers that the Protestant Reformation poses Christian ideas of property in relation to the fundamentals of Christian faith. The problem of property becomes a problem to be approached in terms of first principles. In this respect the Reformation is different from the medieval era, in which property relations were rather systematically regulated in the derivative terms of canon law and moral theology.

Property is that which is owned. This goes all the way from real estate to copyright, from the stuff of the earth to the fruits of the spirit. Ownership is the relation of belonging. It is a dual claim, involving both the things of this world, regarded as goods, and the right to possess and use these goods. Therefore, insofar as property is a problem, the focus of concern is not the goods themselves but the right of possession and use of those goods. Something has gone wrong with the relation of belonging, and the dislocation has been described in various ways. The following proposition and its corollary may, however, help to get at the real nature of what is wrong about property. The proposition is as follows: *The relation of belonging goes wrong whenever the right of possession and the right of use fail to correspond.* And the corollary is this: *The right of possession and the right of use fail to correspond whenever the right of possession determines the right of use; accordingly, the restoration of this correspondence requires that the right of use shall determine the right of possession.*[3] Thus the disposition of goods is the key to the solution of the problem of property, and the critical question is this: What are the presuppositions and conditions in terms of which goods may be said to be rightly disposed?

The answer of the Reformation to this question is that justification by faith defines the presuppositions and the conditions in terms of which goods may be said to be rightly disposed. This answer has a threefold bearing upon the problem of property.

In the first place, it means that the problem of property is part of the problem of sin. It is the fallen world, not the world as it was created, in which the dislocation between the possession and the use of this world's goods has occurred. Sin is the cause of the problem of property because sin is the transgression of the limit set for us in the world by God the Creator, the consequence of which is a struggle over sovereignty that effectively prevents us from discerning what really belongs to whom, and from living accordingly. This struggle is perennially destructive, so that if we are really to find again the limit in terms of which we can know what

3. This is what the medieval writers meant by *occupatio*.

belongs to whom and live accordingly, we must be able to count upon some possibility beyond ourselves and our world. The significance of this correlation between a distorted sense of ownership and the transgression of the constitutive limit of our life in the world is that the problem of property is essentially a religious problem, and not an economic or social one, important as those aspects are.

In the second place, the bearing of justification upon the disposition of goods means that the problem of property is part of the problem of redemption. It is in *this* world — and not some other one — that the possibility of living within such limits as will make ownership a blessing rather than a curse is actually open to us. This possibility is bestowed upon us when God in Christ forgives us our sin. Luther was fond of declaring that the human heart was turned within itself — *cor incurvatum in se* — and he was at one with Calvin in noting that the world, instead of being the plain avenue for the recognition of the nature and the will of God, leads humanity into the most amazing idolatries and into a constant shuttle between intolerable tyrannies and anarchies. The incarnation and the atonement are an attack upon this unhappy curvature and all its works. They mean that justification, although it is not a possibility inherent in humanity or nature, nevertheless occurs in the world of humanity and nature and can be the decisive factor in the practical reckoning of life. To reckon with one's justification is to move into a new order and a new sovereignty, which are not yet triumphant, but which are nevertheless real and effective. The significance of this correlation between the recovery of the proper limit for right ownership and a new order and sovereignty in the world is that the solution of the problem of property is really a christological solution, and only secondarily an educational or political one.

In the third place, when the Reformation defines the presuppositions and conditions in terms of which goods may be said to be rightly disposed with reference to justification by faith, it means that the problem of property is part of the problem of the church. Justification affirms the forgiveness of the sinner, but it does not promise the eradication of sin. Indeed, precisely the converse is true. Justification is the basis for the hope and the resource of meaningful life in the midst of continuing sin. The new order and sovereignty in the world, regarded as the Kingdom of Christ, do not eliminate contending sovereignties but war against them and herald their approaching doom. But meanwhile there is an interim. According to the Reformation, this interim is inaugurated for the world by the resurrection of Jesus Christ, and for the individual in and through justification. This interim is consummated both for the world and for the individual at the Final Judgment. During the interim, the justified strive to make their calling and election sure and to work out their own salvation with fear and trembling. One of the distinguishing marks of this endeavor is the way they possess and use what they own.

The Reformers are clear as can be that this endeavor can be neither private nor profane. If it is private, it begets perfectionistic extremes; if it is profane, it begets ever new perversions of ownership. Consequently, the church is the interim area in which the faith and the duty of the believer concerning property — and not only property — are expressed and safeguarded against both extremes. When the Reformation lifts the problem of property into this interim, it separates itself sharply both from secularism and from Catholicism. Secular thought about property tends either toward a utopian solution of the interim character of the problem or toward a disregard of the interim, in which case the problem is viewed as perennial and without solution. Catholicism, on the other hand, correctly regards the problem of property as a problem of the interim, but it regards the faith and duty of the believer as *defined by* rather than merely *expressed in* the church. This means that for Catholicism the church determines the nature of justification instead of justification's determining the nature of the church. So far as the problem of property is concerned, this distinction makes all the difference in the world. It is the difference between an amelioristic and a revolutionary attack upon the disparity between possession and use in the disposition of goods. The significance of this correlation *ad interim* between the faith and duty of the believer and the disposition of goods is that the problem of property is provisionally (e.g., under any given set of conditions) an ecumenical problem[4] and not a technological or moralistic one.

4. The term *ecumenical* is used here rather than *ecclesiastical* or *institutional* in order to emphasize the dynamic character both of the church and of the problem of property. The church is dynamically regarded when it is viewed as the area in which the faith "once for all delivered" must be related in a new and meaningful, though also continuous, way to the decisions about faith and duty that the believer is perennially called upon to make. The problem of property is dynamically regarded when it is viewed in essentially the same terms under various conditions, and in such a way as to take full account of changed conditions without losing sight of the essential structure of the problem, which is religious. The term *ecumenical* also has the merit of conveying the sense in which the Reformation is the correction and continuation of the true Catholic tradition.

Now these considerations are of particular importance for the understanding of the Reformation teaching about property because of a widespread contemporary misapprehension concerning the Reformation itself. Historically speaking, it is generally held that the Reformation belongs to the modern, rather than to the medieval, period. The grounds for this assumption are obvious. Among them are the facts that the Reformers did effectively disrupt, for their contemporaries and succeeding generations, the authority of the medieval church; that the disruption of ecclesiastical authority was followed by the disruption of political authority with the passing of the Holy Roman Empire; and that the assertion of the independence of the individual religious consciousness was both prelude to and channel for latent individual tendencies that were already chafing for a Renaissance. Thus, sectarianism, nationalism, and individualism, which are so determinative of modern culture, seem directly traceable to the Protestant movement, which disrupted the cultural and collective unity of the Middle Ages. But what is phenomenologically evident is not otherwise self-evident, so that these obvious connections become a little too obvious. The least that can be said is that those who make them do not always show the most desirable familiarity with what the Reformers themselves thought they were doing. It is the great merit of Troeltsch's monumental study of this problem that it so carefully traced the interconnections of the Reformation with the medieval and the modern world, and that it thus demonstrated their essential kinship.[5] The fact that the Reformers ever and again approach the border of sectarian piety and practice without really crossing it explains, according to Troeltsch, the ambiguity as well as the error of the usual historical estimate.

But the error persists, and with it the tendency to judge the Reformation by what are alleged to be its fruits rather than by a serious examination of its roots. Two particularly vexatious consequences of what may be called "this historical dislocation of the Reformation" must be noted if we are rightly to establish its teaching about property. The first is the celebrated thesis of Max Weber that Protestantism fostered the spirit of capitalism.[6] Weber describes rather than defines the spirit of capitalism.

5. Ernst Troeltsch, *Die Soziallehren der christlichen Kirchen und Gruppen*, Gesammelte Schriften, vol. 1, 3rd ed. (Tübingen, 1923), cf. esp. p. 470 n. 214, pp. 611-12.

6. Max Weber, *Gesammelte Aufsätze zur Religionssoziologie*, vol. 1, 2nd ed.: "Die protestantische Ethik und der Geist des Kapitalismus" (Tübingen, 1922).

But what it comes to is, in Professor Tawney's phrase, "the temper of single-minded concentration on pecuniary gain."[7] The net effect of Weber's research has been to provide evidence for the contention that, just as medieval Catholicism supplied the necessary religious sanctions for feudal social economy, so the Reformation supplied the religious sanctions for bourgeois social economy. This is the clue to Luther's unhappy diatribe *Against the Murderous and Thieving Peasant Bands*.[8] Indeed, there would seem to be no better implementation in all history of Antony's remark in *Julius Caesar,* "The evil that men do lives after them, / The good is oft interred with their bones" (act 3, sc. 2, l. 79). It does not alter matters that, earlier in the same year, Luther had written *An Exhortation to Peace in Response to the Twelve Articles of the Swabian Peasants,*[9] in which, with less invective but no less severity, the duties of the princes were outlined.

Protestantism fostered the spirit of capitalism. One need only turn to Calvin's *Institutes of the Christian Religion* for text after text to show it. We read, for example:

> He who shall repose himself . . . on the Divine Blessing, will neither hunt after the objects violently coveted by men in general, . . . nor will he impute any prosperous event to himself, and to his own diligence, industry, or good fortune; but will acknowledge God to be the author of it. If, while the affairs of others are flourishing, he makes but a small progress, or even moves in a retrograde direction, yet he will bear his poverty with more equanimity and moderation, than any profane man will feel with a mediocrity of success, which would merely be inferior to his wishes; possessing, indeed, a consolation in which he may enjoy more tranquil satisfaction, than in the zenith of opulence or power; because he considers, that his affairs are ordered by the Lord in such a manner as is conducive to his salvation.[10]

What else can this mean but that one is advised to accept the material conditions of life, whatever they may be, and however unequal, as the directive of the Lord for one's salvation? And when one does so, what is

---

7. R. H. Tawney, *Religion and the Rise of Capitalism* (London, 1936), p. 320.

8. Martin Luther, *Wider die Mörderischen und räuberischen Rotten der Bauern,* W.A., vol. 18.

9. W.A., vol. 18.

10. John Calvin, *Institutes of the Christian Religion,* 3.7.9, Allen's translation (Philadelphia, 1928).

to prevent the poor from becoming poorer and the rich from becoming richer? In an urban and technological society, in which even the restraint of neighborliness has disappeared, the answer is, Nothing! Calvin's admonition is understandable only as providing religious encouragement for pecuniary gain.

It is beside the point that in an urban and technological society people are seldom influenced by religious opinion anyway. Nor does it really matter that there are texts upon texts both in Luther's and in Calvin's works according to which "the lot of the Lord," far from being offered as the occasion for exploitation, is underlined as the occasion for mutual charity and true community. Their qualifying admonitions on the score of charity and community are seen in what they have to say about the seventh commandment, "Thou shalt not steal." For, as Luther states, "stealing is nothing other than the unjust acquisition of another's goods, and this includes, briefly, every advantage at one's neighbor's expense, in all dealings with him."[11] And as Calvin puts it,

> Let servants show themselves obedient and diligent in the service of their masters; and that not only in appearance, but from the heart, as serving God himself. Neither let masters behave morosely and perversely to their servants, harassing them with excessive asperity, or treating them with contempt; but rather acknowledge them as their brethren and companions in the service of the heavenly Master, entitled to be regarded with mutual affection, and to receive kind treatment. . . . Moreover, our attention should always be directed to the Legislator; to remind us that this law is ordained for our hearts as much as for our hands, in order that men may study both to protect the property and to promote the interests of others.[12]

Now, plainly, Calvin's correlation of the protection of property with the promotion of the interests of others presupposes the religious character of the problem of property. And historical candor compels us to recognize that he and his contemporaries belonged to a culture in which earth and the designs of heaven were vividly and inseparably related. Comparatively speaking, this is certainly medieval, not modern. If one views what the Reformers thought they were doing in relation to our modern social

11. Martin Luther, *Grosser Katechismus*, ed. D. Johannes Meyer (Leipzig, 1914), p. 79; my translation.
12. Calvin, *Institutes*, 2.8.46.

economy, in which the disposition of goods is increasingly enmeshed in the net of rugged individualism and international anarchy, there can be only one conclusion, that is, that the Reformation was on the side of social reaction. Its doctrine of orders, of vocation, of total depravity, of the church as the elect community of the justified — all presuppose and defend a society in which social status is fixed and determines occupation, and in which faith and duty, although derived from the church, are primarily matters of personal conviction and responsibility. The indictments that the Reformers leveled against monopolies and large-scale financial dealings, against usury and the corruption of trade, are matched by their invectives against indolence and begging. Thus their economic judgments would seem to be, on the whole, either bulwarks of the status quo or obsolete.

There is, of course, considerable correspondence in objective fact between these Reformation doctrines and the economic mores of a bourgeois society. So much Weber has painstakingly and persuasively demonstrated. But even Professor Tawney, through whom Weber's thesis became current among us, has not overlooked the oversimplifications involved in it. He calls attention particularly to Weber's ascription to intellectual and religious influences and developments that are traceable to other factors as well, and to Weber's oversimplification of Calvinism itself.[13] At this point, curiously enough, Tawney ranges Troeltsch with Weber, although in fact Troeltsch also challenged the same point.[14] Indeed, it is difficult to see how anyone could fail to make the point, or why there should have been so much ready talk about "Calvinism and capitalism," as though this were the heart of the economic teaching of the Reformation. "That anyone," Weber himself wrote, "could set the purpose of his life's work exclusively in terms of the idea of going to his grave heavily laden with material goods and wealth, seemed to him [the precapitalistic person] purely the fruit of perverse impulses."[15] Certainly the Reformers would have agreed without reservation with this precapitalistic attitude; they would have nothing to do with what Weber means by the capitalistic spirit.

13. Tawney, pp. 319-21.
14. Tawney, p. 319. Tawney alludes to Troeltsch's expressed agreement with Weber in note 381 of the *Soziallehren*. But in note 344 of the same work Troeltsch declares that the distinction between Calvin and Calvinism must be accented even more than Weber does if we are to obtain a correct account of the influence of Protestantism upon the development of bourgeois culture.
15. Weber, p. 55; my translation.

This, of course, Weber also knows. But those who have drawn hasty conclusions from Weber's argument might well recall it. They might recall, too, that Weber very carefully opened his account of the capitalistic spirit with the wisdom of none other than Benjamin Franklin, whose piety was something less than Puritan and whose faith was nourished elsewhere than in Wittenberg or in Geneva![16]

The other tendency to misjudge the Reformation that must be noted if we are rightly to estimate its teaching about property is the one that sets the individual too completely over against the church. A brilliant instance of what can happen, especially when this tendency is combined with the one stemming from the thesis of Max Weber, is offered by Erich Fromm's account of the Reformation in his discussion of the problem of freedom. Fromm's analysis is worth quoting at some length, because it both shows the economic outlook of the Reformation and illustrates the need for caution in appraising religious factors.

> Luther's system, in so far as it differed from the Catholic tradition, has two sides, one of which has been stressed more than the other in the picture of his doctrines which is usually given in Protestant countries. This aspect points out that he gave man independence in religious matters; that he deprived the Church of her authority and gave it to the individual; that his concept of faith and salvation is one of subjective individual experience, in which all responsibility is with the individual and none with an authority which could give him what he cannot obtain himself. . . .
>
> The other aspect of modern freedom is the isolation and powerlessness it has brought for the individual, and this aspect has its roots in Protestantism as much as that of independence. Since this book is devoted mainly to freedom as a burden and danger, the following analysis, being intentionally one-sided, stresses that side in Luther's and Calvin's doctrines in which this negative aspect of freedom is rooted: their emphasis on the fundamental evilness and powerlessness of man. . . .
>
> What is the connection of Luther's doctrines with the psychological situation of all but the rich and the powerful toward the end of the Middle Ages? As we have seen, the old order was breaking down. The individual has lost the security of certainty and was threatened by new

16. See the cynical "success-by-all-means" philosophy in Franklin's essays *Necessary Hints to Those That Would Be Rich* and *Advice to a Young Tradesman*.

economic forces, by capitalists and monopolies; the corporative principle was being replaced by competition; the lower classes felt the pressure of growing exploitation. The appeal of Lutheranism to the lower classes differed from its appeal to the middle class. The poor in the cities, and even more the peasants, were in a desperate situation. They were ruthlessly exploited and deprived of traditional rights and privileges. . . . The Gospel articulated their hopes and expectations as it had done for the slaves and laborers of early Christianity, and led the poor to seek for freedom and justice. . . .

Although Luther accepted their allegiance to him and supported them, he could do so only up to a certain point; he had to break the alliance when the peasants . . . proceeded to become a revolutionary class which threatened to overthrow all authority and to destroy the foundations of a social order in whose maintenance the middle class was vitally interested. . . . As a whole, the middle class was more endangered by the collapse of the feudal order and by rising capitalism than they were helped.

Luther's picture of man mirrored just this dilemma. Man is free from all ties binding him to spiritual authorities, but this very freedom leaves him alone and anxious. . . . By not only accepting his own significance but by humiliating himself to the utmost, by giving up every vestige of individual will, . . . the individual could hope to be acceptable to God. . . . In psychological terms his concept of faith means: if you completely submit, if you accept your individual insignificance, then the all-powerful God may be willing to love you and save you. . . . Thus, while Luther freed people from the authority of the Church, he made them submit to a much more tyrannical authority, that of a God who insisted on complete submission of man and annihilation of the individual self as the essential condition to his salvation. . . .

In making the individual feel worthless and insignificant as far as his own merits are concerned, in making him feel like a powerless tool in the hands of God, he deprived man of the self-confidence and of the feeling of human dignity which is the premise for any firm stand against oppressing secular authorities. . . . Once the individual has lost his sense of pride and dignity, he was psychologically prepared . . . to accept a role in which his life became a means to purposes outside of himself, those of economic productivity and accumulation of capital. Luther's view on economic problems were typically medieval. . . . But . . . his emphasis on the nothingness of the individual was in contrast and paved the way for a development in which man not only was to obey secular authorities but had to subordinate his life to the ends of economic achievements. . . .

Calvin's theology . . . exhibits essentially the same spirit as Luther's, both theologically and psychologically.[17]

Now, this analysis of the teaching of the Reformation and its bearing upon property relations appears to mean *(a)* that the Reformation was part of the social upheaval of the late Middle Ages, an upheaval inspired by a growing conviction of the freedom, worth, and dignity of the individual and by the concern of new and hitherto impotent groups for social recognition and economic status; *(b)* that, initially and superficially, certain doctrines of the Reformation expressed and aided these aspirations for social change, but that the dominant effect of the Reformation teaching was to cut the nerve of effort at social and economic improvement; *(c)* that this result was chiefly due to the isolation of the individual whose "independence" had been asserted; and, finally, *(d)* that the long-range significance of this individualism is the contradiction (in what Calvin and Luther thought they were doing) between their medieval and feudal perspectives and loyalties and their theological and psychological nurture of the capitalistic spirit, which subordinates human life "to the ends of economic achievements." Thus Fromm, like Weber, judges the Reformation by modern rather than by medieval, by bourgeois rather than by feudal, standards, and, owing perhaps to the psychological bent and the more contemporary character of his analysis, underlines the unhappy consequences of Protestant individualism.

But all this must look altogether different to anyone who remembers that Luther and Calvin also had a doctrine of the church. Whatever they had to say about the individual must be understood in relation to this doctrine if it is not to be misunderstood. Whatever they had to say about property must be understood in relation to this doctrine if it is not to be erroneously oversimplified. Thus the isolated and the anxious individual whom Fromm derives from the combination of Luther's doctrine of justification and Calvin's doctrine of election has at best a shadowy and temporary emergence from the polemics against medieval ecclesiasticism. It must be noted that precisely here the Reformers were contending, not for the individual, but for the true, as against the false, church. Indeed,

17. Erich Fromm, *Escape from Freedom* (New York: Rinehart, 1941), pp. 74, 79-81, 83-84.

the independence of the individual that Fromm extols and the isolation that he regrets were well known to the Reformers, quite independently of the nascent struggle between the bourgeoisie and the barons and princes. Their frame of reference was at least as much biblical as feudal, and so they would have called Fromm's kind of freedom "the bondage of autonomy," because they would have known that in a feudal, as well as in a bourgeois society — and also in a socialist society — the independent individual can never really exist except in anxious isolation. Consequently, their remedy was not to replace a tyrannical authority with the authority of a God who insisted on "complete submission of man and annihilation of the individual self as the essential condition to his salvation." Rather, they urged the membership of the individual in a community of believers under the ordering will and saving love of God, a community in which the limits of individuality were embodied in the duties of mutuality.

Moreover, the acceptance of economic production and the accumulation of capital as the dominant ends of individual life are an achievement that is really more complicated than the mere psychological preparation provided by the individual's loss of "his sense of pride and dignity." As a matter of fact, if Fromm is correct at this point, Weber is in error. For Weber's thesis charges Calvinism with having fostered the capitalistic spirit precisely because it connected individual dignity with material well-being. On the other hand, if, as Fromm implies, the Reformers are to be charged with having chastened the revolutionary zeal of the peasants and the poor in the cities, this can be only because they emphasized the significance and dignity of humanity on another level and held out rewards in another world, and certainly not because they encouraged the subordination of life "to the ends of economic achievements." Indeed, the truth is — and in the light of it such confusions ought at last to be disposed of — that the Reformation doctrine of the church preserves individualism from the perils of autonomy, economic processes from the perils of idolatry, and the religious direction both of the individual and of the economy from the perils of clericalism. If such a doctrine seems, from the perspective of a technological society, deficient in revolutionary possibilities, it is worth remembering that on this point Luther and Calvin were themselves divided, and that more is to be gained from a fresh examination of the problem of property as a problem of the church than from the easy supposition that the Reformers had no doctrine of the church as against individualism.

When the Reformation is understood in terms of the religious and social context of the late Middle Ages, instead of the religious and social context of an emergent bourgeois culture, its teaching on property has a relevance for our own time that is not otherwise discernible. In the first place, its teaching on property could not have been formulated except in the religious and social context of the late Middle Ages. In the second place, whatever Reformation precepts and attitudes were entwined in the individualistic and economic aspirations of the middle and lower classes were so entwined because the capitalistic spirit, embodied in bourgeois culture and society, had its antecedents in the Middle Ages, both at their height and in the day of their decline.[18] Third, even the religious precepts and attitudes of the Reformation continued, in spite of bourgeois influence, to be admixed with medieval piety and practice. The sectarian problem, as Troeltsch has brilliantly shown, is the critical case in point. Probably sectarianism could not have flourished except in the soil of the Reformation; nevertheless, nothing proves more conclusively that the Reformers did not wish to be either individualistic or reactionary or revolutionary per se than their repudiation of sectarian inwardness, asceticism, and utopianism. Fourth, we who live in the day of the decline of the bourgeois culture ought to be able to appreciate, sympathetically and soberly, the position of the Reformers in the day of the decline of medieval culture. The task of assessing correctly the bearing of the past upon the future, of articulating a rediscovered faith amid the conflicting pressures and duties of a society in transition, of making immediate decisions with insufficient grasp of their consequences, either near at hand or far removed, and to compel the humbler course of rigorous preoccupation with the fundamentals of the Christian faith and only a halting application of it to the glaring issues of the day often seems too far beyond human wisdom and strength.

Finally, there are at least two medieval conceptions that also informed the teaching of the Reformation and, because of their special bearing upon the problem of property, may serve as instruments for the refashioning of our thinking upon the wider total problem of Christianity and property. These conceptions are embodied in the idea of the *corpus Christi* (body of Christ, the church) and in the idea of the *corpus Christianum* (body of Christians in the world). Let us look first at the substance of the Reformation teaching on property, and then at the ideas of the *corpus Christi*

18. Cf. Hector Menteith Robertson, *Aspects of the Rise of Economic Individualism* (Clifton, NJ: A. M. Kelley, 1973).

and of the *corpus Christianum* as the framework for the understanding of the Reformation teaching in its beginning and today.

The Reformers believed in private property. This is not because they were capitalist but because they were Christian. That is to say, Luther and Calvin both recognized that the ownership of goods is a legitimate condition of human life in a world that belongs to God. But ownership, as they understood it, is never the exclusive right of possession. This is what differentiates the Reformers' conception of private property from the capitalistic view of it. Indeed, one could put the difference sharply by saying that, according to the Reformation, the right to use determines the right to possess; whereas the capitalist doctrine is that the right to possess determines the right to use. Rightly understood, possession is in order to use; use is not in order to possess.

Now the reason for the legitimacy of the ownership of goods is quite simple. It is that ownership is a derived and not an inherent right. The grounds for it are neither in the goods themselves nor in the one who needs and uses them, but rather in God, who bestows the goods and determines their fruitfulness. The householder, not the merchant, is the prototype of proper ownership. "Economics" literally means household management. Calvin declares that God

> appointed man, lord of the world; . . . and hence we infer what was the end for which all things were created; namely, that none of the conveniences and necessaries of life might be wanting to men. In the very order of creation the paternal solicitude of God for man is conspicuous, because he furnished the world with all things needful, and even with an immense profusion of wealth before he formed man. Thus man was rich before he was born. . . . Thus we are to seek from God alone whatever is necessary for us, and in the very use of his gifts, we are to exercise ourselves in meditating on his goodness and paternal care.[19]

And Luther, with characteristic simplicity and directness, amplifies the contention of his contemporary. He seems to cast a somewhat vegetarian eye upon the circumstance that Adam, "in addition to all that food which he had in abundance from all the trees around him and from their fruits, which were nobler and richer than any we now possess or know," should also have been given dominion over the beasts of the field and the fish of the sea. Since rationing was obviously no problem for Adam, Luther is

19. John Calvin, *Commentary on Genesis* (Edinburgh, 1897), vol. 1, pp. 96, 99.

unable to figure out what use he could have made for this enlargement of authority. But rather than yield to the temptation of speculation, Luther is ready to recognize himself with us as "sunk . . . in ignorance of God and his creatures" and to drive home the same point that Calvin has made.

> Nor could he [i.e., Adam] need raiment or money, who had all things under his immediate dominion and power. Nor did he need to regard any avarice or expectation in his posterity. Adam and Eve therefore being thus amply provided with food, needed only to use these creatures to excite their admiration and wonder of God and to create in them that holiness of pleasure which we never can know in this state of corruption of our nature.[20]

Apparently, so long as human life is ordered by God, the right use determines the right of possession of the goods of this world because they belong to God and serve, in Calvin's phrase, "the conveniences and the necessaries of life."

Goods are to be owned *soli Deo gloria*. But according to the teaching of the Reformation, ownership is a legitimate condition of human life after as well as before the Fall. Luther and Calvin seem to accept private property as a desirable condition of both the sinful and the created (unfallen) orders. It is, however, not always clear why they do so. Consequently, it is at this point, perhaps more than at any other, that the greatest confusion about the Reformation teaching gathers. A telling instance is supplied by the fate of the word *stewardship*. What was originally a high word of trust became a byword of suspicion. In original fact, stewardship really designates the kind of ownership in which possession is in order to use, because the goods of this world are and remain the gifts of God. The Christian mind has thus almost naturally found its way back to it again and again. But stewardship makes the sinful distortion of ownership equally vivid, and nowhere more so than when joined with certain aspects of the Reformation teaching. What has happened is that, although Luther and Calvin never tire of insisting that stewardship is a duty as well as a privilege, the privileges attaching to such stewardship have always outrun the corresponding duties.

Some explanation of this ambiguity, however, lies in the sense in which the Reformers recognized the problem of property as a part of the problem of sin. The matter can, perhaps, be put like this: A sinful order is a radical

20. Martin Luther, *Commentary on Genesis,* trans. Lenker (Minneapolis, 1904), p. 128.

distortion, but not a complete destruction, of the created order. Consequently, the ownership of goods is still an expression and acknowledgment of the benevolence of the Creator. But a sinful order bears within itself the seed of anarchic self-destruction. The ownership of goods, therefore, is one of the ways in which the sustaining limits of the Creator's order are asserted and obeyed. Luther, for instance, could argue with equal candor, and almost equal intensity, against both usury and the peasants on this ground. Dealing in incomes or rebellion is alike destructive of private and public well-being. This is inevitable since they violate both natural law and Christian love.

> Natural law says, what we wish and desire for ourselves, we shall wish and desire for our neighbor also; and it is the nature of love . . . not to seek its own profit or advantage, but that of others. But who believes that in this business, anyone buys income . . . with a view to giving his neighbor, the seller, a profit and advantage equal to his own? Thus it is to be feared that the buyer would not like to be in the seller's place as in other kinds of trade.

> The Gospel does not make goods common, except in the case of those who do of their own free will what the apostles and disciples did in Acts iv. They did not demand as do our insane peasants in their raging that the goods of others . . . should be common, but only their own goods. Our peasants, however, would have other men's goods common and keep their own goods for themselves.[21]

But the function of property as an instrument of order against the anarchy of sin can never justify the use of property in such a way as to give the right of possession precedence over human need.

Luther declares, in commenting upon the text of Matthew 5:40,[22] that this is the highest precept concerning what our Lord teaches about the disposition of goods. "Some think," he says, that this precept

> is recommended, not commanded, and regard it as a matter of indifference that everyone sets out to recover what belongs to him and to protect it by force, as best he may. The command, they say, applies to the perfect only. The defense is that if this were true, the evil-minded would be

---

21. Martin Luther, *Von Kaufhandlung und Wucher,* W.A., vol. 15; Wider die mörderischen und räuberischen Rotten der Bauern, W.A., vol. 18. My translation.

22. "And if anyone wants to sue you and take your coat, give your cloak as well."

free to take and to steal at will, and finally nobody would have anything. This excuse is irrelevant. The precept is a command, not to be disregarded because of wicked men.[23]

In other words, private property is a defense against the perils of anarchy; but the perils of anarchy are no defense of private property. It is precisely this inconsistency that makes the teaching of the Reformation fruitful for our own time. For it means that the insights of the Reformers into the blessings and the dangers of property are valid, even though they did not push them beyond the socioeconomic boundaries of a feudal society.[24]

And from another context we may add a further check. Concerning the commandment "Thou shalt not steal," Calvin declares:

> We will duly obey this commandment, then, if, content with our lot, we are zealous to make only honest and lawful gain; if we do not seek to become wealthy through injustice, nor attempt to deprive our neighbor of his goods to increase our own; if we do not strive to heap up riches cruelly wrung from the blood of others; if we do not madly scrape together from everywhere, by fair means or foul, whatever will feed our avarice or satisfy our prodigality. On the other hand, let this be our

---

23. Martin Luther, *Kleiner Sermon vom Wucher,* W.A., vol. 15.

24. Calvin, in a somewhat wider context, makes a similar analysis of the function of property in relation to its use. He is talking about the ascetic reaction to the fact that property is necessary. Again, the argument turns upon property as an order of creation.

> Let this be our principle: that the use of God's gifts is not wrongly directed when it is referred to that end to which the Author himself created and destined them for us, since he created them for our good, not for our ruin. Accordingly, no one will hold to a straighter path than he who diligently looks to this end. . . . Did [God] not . . . render many things attractive to us, apart from their necessary use?
>
> Away, then, with that inhuman philosophy which, while conceding only a necessary use of creatures, not only malignantly deprives us of the lawful fruit of God's beneficence but cannot be practiced unless it robs a man of all his senses and degrades him to a block.
>
> But, no less diligently, on the other hand, we must resist the lust of the flesh, which, unless it is kept in order, overflows without measure. . . . [O]ne bridle is put upon it if it be determined that all things were created for us that we might recognize the Author and give thanks for his kindness toward us. (*Institutes,* 3.10.2-3, trans. Ford Lewis Battles [Philadelphia: Westminster Press, 1960], vol. 1, pp. 720-21) .

constant aim: faithfully to help all men by our counsel and aid to keep what is theirs, in so far as we can; but if we have to deal with faithless and deceitful men, let us be prepared to give up something of our own rather than to contend with them. And not this alone: but let us share the necessity of those whom we see pressed by the difficulty of affairs, assisting them in their need with our abundance.[25]

Here again, possession is in order to use, for the glory of God and the well-being of humankind, both body and soul.

But if the Reformers were right about the necessity and the obligations of property as part of the problem of sin, they were children of their time in dealing with the problem of property as part of the problem of redemption. The bad men to whom Luther refers in the "Brief Sermon on Usury" he turns over to the powers that be. And what is so annoying about Calvin is that, every time he wins the reader's assent to his account of the function and the use of property as fundamentally a religious problem, he bluntly draws some consequence that, for a socially sensitive conscience, is inadmissible. For instance, the very passage already quoted includes this among the rules for avoiding licentiousness: "That persons whose property is small should learn to be patient under the privations, that they may not be tormented with an immoderate desire of riches." Now that is too much! Calvin may not have been able to see beyond a doctrine that has the net effect of weighting the issue on the side of the *status quo ante*. We, however, not only can but must see farther!

In the teaching of the Reformation about property, this issue focuses squarely upon the doctrine of vocation. The function and the use of property as an order of creation are concretely expressed for everyone in the exercise of his or her calling. One's calling is the work that one does in the world, regarded as God's assignment. Such a doctrine has the merit of preserving the intricate network of social responsibility from sectarian perfectionism and from the kind of inertia that never does anything at all because it never can discover a point to take hold. But it has had the great defect of providing a religious sanction for every individual's lot. The affluent are content and energetic; the indigent are content and frustrated; and when the inevitable moment comes, the moment in which the sinfulness of the sinful order can be tolerated no longer, the outbreak bursts all bounds in a struggle for power that defies both God and humanity.

25. Calvin, *Institutes*, 2.8.46, trans. Battles, vol. 1, pp. 409-10.

The real mistake of the Reformation was that its doctrine of justification provided the believer with a personal reorientation but no social one, so that the vocation in which a person expressed justification left the believer more anxious about the sin from which he had presumably been delivered than about the freedom for which Christ had presumably set him free. This seems all the more unfortunate since both Luther and Calvin had replaced the rule of self in the conduct of affairs.

Nevertheless, this unhappy error is not inherent in the Reformation doctrine of vocation. This may be seen from the fact that for the Reformers the problem of property was also a problem of the church. They believed in the body of Christ and in a body of this world. The framework of all their thought and energy was supported by the conviction that the world must become a Christian order because there was an order of Christians in the world. When, then, the doctrine of vocation is seen in relation both to the *corpus Christi* and to the *corpus Christianum,* it can provide a positive approach to the problem of property that the Reformers themselves did not explore.

Troeltsch has shown that Luther's ready reliance upon existing authority and the fateful duality in his thought, which separated personal faith from public action, was not due to any desire to sanctify the powers that be or to the view that what happened in the world was no concern of the justified believer. In both instances, Luther's attitude was governed by the circumstance that, having rejected the hierarchical order of salvation and virtue that had made possible the Catholic correlation of the *corpus Christi* and the *corpus Christianum,* he adopted instead the view that Christian faith and duty were incumbent upon the whole person in the totality of existence at every moment. Having thus carried the tension between the demands of the gospel and the recalcitrance of the world into the soul of the believer, Luther could only despair of the world in the certain hope of the eventual triumph of the rule of Christ! In Luther's judgment, both the order of creation and the second coming of the Lord were violated by the sects, which tended to regard the "eventual triumph" as already accomplished — so that the gospel could be regarded as more perfectly expressed in human life than it actually was, or the world more completely abandoned than it ought to be. His way of avoiding both Catholicism and sectarianism was to recommend vocational faithfulness in acknowledgment of the Creator's order and in dutiful service to that order until the day of its deliverance. For Calvin, on the other hand, one's calling was not one's way of being faithful in two realms, but a way of making one's election sure. Not least among the brilliant aspects of Troeltsch's analysis is his demonstration that, for Calvin, the doctrine of predestination avoided the separation of the church and the world that was induced by Luther's emphasis upon the saving love of God.

Calvin encouraged the believer to make an aggressive effort to conform the world unto the body of Christ, that is, to establish the *corpus Christianum*. Those who think that belief in predestination and ethical vigor are incompatible ought to study this analysis with care. Calvin's thought thus had certain affinities with that aspect of sectarianism which insisted that the *corpus Christi* could be implemented in a *corpus Christianum* and that such activity was the evidence of salvation. But with that other aspect of sectarianism, which insisted that the gospel could be more perfectly expressed in human life than it was, Calvin had no patience. The body of Christ, the church, was located in the world and was consequently involved in the sinfulness of the order of creation, even though it expected the consummation of redemption. Calvin rejected Catholicism on the same grounds that Luther did. Like Luther, Calvin recommended vocational faithfulness in acknowledgment of the Creator's order and in dutiful service to that order, against the day of its deliverance. But, unlike Luther, vocational faithfulness was for Calvin a master of working against the day of deliverance, rather than working until the day of deliverance. This explains why Calvinism rather than Lutheranism became the religion of the bourgeoisie insofar as the bourgeoisie was at all Protestant and religious. For when you are working against the day of deliverance you are more likely to work so hard as to find in material well-being the mark of piety; whereas if you are working until the day of deliverance, you are more likely to find contentment with whatever favors have fallen to your lot, as the surest clue to pious duty.

But this is not the only possibility. Suppose one recognized with Luther and Calvin that the problem of the goods of this world is to be completely tackled at the point of one's vocation. Suppose further that one combined Luther's despair of the world with Calvin's predestinate affirmation of the world in such a way that in despair one would hold all things as not having them, and in confidence one would use all things as having to dispose of them. In this way one might avoid the historical perils both of Lutheranism and of Calvinism. In order to do this, however, one would need to bring the doctrine of vocation more directly into relation with the rule of Christ. Thereby the problem of property, as a problem of the church, would be first and foremost a problem of redemption. The attack upon the sinful use of property would then proceed from the kingship of Christ, not from the acknowledgment of the Creator in the order of creation. This would mean that the right of use would really determine the right of possession, and that insofar as the structure of society resisted that determination, the justified believer as a member of the body of Christ would be under orders to alter it.

Telling the Truth

The Eighth Commandment:

"YOU SHALL NOT BEAR FALSE WITNESS
AGAINST YOUR NEIGHBOR"

According to Luther there is one more indispensable treasure beyond our body, wife or husband, and property, and that is our honor. "It is," Luther declares, "intolerable to live among men in public disgrace and contempt. Therefore God will not have our neighbor deprived of his reputation, honor, and character any more than of his money and possessions" (p. 43). Hence, we arrive at the eighth commandment: "You shall not bear false witness against your neighbor."

Luther describes three ways in which this commandment applies to the Christian life. First, he says, the commandment condemns the courts of justice, which, rather than defending the poor, falsely accuse and punish them. Believing that it is "the universal misfortune of the world that men of integrity seldom preside in courts of justice," Luther points out that it is the poor and powerless who inevitably suffer from false charges. From this situation Luther claims that "the first application of this commandment, then, is that everyone should help his neighbor maintain his rights. He must not allow these rights to be thwarted or distorted but should promote and resolutely guard them, whether he be judge or witness, let the consequences be what they may" (p. 44). Hence, according to Luther, the commandment points initially to the public responsibility for justice.

Second, Luther claims that the commandment applies to "spiritual jurisdiction or administration." Here Luther points to the false witness that is often borne against "godly preachers and Christians," who are frequently accused of heresy and apostasy. According to Luther, "the Word of God must undergo the most shameful and spiteful persecution and blasphemy: it is contradicted, perverted, misused, and misinterpreted"

(p. 44). Nevertheless, he counsels Christians to "let this pass," knowing that such condemnation of God's truth and God's people is inevitable in this sinful world.

The third way in which the commandment against bearing false witness against the neighbor applies to us, according to Luther, is that it "forbids all sins of the tongue by which we may injure or offend our neighbor." In other words, Luther condemns the vice of gossip, noting "the common vice of human nature that everyone would rather hear evil than good about his neighbor" (p. 44). Even though the content of a particular piece of gossip may in itself be true, Luther's understanding of truth, much like that of Bonhoeffer after him, encompasses more than the mere equivalence of words with facts. Where and when and how one speaks what one knows is also part and parcel of how we define the truth.[26]

Whereas all three of these applications of the eighth commandment hold importance for us today, our attention here will focus on Luther's first application of this commandment, that is, the fact that courts of justice often falsely accuse and punish the poor. In this regard the trial and execution of Julius and Ethel Rosenberg forty years ago as well as the ongoing ill-treatment of the Haitians in the United States today provide powerful cases in point. Here the innocent have indeed been oppressed at the hands of the courts, their cases have been lost, and their punishment has been severe and sometimes irreversible. Here indeed we see further evidence of the need for us to take responsibility for our neighbors in part by seeking to uphold their civil rights.

The Rosenbergs [27]

The year was 1953. The day was Friday, the 19th of June. The time was between 8:04 and 8:16 p.m. The hour had been advanced from the customary final hour of the day, set — tauntingly, and even blasphemously, as it seemed then (ironically, and even cynically, as it seems in retrospect) — to take account of the start of the Jewish shabbat at sundown. Julius

26. See Dietrich Bonhoeffer, "What Is Meant by 'Telling the Truth'?" in *Ethics* (New York: Macmillan, 1965), pp. 363-72.

27. These reflections, part of a speech given at an ecumenical memorial service for the Rosenbergs held at Union Square in Manhattan on June 19, 1978, were first published under the title "History's New Light: The Rosenbergs, Then and Now," in *Christianity and Crisis*, 17 July 1978, pp. 185-87.

went first to his death in the electric chair in Sing Sing Prison at Ossining, New York. Ethel followed her husband in the same manner. Both were steadfast in their unwavering insistence that they were innocent of the crime of espionage with which they had been charged and dubiously tried and sentenced to death. This claim of innocence is yet to be convincingly disproved in conscience and in law.

There was at the time a gathering outcry both of conscience and of law, a stirring among the people, both across this land and around the world, because a denial of right and justice had occurred that — in its very haste to deny itself and claim the name both of right and of justice — had the more ineradicably acquired the guise and the guilt of the oppression of the poor. For the poor, in our society just as in Luther's, are those who are either defenseless or whose defense has been trampled by the callous intrigue of privilege and power; who have no sustaining place or protection or opportunity or guardianship in the land; who are, in the most dehumanizing sense of the phrase, "strangers within the gate."

On Wednesday, June 17, 1953, Justice William O. Douglas granted a stay of execution. However, as some knew but most did not, an arrangement had already been agreed upon between Chief Justice Fred Vinson and Herbert Brownell, the Attorney General of the United States, according to which the Chief Justice would take the unprecedented step of summoning the full membership of the Court into special session for the purpose of vacating the stay that Justice Douglas was expected to grant. On Thursday, June 18, 1953, the full Court convened, and on Friday, the 19th, the Court vacated the stay, and thus deprived Ethel and Julius Rosenberg of the remaining legal preemption of the awesome sentence condemning them to death.

Appeals for commutation of the sentence by President Eisenhower included an appeal by His Holiness, Pius XII, attesting the intense concern around the world with the Rosenberg trial and its grim conclusion. In spite of all their efforts, the people who in 1953 gave first priority in conscience and law to right and justice, to humane apperception and compassion — in public as in private affairs — experienced defeat at the hands of the Court.

Consistent with Luther's claim that the courts overlook the rights of the poor and innocent, Julius and Ethel Rosenberg were victims of injustice played out in the courts of justice. They were the victims of a proceeding in the judicial court of Manhattan, presided over by Judge Irving R. Kaufman. To many people it was evident then — as has become increasingly evident since — that Judge Kaufman's mind was made up even before the trial began on the question of the sentence he would impose. The shocking series of *ex parte* judicial actions, with regard to both the Rosenbergs and Morton Sobell, who was also charged in the case, seemed already then to be in tandem with the career ambitions of the prosecutorial staff and, indeed, of the judge himself. These actions ill-concealed the lurking kangaroo character of the court in which the Rosenbergs and Sobell were tried and convicted. Justice, as the prophet Habakkuk once put it, was coming out perverted (Hab. 1:4) because the law was being used to victimize those who had been brought before the bar of judgment, not to adjudicate the cause that had so bitterly set enmity between the accusers and the accused.

It was, indeed, "a dread and awful time." The frenzy with which those in high places, at a mounting tempo approaching hysteria, sought to ensnare those in low places in a conspiracy of fear and suspicion and mistrust, so that everyone should be set against his or her neighbor, concealed more than the self-justifying ambitions of the powerful and the privileged in this land. It concealed a fundamental loss of confidence in the vision, the hopes, and the principles that informed and shaped the founding of our country, and that, in the course of human events, had made the United States of America a harbinger of human freedom and opportunity, possibility and fulfillment, for all the peoples and nations of the earth.

In retrospect, the wonder is not at the fact that the love of so many for freedom and justice and "a civil body politick" (in Jefferson's phrase) grew cold. The wonder is rather at the more than considerable number of people in our country and around the world who did not bow the knee before self-justifying power; who were not driven into silence by the institutionalized suppression of dissent; who held firmly to the conviction that the integrity of innocence, until guilt be proven beyond reasonable doubt, is the sign that justice is the criterion and purpose of law, not law the criterion and purpose of justice.

For these people, a humane apperception nurtured the discernment that, beyond and over and above the question of the guilt or innocence of Ethel and Julius Rosenberg and Morton Sobell, there was the question of whether the state is the master or the servant of the people. At stake is the fateful difference between a state in which the power of the law has been surrendered to the law of power and a state in which freedom is the indispensable condition of order and justice is the criterion of law. For any state in which the power of the law has been surrendered to the law of power has abandoned the way of freedom, justice, and right and has embraced the course of tyranny. So Ethel and Julius Rosenberg were the victims of a court, of a state, and of a society whose confidence in freedom, justice, and right was in disarray. The same, as we will now see, can be said of refugees fleeing the injustice of Haiti and seeking asylum in the United States, but not always finding a nation as committed to truth and justice as they expected.

The Haitians [28]

On August 19, 1979, *The New York Times* carried a special dispatch from reporter Wayne King in Miami that read in part:

> A woman and five small children drowned, allegedly forced overboard into 20 feet of dark water by two men smuggling them and others into the country, part of a stream of Haitians fleeing their homeland.
> Nine made it to the shore alive. One is missing. The body of 31-year-old Elaine Lorfils washed onto the beach. The bodies of the five children, 4-11 years old, were found bobbing in the sea.

On July 2, 1980, in a class-action suit in Miami Federal District Court, Judge James Lawrence King (no relation to reporter King) ruled that more than 4,000 Haitians seeking asylum in the U.S. had been denied due process of law and equal protection of the laws, and had been victims of "systematic and pervasive" discrimination by immigration authorities who had "pre-judged Haitian asylum cases as lacking any merit." Judge King found that the manner in which the Immigration and Naturalization Service (INS) had treated these Haitians "violated the Constitution, the immigration statutes, international agreements, INS regulations and INS operating procedures." And he declared, "It must stop!" More than fourteen years later, however, it has not stopped, and until it does, Dieumerci Lorfils — husband of Elaine and father of the five drowned children — is, along with countless others,

---

28. Portions of this section were first published in an essay entitled "The Haitian Struggle for Human Rights," *The Christian Century* 97 (8 October 1980): 941-43, and in an article entitled "The Stranger Within the Gate: Two Stories for the American Conscience," by Paul Lehmann and Ira Gollobin, *The Christian Century* 89 (15 November 1972): 1149-52.

the silent witness to the almost genocidal inhumanity that characterizes the treatment of the Haitian refugees by past and now present government officials of the U.S. through its Departments of Justice and State.

The present plight of the Haitians began in 1957, when Francois ("Papa Doc") Duvalier assumed power in Haiti. From then until his death in 1971, he ruled this small Caribbean country with a cruel dictatorial power, torturing political opponents and arbitrarily placing citizens in prison without trial or hearing. As he lay dying in 1971, "Papa Doc" Duvalier, as "president for life," proclaimed his son, Jean Claude ("Baby Doc"), his successor with the same title. The principal instruments of presidential repression and suppression of human rights in Haiti remained the Tontons Macoutes, the dreaded secret police force of the Duvaliers — 30,000 strong. Even now, though Jean Claude Duvalier is gone and a duly elected president, Jean-Bertrand Aristide, shows hope for political reform, the country continues to be in political disarray as Aristide is prevented from exercising his office.

Haiti is as miserable economically as it is politically. Long before the present situation erupted, poverty was notorious. The population is largely peasant, subject to the vagaries of precarious small-farm and village existence. Economic deprivation has contributed to a population mobility that has made the Haitian people the wanderers of the Caribbean. They have provided cheap labor, chiefly for the Dominican Republic and the Bahamas — and on this account they have endured the humiliating discovery that the attempt to break free of a subsistence level of existence at home serves but to make them victims of exploitation abroad. On the other hand, this same search for a viable economic level of existence has made them victims of the judgment, by their own government as well as by foreign ones, that they are economic migrants and in no sense political refugees. Since December 12, 1972, when the first boatload of Haitians arrived in Florida after an eight-hundred-mile journey of indescribable torment and danger, this fiction has functioned as the cornerstone of U.S. policy toward the Haitians.

From the first, the Nixon, Ford, and Carter administrations treated the Haitians with hostility instead of hospitality. Prejudged to be economic and not political refugees, they were given cursory "interviews" upon their arrival, with no attorney permitted. They were imprisoned, often on a $1,000 bond, and those released were denied work authorization. They have fared no better under the Reagan, Bush, and now Clinton administrations, campaign promises to the contrary.

After welcoming Cubans for twenty years, Washington is hard pressed to justify its ill-treatment of the Haitian refugees without being accused of racial bias, since the Haitians, unlike most Cubans, are black. As far back as February 1974, a resolution of the Governing Board of the National Council of Churches noted this racial aspect and called attention to its "divisive" potential. From the beginning of the controversy the congressional Black Caucus, the National Urban League, and, above all, Haitian communities and the black community in Florida have been in the forefront of the struggle to win political asylum for the Haitians, as a minimal and just recognition of their human rights. Innumerable religious groups (Protestant, Catholic, and Jewish), many labor organizations, and government officials have at various times joined in supporting asylum. This escalating pressure, along with favorable television coverage and major newspaper editorials favoring asylum, has to some extent eroded Washington's opposition to the recognition of Haitians' human rights, but the abusive treatment continues.

The Haitians' struggle calls into question the commitment of the U.S. government to the achievement of human rights in this land and in every land. It exposes the need for a foreign policy in and through which justice is discerned and practiced as the surest safeguard of security, peace, and freedom in the Caribbean and anywhere else in the world. The struggle unmasks the specter of racial discrimination that haunts the refusal to treat the Haitians in the same way as Cubans, Vietnamese, and others in flight from political repression and economic despair.

Luther's insistence that the eighth commandment condemns the courts of justice for falsely accusing and punishing the poor prods us to remember that deeply rooted in the Hebrew-Christian faith is concern for the "stranger within the gate." Under the covenant between Yahweh and the people of Israel, care of the poor, the widows, and the aliens is a fundamental way of signalizing recognition of Yahweh as sole and righteous God whose continuing presence in the midst of his people liberates them. Thus the strongly mandatory Book of Deuteronomy specifies that "cursed be anyone who deprives the alien, the orphan, and the widow of justice" (27:19). Concern for the stranger witnesses to the justice intrinsic to God's nature and will and to the integrity of the people's faith.

Jesus of Nazareth was brought up in the piety of the covenant of God with humanity and of human beings with one another. What Abraham had launched and Moses had given political form in the historical consciousness of the Hebrew people, Jesus affirmed as the secret of human community and fulfillment — a community long awaited and worked for, and suddenly, with his life and teaching, giving present reality to the shape of the future. "The kingdom of God," Jesus called it; and in the powerful parable summarizing what the kingdom of God was all about, he made it plain that the future belongs to those who welcome the stranger. "I was a stranger," he said, "and you welcomed me" (Matt. 25:35). With Jesus, an ancient responsibility was brought under the liberating impulse of a community of discipleship. This community was born in the transformation of the babel of languages, which turn strangers into enemies, by a Pentecostal gift through which each understands every other. The people were "amazed and astonished, [and] they asked, ' . . . how is it that we hear, each of us, in our own native language?' " (Acts 2:7-8).

If "fantastic" designates a basic and humanizing connection between fantasy and experience, it is fantastic to suggest that the story of civilization is the story of the stranger made to feel at home. Yet it can be said that, from Abraham and Moses to Jesus and the community of his presence and spirit, the good news is that the freedom to be and to stay human in the world is expressed and nurtured by the gift of hospitality to the stranger and that societies gain or lose sense and stability according to how they make room for the stranger within their gate. By the same token, the bad news is that persons and societies who turn out the stranger turn in upon themselves and sooner or later wither and die.

In the United States of America today, however, this saving story and the saving reality it points to are in high disregard, signaled by the mounting temptation to convert the stranger among us from a neighbor into a scapegoat. The many urgent and complex problems that beset the nation — poverty, population explosion, environmental pollution, and the liberation of oppressed groups — are almost all-absorbing, and amid the furious clamor and confusion of attempts to set them right the voice of the strangers within our gates goes unheard, their plight unnoticed. This disregard of the eighth commandment allows the principalities and powers that shape our nation's policies to pursue their subtle violation of the conscience of a people rooted in and nurtured by the saving story.

There was a time when immigrants to this country were welcomed. But today many of our government officials and much of our press call them "aliens" — a word implying not only that they are noncitizens but that their way of life is inferior and even hostile to ours.

The Bill of Rights makes no distinction between "persons" and "citizens." It guarantees to all "persons" certain rights, such as freedom of speech and assembly, due process of law, and equal protection under the laws. Invasion of the constitutional rights of noncitizens endangers the constitutional rights of citizens; for as "persons," neither of these has greater stature than the other. There is no way to breach the constitutional wall protecting noncitizens without simultaneously opening the floodgates to erosion of the rights of citizens. The choice before us as a people lies between the politics of death and a politics of humanity. In America today, the story of the stranger is one concrete point of entry into the saving story, and conversely, the saving story is the point of entry into the experience and the power that bring memories and hopes together in the liberation of the present. Together, the two stories are a tale of hope for a politics of humanity, which those who practice the politics of death among us can neither match nor prevent. Here is a legacy for an America that has neither the need nor the desire to be supreme in the earth, but an America that is in truth a land of promise. Those of us whose apperception is nurtured at the intersection of these two stories do well to remember Luther's claim that the first application of the eighth commandment regarding the prohibition against bearing false witness against the neighbor lies in positive instruction to help our neighbors maintain their rights.

A Question of Belonging

The Ninth and Tenth Commandments: "You Shall Not Covet"

Although Luther splits the prohibition against covetousness into two commandments, he discusses them together. According to him, these last two commandments do not have to do either with theft (the ninth commandment) or with unchastity (the tenth commandment), since these two vices have already been covered in the seventh and sixth commandments. Rather, he claims that the ninth and tenth commandments are meant "to forbid anyone, even with a specious pretext, to covet or scheme to despoil his neighbor of what belongs to him, such as his wife, servants, house, fields, meadows, or cattle" (pp. 48-49). Whereas theft, prohibited in the seventh commandment, involves the illegal taking of what does not belong to you, the ninth and tenth commandments deal with actions whereby one might *legally* and even *with honor* entice something or someone away from the neighbor. Hence, these last two commandments are not addressed "to those

whom the world considers wicked rogues, but precisely to the most upright
— to people who wish to be commended as honest and virtuous because
they have not offended against the preceding commandments" (p. 49).

Vocation and the Ninth Commandment:
"You Shall Not Covet Your Neighbor's House"

The legally minded have always fallen into two traps. On the one hand, they
hold themselves and others to such strict adherence to the literal wording of
the moral law that following God's will becomes an unbearable burden rather
than an act of gratitude. On the other hand, legalism also opens the way for
getting *around* the spirit of the law while still claiming to follow the law.
Luther believes the ninth commandment speaks against this second error,
for it addresses those who seek to follow the letter of the law, all the while
scheming to acquire their neighbor's goods without guilt or fear of reprisal.

> Such is nature that we all begrudge another's having as much as we have.
> Everyone acquires all he can and lets others look out for themselves. Yet
> we all pretend to be upright. We know how to put up a fine front to
> conceal our rascality. We think up artful dodges and sly tricks (better
> and better ones are being devised daily) under the guise of justice. We
> brazenly dare to boast of it, and insist that it should be called not rascality
> but shrewdness and business acumen. In this we are abetted by jurists
> and lawyers who twist and stretch the law to suit their purpose, straining
> words and using them for pretexts, without regard for equity or for our
> neighbor's plight. (p. 49)

Such is the nature of hypocrisy, whereby one is righteous according to the
law though deceitful in human relationships. We are reminded that ethical
demands acquire meaning and authority *only* from the specific moral
relationships that precede and shape these demands. The first relationship
we bring to each ethical situation is that defined by the first commandment, "You shall have no other gods," which according to Luther simply
means, "You shall fear, love, and trust me as your one true God" (p. 53).
Luther's reflections on the ninth commandment bring us back to the first
as a reminder that we do not "keep" the Commandments; we obey the
One whom the heart can trust completely. To *keep* the Commandments
means that we can find ways to deceive our neighbor and take what belongs
to him or her even if we never technically break the law. To *obey* the One

who gives the Commandments and the One in whom we trust completely leads to responsible relationship with our neighbor.

> God does not wish you to deprive your neighbor of anything that is his, letting him suffer loss while you gratify your greed, even though in the eyes of the world you might honorably retain the property. To do so is dark and underhanded wickedness, and, as we say, it is all done "under the hat" so as to escape detection. Although you may act as if you have wronged no one, you have trespassed on your neighbor's rights. It may not be called stealing or fraud, yet it is coveting — that is, having designs upon your neighbor's property, luring it away from him against his will, and begrudging what God gave him. The judge and the public may have to leave you in possession of it, but God will not, for he sees your wicked heart and the deceitfulness of the world. (p. 50)

While the seventh commandment (against stealing) teaches us that we are to *own* and *use* property to the glory of God, the ninth commandment (against coveting our neighbor's goods) teaches us that we are to *acquire* property (whether by purchase or production or any other means) to the glory of God. The ninth commandment, therefore, leads us to examine the doctrine of vocation and the vocational predicament of our time as one avenue for discovering what it means to acquire property to the glory of God.[29]

An eminent professor of history once remarked that he had reflected a good deal upon the first question of the catechism, "What is the chief end of man?" The professor's own formulation of the answer was quite uncatechetical, but his orientation was sound and underlined a basic predicament of democratic society. The professor replied to the catechism, in effect, in this way: "The chief end of man is to achieve the maturity necessary for making responsible and adequate decisions." He then went on to say that he had become much concerned about the prospects for maturity of citizens in a democratic society, owing to the overwhelming influence upon that society of technological industry. The professor was not suggesting, he declared, that there was anything like a one-to-one correlation between personal immaturity and mechanized industry. His concern had been aroused by the observation that in such a society, for

---

29. The following reflections were originally published as "Biblical Faith and the Vocational Predicament of Our Time," *The Drew Gateway* 23, 3-4 (1952-53): 101-8.

countless people, the meaning of what they are doing is either lacking or obscure, and there is a consequent paralysis of motivation and personal fulfillment.

This observation has, of course, long preoccupied many people, none more incisively than the artists whose gifts and tasks are to look deeply and totally into what is going on. In Eugene O'Neill's play *Dynamo*, the plot concerns a young son of the manse, whose father's narrow and rigid conception of God and of religious living has reduced the heritage of faith and pity to irrelevance and left a vacuum to be filled by new and more lively deities. The son finds in the whirring dynamos of the nearby hydroelectric plant the meaning that overwhelms and fills his life. Near the end of the play there is a hymn to electricity that expresses the faith and hope of a contemporary youth in search of maturity. It is the machine that provides the compelling and creative answer to his quest.

> It's so mysterious . . . and grand . . . it makes you feel things. . . . you don't need to think . . . you almost get the secret . . . what electricity is . . . what life is . . . what God is . . . it's all the same thing. . . . It's like a great dark idol . . . like the old stone statues of gods people prayed to . . . only it's living and they were dead. . . . Listen to her singing . . . that beats all organs in church . . . it's the hymn of electricity . . . "always singing about everything in the world" . . . I feel like praying now![30]

These expectations have, of course, not been sustained. The same theme was treated in another medium by Charles Chaplin. His *Modern Times*, it may be recalled, is the account of the confusion, futility, and ultimate loss of humanity that have overtaken the citizens of a society dominated by the mechanization and the monotony of the machine. That society has become not a "human" but a "commodity" society. This transformation has been accompanied by a correspondingly profound and subtle change in what people expect out of life and in the way in which people think about themselves.

Perhaps the most powerful and penetrating epitomization of the commodity character of our society and its impact upon the effort of people to express and to retain their humanity is Arthur Miller's Pulitzer prize–winning play, *Death of a Salesman*. Willie Loman lives out the whole of his adult life always being somebody else. He is a salesman and so is caught in a critical web of our economic life, the network of processes,

---

30. Eugene O'Neill, *Dynamo*, act 2, sc. 3.

values, and relationships by which the goods that are produced find their way into adequate channels of distribution and consumption. Willie Loman's equipment for his job is his obvious and average humanity, with a considerable edge over most of his fellows in congeniality and communicativeness, those traits which make it the easiest to get along with people. But Willie Loman is never able to accept himself as he is and for what he is. The values that he cherishes — or covets — lie elsewhere. They pivot about the "big deal" that will give him the big promotion, the big commission, the big house and car in the right neighborhood and with the right people. Willie Loman's passion (one could say "covetousness") for these values is so intense that he is able to translate himself into a world of fantasy and of the future that destroys his wife and children and himself. The deep and subtle pathos of the Loman family is that the father's affection for his wife and children is second only to his passion for success, so that it is always for the sake of those he loves that he pursues the values that undo them all. The work that Willie Loman does and the values that surround and sustain him in the doing of his work are so alien to his humanity as to destroy it.

Willie Loman's story and the story of all who are like him is consistent with Eric Fromm's description of how the contemporary marketing mentality has turned persons into commodities:

> In our time the marketing orientation has been growing rapidly, together with the development of a new market that is a phenomenon of the last decades — the "personality market." . . . The principle of evaluation is the same on both the personality and the commodity market: on the one, personalities are offered for sale; on the other, commodities. Value in both cases is their exchange value. . . . Success depends largely on how well a person sells himself on the market, how well he gets his personality across, how nice a "package" he is; whether he is "cheerful," "sound," "aggressive," "reliable," "ambitious"; furthermore what his family background is, to what clubs he belongs, and whether he knows the right people. . . . A stockbroker, a salesman, a secretary, a railroad executive, a college professor, or a hotel manager must each offer different kinds of personality that, regardless of their differences, must fill one condition: to be in demand.

Fromm anticipates the objection that his account of the economic function of the market and its influence upon personal values and behavior is oversimplified. "Nevertheless, the regulatory function of the market has been, and still is, predominant enough to have a profound influence on the character formation of the urban middle class and, through the latter's social and cultural influence, on the whole population."[31] In a similar way, the objection may be anticipated that not everybody is involved in the vocational predicament of our time. Certainly there are many people whose work is meaningful and who find human fulfillment in it. Nevertheless, to adapt a phrase of Fromm's, the regulatory role of industrialism has profoundly affected the nature, conditions, and meaning of work — so profoundly that those who are beyond the range of this influence may be regarded as negligible in an analysis of the problem of work in our time.

The vocational predicament of our time is that work has lost its vocational significance. To put it another way, the vital link between vocation and occupation in the work that people do has been severed. The occupational element in work denotes that which principally engages the time, interest, and energy of the person who works. The word itself (*occupatio,* from *ob* and *capio*) refers to the taking over of a place or an object by getting, so to say, on top of it — that is, by mastery. The vocational element in work denotes the human context in which the work is done. The word itself (*vocatio,* from *voco,* to call) was apparently first used of an invitation to table, a usage that vividly underlines the social and human relationships involved. It is not difficult to see how the range of social and human relationships could be extended to include the values and purposes for which people come together and which give meaning to their common life. Thus, whenever the vocational context of the occupational life is plain and operative, work is meaningful. Furthermore, its meaning is essential and clear: work is the principal activity of men and women, in the doing of which their humanity is filled out and filled up. Conversely, whenever the vocational context of the occupational life is obscure or inoperative, work not only loses its meaning but becomes the principal and effective occasion for depriving men and women of their humanity. The simple fact is that too many people today are principally engaged in doing what they do without an effective sense of having been called to do it and without an effective sense that what they do serves a creative human purpose.

It is impossible to say whether or not this has always been true of work in the world. Let us assume that work has always been involved in

---

31. Eric Fromm, *Man for Himself: An Inquiry into the Psychology of Ethics* (New York: Rinehart, 1947), p. 68.

a tension of greater or less intensity between its vocational and its occupational elements. Nevertheless, we need to understand why we live in a time of greater rather than less vocational tension if we are to bring the insights of biblical faith effectively to bear upon the problem of work and covetousness.

The genesis of the vocational predicament of our time is complex. Its social and economic phases may be dated from the transformation of the economic activities of human workers by the machine. The machine did achieve an "industrial revolution," which not only altered the processes of production and distribution of goods and services but basically changed two important human relations of economic life. The first of these human relations has to do with the possession and control of economic goods and processes — that is, with ownership. One has only to consider the difference between a factory and a farm, on the one hand, and between a factory and a shop on the other, to become vividly aware of what has happened to the relation between the *people* who own the economic goods and processes to which they have title and control and the *operations* by which goods and services are produced and distributed. The difference has, of course, been effected by the machine. Basically, what has happened is that the people who own economic goods and services have come to be less and less directly involved in the actual operations by which these goods and services are produced and distributed. The actual operation of industry today is dependent upon the *managers* and not the *owners* of the economic goods and processes involved. The consequences of this shift in the relations between ownership and operation for the attitudes, values, and responsibilities in terms of which people "operate" an industry have not yet become fully clear or been fully explored. Their range and depth, however, cannot be easily overestimated.

The second important shift in the *human* relations of economic life has to do with those whose chief connection with economic goods and processes is their physical energy and/or their manual or mental skill — in short, their labor. Here, too, the industrialization of economic life has wrought deep and as yet not fully explored or understood changes. One has only to consider, for instance, the extent to which the United States has become a nation of jobholders rather than of property-holders to become vividly aware of what has happened to the relation between the *people* who "work" and the economic *process* by which they work and the goods that are the fruit of their labor. Certainly, there is a distance, if not an alienation, between the workers and their work, which has greatly affected the personal satisfactions and responsibilities that relate individuals to the work which they do. It is not too much to say that two important human relations of economic life (if not the two most important) have been depersonalized as the industrial revolution has developed, and that this depersonalization is a basic obstacle to the recovery of the vocational significance of the work that people do.

Two instances of this depersonalization will show how axiomatic it has become. Many years ago, I was riding from Omaha to Chicago on the Burlington Railroad's diesel-powered streamliner. It was the second trip of the much-heralded innovation in railroad passenger transportation. Sitting in the diner at breakfast while trying vainly to steady the coffee against the phenomenal speed of the train, I could not help overhearing a conversation of two gentlemen who appeared to be executives of the railroad. One was explaining to the other that the management was not altogether satisfied with the performance of the train. Indeed, there were engineering problems that should have been more carefully worked out before introducing the train to the schedule, and the existing track was not at all points suited to the operation of a train at such high speed. These hesitations had all been set aside, however, owing to the pressure of competition from other railroads.

Some ten years after that sobering experience, my small son received a tricycle as a gift. It came directly from the factory but could not be assembled because the steering shaft had not been welded with sufficient care and had become detached from the axle joining the two smaller wheels. I commented upon this curiosity to the welder, who sought to reassure me by explaining that the week before he had had to perform exactly the same kind of operation upon two brand-new Fords!

In the years since then we have all come to learn that these experiences are not isolated ones. Auto companies have on occasion knowingly put faulty and dangerous products on the road, having calculated that settling insurance claims will be cheaper than a total recall. The building industry, toy makers, and many other producers of goods can be similarly charged. Under the pressure of competition, the speed of production in our technological economy tends to subordinate personal and human relations — not to mention safety — to the productive process itself. It is not difficult to see in such a context how extensively the constructive relationship between work and human creativity and personal fulfillment has been undermined, if not destroyed. It is also not difficult to see how human covetousness leads to disregard of human welfare.

It would be easy to claim that the machine is the cause of the vocational predicament of our time, but this conclusion would be false. It would mean that some particular factor in the economic life of our time could be singled out as a kind of scapegoat for our vocational ills. The scapegoat is never a sign of personal maturity. It is instead a socio-psychological sign of frustration and defeat. The machine, moreover, is here to stay. The problem of the recovery of the link between vocation and occupation in the work that people do must be solved, if at all, with reference to the machine, not in disregard of it. At least from the standpoint of biblical faith, no problem of human life in this world is to be solved by excluding or by oversimplifying the factors that make the problem a problem. Biblical faith sets out to transform the world, not to unmake it. The Bible has certain elemental suggestions to make toward the recovery of the vocational significance of work that are particularly relevant to the vocational predicament that has been described.

It is no accident that, according to the early chapters of Genesis, one of the fundamental dislocations of a fallen world is the dislocation of the significance of work. Work, along with nature and the birth of one's own kind, belongs to the elemental enmities in which human life is involved as a consequence of sin. If one thinks of these enmities in contrast to the Creator's original arrangements of creation, the differences are instructive. Humanity's original uniqueness in creation is marked by the service of God in the fellowship of creatures. Nothing in this world is outside the range of the divine purpose. Everything in this world is an instrument of the divine will. There is no limit to the extent to which creation and all things in it can express the divine will and serve the divine purpose. Things are subordinate to human beings, but things are also indispensable to one's own performance of one's responsibilities in creation and to the fulfillment of one's life in fellowship with God. Everything in creation does, so to speak, the work peculiar to its own God-given existence in the enjoyment of God through all the things that God has made.

And then the fatal dislocation occurred. The theologies have varied in their formulation of the precise cause and nature of the Fall. So much at least is plain from the account of the temptation of the serpent and the lapse of human beings. The temptation unfolded the possibility of a world more promising for humanity than the world that God had made. For a split second, as it were, the issue was posed whether humanity trusted God and God's divinely appointed conditions for the fulfillment of human life in the world or not. And in the wake of the disobedience of distrust, the mortal enmities to the expression and achievement of our humanity in the world followed. Joy in the birth of humanity's own kind was subdued and overshadowed by pain. The secrets of all living things unlocked themselves to humanity's own hurt as well as to humanity's divinely ordered good. Work done without trust was transmuted into toil.

As regards the vocational predicament of our time, these biblical insights into the dislocation and the fulfillment of human life in the world point at least to this: The vocational and occupational elements in work are creatively joined whenever and insofar as it is possible for human beings to work in a context of trust derived from the service of God in the fellowship of creatures. Those of us who accept these biblical insights as the working faith of our lives have here a way of opening up the work that we do to fresh and unlimited personal resources and practical experimentation. There is no room here for uniformity or regimentation. Each industrial situation can and must be explored in terms of the bearing of these biblical insights upon its own special technical and personal problems. It could be that such a biblical reexamination of the problem of work would carry us beyond the ideological impasse that now divides the world into two and stultifies us all. It could be that such a biblical reexamination of the problem of work would add a fresh and regenerative possibility to each Christian congregation — namely, the possibility of being an experimental laboratory for the recovery of the vocational significance of work.

Belonging and the Tenth Commandment: "You Shall Not Covet His Wife, Man-servant, Maid-servant, Cattle, or Anything That Is His"

While the tenth commandment prohibits coveting the neighbor's wife, it more positively leads to the description of human belonging. It allows us, therefore, to look at the meaning of marriage as a parable of human relatedness representing neither hierarchy nor egalitarianism, but reciprocal responsibility.[32]

32. Portions of the following reflections were originally published as "A Christian Look at the Sexual Revolution," in *Sexual Ethics and Christian Responsibility*, ed. John Charles Wynn (New York: Association Press, 1970), pp. 51-82.

Luther rightly points out that in the time of the Old Testament a man could issue his wife a certificate of divorce quite readily. She was, therefore, subject to his capricious whims. She did in fact "belong" to him almost in the sense of ownership. This could present an intolerable situation, to which this commandment against coveting another's wife is meant to speak. The same commandment can speak to our situation today if we come to it and bring from it a radically different interpretation of "belonging." We come to our understanding of belonging via the Christian's search for sexual meaning.

In its depths, and in the last analysis, the search for sexual meaning is the search for a relation of fundamental, dependable, and liberating belonging, a relation in which freedom and fidelity accompany the gift of identity, that is, of self-accepting selfhood. In its depths, and in the last analysis, the Christian assessment of the bond between sexuality and humanity focuses upon and is derived from precisely such a relation. As Karl Barth has put it in a somewhat lengthy passage:

> the account of the creation of man as male and female is the climax of the whole history of creation. . . . In this . . . there is a radical rejection of isolation. And the point of the whole text is to say and tell . . . who and what is the man who is created good by God. . . . This man . . . must have a partner like himself, and must therefore be a partner to a being like himself; to a being in which he can recognize himself, and yet not himself but another, seeing it is not only like him but also different from him; in other words a 'help meet.' This helpmeet is woman. . . . God the Creator knows and ordains, but He leaves it to man to discover, that only woman and not animals can be this helpmeet. Thus the climax of the history of creation coincides with *this first act of human freedom.* . . . In the first instance, [man] exercises his human freedom, his humanity, negatively. He remains free for the being which the Creator will give him as a partner. He waits for woman and can do so. *He must not grasp after a false completion.* But who and what is woman? She is not [man's] postulate, or ideal, let alone his creation. Like himself, she is the thought and work of God. . . . *She is not merely there to be arbitrarily and accidentally discovered and accepted by man.* As God creates both man and woman, He also creates their relationship and brings them together. But this divinely created relationship — which is not just any kind of relationship, but the distinctive human relationship — has to be recognized and affirmed by man himself. . . . Here we have *the second and positive step in the act of freedom,* in the

venture of thought and speech, of man exercising his humanity in this freedom. *At the heart of his humanity he is free in and for the fact that he may recognize and accept the woman whom he himself has not imagined and conjured up by this desire, but whom God has created and brought.* With this choice he confirms who and what he is within creation, . . . the particularity of his creation. . . . *Human being becomes the being in encounter in which alone it can be good.* . . . 'Therefore shall a man leave his father and his mother, and shall cleave unto his wife' means that because woman is so utterly from man he must be utterly to her, because she is so utterly for him he must be utterly for her; because she can only follow him in order that he should not be alone he must also follow her not to be alone; because the first and stronger can only be one and strong in relationship to her he must accept and treat her, the second and weaker, as his first and stronger. It is in this inversion that the possibility of the human, the natural supremacy of the I over the Thou, is developed in reality. It is in this way that the genuinely human declares its possibility. . . . The human is the male and female in its differentiation but also its connexion.[33]

This is what the mystery of belonging really is. It is the mystery wherein and whereby the sexual relation between male and female is the basis and the bearer of the self-identity of humankind and of the freedom and fidelity to be human in the world. The identity-freedom-fidelity syndrome defines the structure and the dynamics of belonging and exhibits the intimacy and the ultimacy of the bond between sexuality and humanity.

Belonging is the experience of a relation through which one knows who one is, as and where one is, in what one does. What one does is respond, from a center of unified and stable selfhood, in a free act of self-giving to another self, similarly centered, unified, and stable. Belonging is being with and for another, through whom the gift of identifiable selfhood has come — really, that is, without dissimulation and self-justification. Belonging is the experience of receiving yourself, as and where you are, as a gift from another who has similarly received you, and finding in everything around you so many different ways of saying "Thank you." Thus belonging is the human and humanizing presupposition and power of involvement. And this is why sexuality is fundamental to human fulfillment.

Long before the epoch-making Freudian discovery and documenta-

33. Karl Barth, *Church Dogmatics,* III/2, trans. G. W. Bromiley et al. (Edinburgh: T. & T. Clark, 1960), pp. 291-92; emphasis added.

tion of the dynamics of selfhood, Christian faith had been put by its biblical basis and perspectives upon the track of what Freud explored with consummate precision and care. However persuasively post-Freudian corrections of the master's overextended concentration upon the role of sexuality in personality may have been established, it is still notable that Freud and the Bible are in agreement about the sexual basics and beginnings of the freedom and wholeness of human beings as persons — that is, of what being human means. Just as "one does not live by bread alone, but by every word that comes from the mouth of God" (Matt. 4:4; cf. Deut. 8:3), so one does not live by sex alone but by every word that illuminates the human meaning of life from birth to death and of insistent hopes and visions of life beyond death. One does, however, also live by bread; just so, one also lives by sex. And just as life by bread, apart from the "bread of life," if left to itself becomes a destructive occasion of idolatrous conflict, so also life by sex, apart from its eucharistic nourishment, becomes a "battle of the sexes" in the course of which each dehumanizes the other. The mystery of belonging is sustained and renewed by the presence of Christ against the threat of belonging. This is why in the Catholic Church marriage is a sacrament and a nuptial mass is its proper celebration. This is also why it is regrettable that in the Catholic Church Reformed a proper faithfulness to Jesus' indications of his sacramental presence has rightly insisted upon marriage as a holy ordinance rather than a sacrament, but has wrongly divorced the celebration of marriage from its eucharistic culmination. A wedding without a celebration of the eucharist is simply a romantic disregard of the human fact that sexuality aims at belonging, that belonging involves threat as well as mystery, and that marriage is a sign that the bond between sexuality and humanity must again and again be forged anew in and by the presence of Christ.

The threat of belonging (which the tenth commandment seeks to overcome) is the libidinal domination of the self by the other. It means that the mystery and wonder of the sexual relation has come under the ominous shadow of frustration and fear. The structure of belonging, according to which the identity-freedom-fidelity syndrome expresses and sustains the experience and power of selfhood, has become a syndrome without sustaining structure, a syndrome of anonymity, diversion, and mistrust, which transmutes the other from the bearer of selfhood into the enemy who enslaves and ultimately destroys the self. The pathos of the search for sexual meaning that characterizes our time is that it is a search for a sustaining structure of belonging that has both abandoned and been deprived of the perspective and power by which the purposed basics of sexual experience and behavior nourish sensitivity to what it takes to keep the threat of belonging from destroying the mystery and wonder of it.

This pathos pervades every level of sexual behavior. The high school or college adolescent making his or her initial and intermittent discoveries of the pleasure and fascination of participation in the physical and emotional responsiveness of the sexually other finds himself or herself caught between what used to be called ecstasy and shame, but with the increasing distance between the sexual and the human in sexual experience, it has come to be taken for granted as a private satisfaction with the self-evidence that goes with "being with it." More and more young adults are eschewing marriage while living together, endeavoring in this way to find sexual and human fulfillment without making ultimate commitments prematurely, in the quiet hope that growing together sexually and humanly will be more promising under the freedom to abandon the relation without reciprocal hurt and without the costs and complications involved in divorce. Spouse-swapping, with or without the formalities of divorce, is a sufficiently discernible pattern of life in suburbia to notice that the practice is no respecter of baptismal covenants or of the responsibilities of church membership or of family and community status, with or without church connections. The question posed by the practice is whether the dubious reciprocity between ennui and excitement is a tolerably satisfying alternative to a marriage relationship that has steadily declined in sexual and human meaning. When parents are unable to share a wisdom born of their own participation in the structure of belonging because they are caught up in "sexual affairs" of their own, age and youth would seem to have been joined in a poignant companionship occasioned by the surrender of the mystery and wonder of belonging to the threat of belonging.

Some fifty years ago James Thurber caught the spirit of this threat of belonging in his book *Men, Women, and Dogs: The Battle of the Sexes.* In Thurber's view, the threat of belonging is so destructive of the mystery and wonder of it as to have transformed the bond between sexuality and humanity into a battleground of relentless and interminable warfare. Thurber seems to be saying that dogs are at an enviable advantage over men and women because they have been spared this devastating and de-identifying conflict. He would give his life to be a dog, but he is condemned to live with and live out his frustrating humanity. We can draw from his pictorials as well as from our own experience that patriarchal and matriarchal tyrannies respectively destroy the humanity of sexual partners, who can neither escape each other nor bear to each other the identity of selfhood through a sexual relationship at once basic, dependable, and humanizing. Hence the question arises whether the conflict between the mystery and the threat of belonging is the sign of a dehumanizing fate foredooming sexuality to frustrations and fear or of a frontier across which the possibility of joining freedom with responsibility in sexual experience and practice is at hand. If the latter, at hand would be the possibility of the transfiguration of sexuality through the grace and truth of a humanizing faith.

It will occasion no surprise that a Christian look at sexual meaning should sooner or later take a look at Jesus Christ. In doing so we do not affirm that the dynamics of sexual meaning find their culmination in Jesus Christ. Too often, Christian faith and thought are offered as a simplistic answer to historical and human problems. The implication is that if everybody were Christian the problems would disappear. The facts are that nobody can be compelled to become Christian, that everybody will not take up Christianity, that other humanizing answers to the search for sexual meaning must be recognized, and that Christians are themselves not free of the perplexities and complexities of sexual experience and behavior. Our present concern is to follow the long biblical journey from the "image of God" to the "image of Christ," from creation to redemption, and to try to suggest how the search for sexual meaning may find in that journey a perspective and power through which freedom may be joined with responsibility in sexual experience and behavior. This perspective and power frankly involve the risk of believing as the companion of the risk of belonging. The risk of believing is the risk of openness to the presence of Christ in the heights and depths, the perplexities and complexities of human experience, and the risk of taking the risk of belonging in the context and the power of that commitment.

What, then, does the presence of Jesus Christ, in the experience of the Christian, offer to the experience and practice of human sexuality? The answer is: the transfiguration of that experience through the transfiguration of the participants in it, as they participate in it. Thus sexual experience and behavior, as basic to humanity, become integral to discipleship. The ultimate escape, according to which experience is transfigured because people are transfigured, is blocked. Transfiguration joins experience and participants in a reciprocity that makes the sexual act the basic occasion of human renewal. Transfiguration is the overshadowing of the threat of belonging by the gift of the mystery and wonder of belonging, owing to the presence of Jesus Christ in the search for sexual meaning. The presence of Jesus Christ is involved with sexual experience and behavior — from coitus to fulfilling companionship — not as a conscious awareness but as the experience of joy and peace in belonging, which seals and celebrates the giving and receiving of identity in faithfulness and freedom.

In an early and not sufficiently heeded essay by Bonhoeffer, a penetrating and succinct description of this experience occurs. It connects Adam and Christ, the image of God in its creation and in its restoration, and the sense in which the transfiguration of humanity has occurred.

> To be in Adam is to be in untruth, in culpable perversion of the will . . . inwards to the self. . . . Man has broken loose from communion with God, thus also with men, and now he stands alone, which is in untruth. Because he is alone, the world is "his" world, his fellow-men have sunk into the world of things . . . for he is utterly "by himself" in the false-hood of self-lordship. . . . The everydayness of man in Adam is guilt. It is the option for self-isolation. . . . It is the creature's wilful and compulsive quest for enjoyment, and as such it is constantly in flight from matters whose acknowledgement sets bounds to the business of enjoyment: death and oneself, as rightly known. But because flight is hopeless . . . the everydayness of Adam is desperation — and that all the more, the wilder the flight and the less man is conscious of despair. Superficiality is the mask of lonely isolation; it is directed lifeward, but its beginning and end is death and guilt.

To be in Christ, on the other hand, is

> man . . . torn away from the attempt to remain alone with himself and turned towards Christ. This is the gift of faith, that man no longer looks on himself but on salvation . . . which has come to him from without. . . . If, through man's self-incapsulation, existence *(Dasein)* in Adam was in subjection to the quality *(Wiesein)* of existence, the sight of Christ brings the loosening of the bonds: existence becomes free, not as if it were able to stand over against the quality of existence as independent being, but in the sense of escaping from the I's domination into the lordship of Christ, where for the first time in original freedom it recognizes itself as the creature of God. . . . [To be in Christ is to be a] person whose existence has been affected, redirected or re-created by Christ.[34]

34. Dietrich Bonhoeffer, *Act and Being* (New York: Harper & Row, 1956), pp. 155-56, 166, 170-71, 174.

This shift from "self-incapsulation" to the freedom of creaturehood, applied to sexuality, means that the identity-freedom-fidelity syndrome has begun to give shape to a structure of belonging in which the sexual relations between male and female begin to function once again as the basis and bearer of what it takes to be human in the world. The risk of belonging, being deprived of its threat, becomes the beginning of meaningful participation in all life's creative occasions: "To fill the earth and subdue it" (Gen. 1:28). In the context of this shift, sexual experimentation finds its appointed place and limit in the finding, by male and female, each of the other. Sexual experimentation belongs to the dynamics of identity in freedom. It does not mean, in and of itself, that promiscuity has made a sexual goal of passion. Nor does the limit appointed for sexual experimentation mean the surrender of the mystery and wonder of belonging to arbitrary social, moral, and religious attempts to safeguard the sexual relation against the threat of belonging. The limit set for sexual experimentation is the limit set by the structure of belonging upon the search for sexual meaning. This search is perennially imperiled by a double desperation. On the one hand, there is uncertainty about belonging; on the other hand, there is disillusionment with belonging. The first leads to confusion and doubt about the possibility of finding the other; the second leads to bitterness and self-deception about the possibility of fulfillment with and through the other. Broadly speaking, the first is a form of sexual despair before the commitments involved in marriage have become part of sexual experience and behavior. The second is a form of sexual despair that finds in marriage the futility and not the fullness of sexual experience and behavior. The fundamental mistake of the moralization of sexual behavior is that it hopes to prevent the futility and failure of marriage by preventing the experimentation that is prerequisite to the sexual commitments that make for belonging. Thus the antidote to sexual despair is sought in the displacement of gospel by law, of freedom by conformity. And all the while, the human meaning of sexuality is being exiled from sexual experience and behavior.

But suppose the shift from being "in Adam" to being "in Christ" were made. How, then, would one deal with these questions: How do I know when I have found the other to whom I belong? How does one avoid disillusionment and find fulfillment in marriage? The answer to the first question is that when the attraction to and by another is transfigured through the structure of belonging into the finding of the other, then the risk of belonging may be made because the threat of belonging has been enveloped and nourished by its mystery and wonder. The answer to the second question is that when marriage is entered upon with the singleness of commitment rooted in the singleness of an ultimate faith, its disillusionments lose their ultimacy and its expectations become the source of ever fresh discoveries that the threat of belonging has been transfigured by its mystery and wonder. As the tenth commandment knows, monogamy without monotheism is precarious; and marriage without monogamy falls short of fulfillment.

These answers do not mean that sexual experimentation will unfailingly lead through the structure of belonging to the other or that the shift from being "in Adam" to being "in Christ" excludes the dissolution of marriage through separation or divorce. There are no securities in sexual experience and behavior against the pain of failure or the suffering occasioned by the shattered possibility of sexual meaning and fulfillment. The transfiguration of sexuality by the presence and power of Christ means that the inheritors of the sexual revolution can understand that sexuality and humanity belong together. Joy and peace in belonging are the fruit of joy and peace in believing. For, as E. E. Cummings put it,

> one's not half two. It's two are halves of one:
> which halves reintegrating, shall occur
> no death and any quantity; . . .
> . . . .
> one is the song which fiends and angels sing:
> all murdering lies by mortals told make two.
> Let liars wilt, repaying life they're loaned;
> we (by a gift called dying born) must grow
>
> deep in dark least ourselves remembering
> love only rides his year
>
> all lose, whole find.[35]

Concluding Comments

The 450th anniversary of the date when Martin Luther's Large Catechism was first published, which occurred some years ago now, has made it seem

35. E. E. Cummings, *Poems: 1923-1954* (New York: Harcourt Brace Jovanovich, 1954), p. 398.

fitting to look again at what Luther has to say about the Ten Commandments. This is the more the case since Luther regarded the Commandments as expressing the quintessence of Christian faith and life, and since a fresh examination of what Luther said discovers to us a perspective and a direction for a responsible and fulfilling participation in the common life and human future promised by Christ that shapes its vision. The significance of this discovery is particularly striking when pursued in relation to some of the most critical questions confronting Christians — and not only Christians — from the depths and range of the common life today.

For Luther, the Decalogue is, in fact and in sum, an apperceptive description of what the gospel — and indeed, the Bible — affirms about life in this world and about what a realistic assessment of life in this world involves. The line between keeping the Commandments and obeying them is drawn by apperception. As we have explored throughout these pages, apperception is the singular human felicity and facility for bringing to what one has come to know that which one knows without knowing that one knows it, and in so doing, discerns whether what one knows is humanly true or false. The Commandments are apperceptive affirmations. As such, they are not prescriptive statements of duties toward God and one's neighbor in a world that God has created, redeemed, and will make new. They are, on the contrary, descriptive statements of what happens behaviorally in a world that God has made and has made fit for being human in. The world — as a fit place for being human in — stands or falls by the Commandments.

In this volume we have seen that Luther's innovative stress upon apperception combines with a dynamic relational sociology of the common life. But just as the Commandments have been deprived of their accent upon responsibility, in freedom and for freedom, by heteronomous interpretation, so the dynamics of reciprocal responsibility, which is indispensable to social interaction as human interaction, have been surrendered to an increasing preoccupation, both inside and outside the church, with an egalitarian displacement of hierarchy, as the necessary precondition of the freedom to be human in the world.

As I have tried to suggest, the egalitarian rejection of a hierarchically ordered society derived its own proper warrant from the manifest failures of hierarchies in church, state, and families to bring inequalities into line with equalities, which are also indispensable to freedom. But although the displacement of feudalism by mercantilism and industrialism was accompanied by a displacement of certain inequalities by equality — particularly in political theory, family relations, and philosophic expectation — the polarization between the hierarchical and the egalitarian realities of social existence intensified to such a degree that hierarchy came to be regarded as the nemesis of the egalitarian vision. In consequence, the question of a third option, beyond hierarchy and equality, is haunting the common life today.

This third option has emerged as the principal thesis of this volume. The thesis is that Luther's interpretation of the Decalogue is unexpectedly congruent with certain significant theoretical sociological attempts to get beyond positivism and quantification, through anthropological and macrosociological analyses of traditional and modern societies. Luther's interpretation of the Decalogue revises the relations between authority and freedom in a move beyond heteronomy and autonomy, toward a theonomously based relational sociology of reciprocal responsibility. Contemporary sociological theory, in turn, revises the relations between hierarchy and equality in a move that transposes their structural polarity into inequality and heterogeneity. Hierarchy, once regarded as the nemesis of equality, is vertically described in terms of graduated parameters, chiefly characterized by inequality. Equality, once regarded as the displacement of hierarchy by identity, is horizontally described in terms of nominal parameters characterized by heterogeneity. Both status groups (graduated parameters) and attribute groups (nominal parameters — i.e., people drawn together by one or more in-group forming variables, such as sex, race, language, etc.) are thus open to a mobility that is insufficiently operative when hierarchy and equality are structurally opposed. The optimum direction and aim of social mobility between inequality and heterogeneity may be expressed by Peter Blau's maxim: "There is too much inequality, but there cannot be too much heterogeneity."

As I have tried to show, the correlation of inequality with heterogeneity expresses in sociological terms exactly what the Commandments express in theological terms. The Commandments recognize heterogeneity as the sign of the world as creation, since creation is the celebration of differentiation, and inequality as the sign of that vertical dimension apart from which the freedom to be and to stay human in the world cannot generate the mobility necessary to the reduction of inequality through heterogeneity. The third option beyond heteronomy and autonomy, indicated by Luther's understanding of the Commandments, is reciprocal responsibility in a relationally ordained sociological world. Reciprocal responsibility is also the middle term between inequality and heterogeneity in a structurally determined society as a human society. Thus reciprocal responsibility as described in the Decalogue and reciprocal responsibility as indispensable to a structurally determined society as a human society intersect. Beyond heteronomy and autonomy and beyond hierarchy and equality, reciprocal responsibility, along the parameters delineated by inequality and heterogeneity, emerges as the necessary condition of the freedom to be human in a world made, and made fit for being human in, by the only authority there is, the authority who means freedom.

When, then, we turn from the principal thesis derived from Luther's interpretation of the Commandments to the question of the significance of the Commandments for the common life, a corollary thesis commands attention. This thesis is that reciprocal responsibility reverses the priority in the relations between rights and responsibilities presupposed by the questions urgently perplexing and pressing upon the common life today. These questions exhibit the priority of rights over responsibilities as crucial. The reciprocal responsibility intrinsic to the structural realism of the Decalogue, however, reverses the relation between rights and responsibilities, so that responsibilities take priority over rights. Rights and responsibilities are neither contradictory nor mutually exclusive of each other. It is the priority that makes all the human difference in the world.

When rights take priority over responsibilities, politicization takes priority over humanization in and of the common life. For rights tend to focus upon limits as hindrances or obstructions to be removed. When responsibilities take priority over rights, humanization takes priority over politicization in and of the common life. For responsibilities presuppose limits as the boundaries within which the freedom to be human in the world is experienced as a foretaste of fulfillment. In this volume we have seen that the Decalogue provides us with the limits that point us toward the freedom for a human future coming our way.

Index